Conspiracy Theories

Conspiracy Theories

Secrecy and Power in American Culture

NATIONAL UNIVERSITY
LIBRARY   SAN DIEGO

Mark Fenster

University of Minnesota Press
Minneapolis
London

The publication of this book was assisted by a bequest from Josiah H. Chase to honor his parents, Ellen Rankin Chase and Josiah Hook Chase, Minnesota territorial pioneers.

Published by the University of Minnesota Press
111 Third Avenue South, Suite 290
Minneapolis, MN 55401-2520
http://www.upress.umn.edu

Library of Congress Cataloging-in-Publication Data

Fenster, Mark.
    Conspiracy theories : secrecy and power in American culture / Mark
Fenster.
        p.   cm.
    Includes bibliographical references and index.
    ISBN 0-8166-3242-1. — ISBN 0-8166-3243-X (pbk.)
    1. Conspiracies — United States.   I. Title.
HV6275.F45   1999
973 — dc21   98-50100

Printed in the United States of America on acid-free paper

The University of Minnesota is an equal-opportunity educator and employer.

11 10 09 08 07 06 05 04 03 02 01 00 99   10 9 8 7 6 5 4 3 2 1

Contents

Preface

Secrets and conspiracies have long interested me. I especially remember enjoying as a child a conspiratorial children's book called *The Secret Three*.[1] Ostensibly the story of three boys who form a secret club, the book's banal description of the boys' adventures was overshadowed by the intrigue through which the boys meet. Two of them, Mark and Billy, learn of Tom's arrival on the island where they all live by finding an encrypted message that Tom had placed inside a bottle and tossed out to sea. Mark and Billy decode the message, meet Tom, and continue to develop new secrets and codes. Wherever you turn, the book implied, you might find a possible sign of some secret, decipherable existence that promised the fulfillment of a deep, perhaps unrecognized desire. Ironically, the book itself was advertised as part of its publisher Harper & Row's I Can Read series; while clearly an allusion to its simple language, large typeface, and pictures representing the action contained in the written story, the series name took on a second meaning for a book that noted the proliferation of secret signs scattered about the world. Within this book, learning to read was a process not only of understanding the plain meaning of writing, but also of discerning the existence and correct interpretation of secret writings and messages.

The club's secret was not its mere existence. Rather, its secret, its "position of exception" in Georg Simmel's phrase,[2] was its infantile but resonant source of power: its exclusivity of membership and language. This exclusivity lent meaning to the otherwise banal boyhood utopia that the book presented, and caused me grave envy, concern, and longing. I remember wanting at once to join the group, to replicate it in my own lonely childhood, and to expose it.

My contradictory response to *The Secret Three* is analogous to the conception of power held by a particular strain of contemporary American populist discourse, conspiracy theory. Imagine the experience of "finding" evidence of a "conspiracy" — not especially difficult, given the circulation of novels, films, and nonfiction narratives that represent such an event. It is a moment of cathexis, especially for the individual who "desires" to find such evidence, to find proof of the existence of a secret group that he or she wishes did not exist and therefore wants to expose and destroy, and, in order to do so, will join a group that replicates the conspiracy's exclusivity. The evidence and its implications are a source of endless further consideration, interpretation, and investigation, of finding and uncovering the plot that constitutes the subject's powerlessness.

This book seeks to interrogate this social and psychic relationship between "conspiracy" and "theorist," between individual and group interpretation and narrative strategies, between populist notions of "the people" and "the powerful." Ultimately, I propose that the utopian "plot" to be uncovered is not composed of the exclusivity and secrets of conspiracy, but of the open-ended political struggle for equality, solidarity, and a transparent, participatory democracy that conspiracy theory might assume but can hardly imagine and cannot attain.

Because I was living an institutionally and geographically itinerant life during my work on this project, I have many to acknowledge and no one to blame for the results. In some ways, this project wove its way through the entirety of my education, and I am thus indebted to some wonderful teachers, including but not limited to the following: at the University of Virginia, where I was introduced to the joys of modern contemporary fiction by Jon Megibow and to the wonders of cultural theory and studies by Joli Jensen; at the University of Texas, where I had the pleasure of working with Janet Staiger, Horace Newcomb, and Tom Schatz; and at the University of Illinois, where Larry Grossberg and Jim Carey were inspirational figures, and where I also had the opportunity to work with Tom Turino, Jim Hay, and Meaghan Morris. Equally important were graduate school friends and cohorts including Chris Anderson, Barbara Burton, Steve Lee, Jeff Sconce, and Jim Wehmeyer at Texas, and Charles Acland and Ann Balsamo at Illinois. Colleagues during brief stays at Indiana and Shenandoah Universities who provided intellectual and moral support include Michael Curtin, Kathy Krendl, and Elizabeth Colton. The "Discerning the Right" conference at the University of Wisconsin-Milwaukee in March 1996 provided an inspirational shot in the arm at the right moment, and my thanks go to the organizers, participants, and especially Matt Wray for the enthusiasm engendered there. Thanks to Chris Anderson, Carol Stabile, Eric Hayot, Barry Penn Hollar, and especially Charles Acland for reading and providing invaluable comments on parts of this manuscript, as well as to audience members at various conferences where parts of it were read. I also want to thank the editors at the University of Minnesota Press with whom I worked, including Janaki Bakhle, Lisa Freeman, and especially Micah Kleit. Jennifer Moore made the publication process move smoothly and transparently, and David Thorstad provided thorough and essential copyediting.

Finally, this book could not have been completed without the help of those closest to me: Holly Kruse, whose love, companionship, and ideas have meant more to me than I can say; my father, Marvin Fenster, whose unflagging support I likely didn't deserve; and my mother, Louise Rapoport Fenster, whose passing during the writing of this book I am still learning to live with. And last but not least my dogs, Wilver and Cali, who are probably just happy to see this darned thing finished once and for all.

Introduction

A word slips out of Dallas in 1963,
Spawns an industry: conspiracy.
Initials ten feet tall just reinforce
And underline: insignificance.
        —Mekons, "Insignificance"[1]

In political discussions with friends and opponents, one can hurl no greater insult than to describe another's position as the product of a "conspiracy theory." The characterization groups its victim with such unsavory characters as militia members, Oliver Stone, computer hackers, and the John Birch Society, and accuses him or her of believing in a secret, omnipotent individual or group that covertly orchestrates the events of the world. According to numerous political and cultural commentators, however, the characterization also places its victim in the increasingly dysfunctional and bizarre mainstream of American political culture. Reporters and editorialists have regularly filled print publications with dispatches concerning the increasing proliferation of conspiracy theory, which is carried forth to youngsters in comic books; to adults in movies and television shows; to all America through an increasingly susceptible news media; and to the frontiers of "cyberspace" through the Internet.[2] These concerned commentators assert that although it has both historical roots and international counterparts, conspiracy theory in the United States has poisoned our political system, culture, and public sphere to an unprecedented degree.[3]

Except for occasional instances, accusations of conspiracy are typically met in the mainstream media by incredulity, if not downright hostility.[4] Consider, for example, the reaction to allegations in the *San Jose Mercury News* in 1996 that Nicaraguan contra agents with ties to the CIA played a central role in the introduction of crack cocaine to American cities.[5] The nation's most-respected newspapers considered both the allegations and the outrage they aroused among African-Americans either to be the result of pathological conspiracy theorizing or as "fueled" by a black community whose indigenous "rumor mill" was particularly susceptible to conspiracy theories.[6] One book on conspiracy theory considered the episode to represent the "overtly conspiracy minded" nature of "the black community," who refused to believe the media investigations that claimed to uncover no evidence of direct CIA involvement in cocaine trafficking. The book's author, Daniel Pipes, blamed black journalists and leaders, all of whom apparently "dislike the existing order and offer radical ideas about changing it," for the vulnerability of African-Americans to reports that the responsibility for the tragic circumstances of the African-American urban poor is not their own.[7] Conspiracy theory is not only destructive in and of itself, according to Pipes, but is a tool that the devious can use on the disaffected — or, as he later refers to the "black community," an "organized group of malcontents"[8] — to raise suspicions of, if not downright hostility toward, the American social and political order.

Employing the term "conspiracy theory" serves as a strategy of delegitimation in political discourse. Conspiracy theory has come to represent a political Other to a "proper" democratic politics — a set of illegitimate assumptions that seem to question that the United States is a benign, pluralistic democracy, and that seem to reject the notion that history moves through the triumph of progress and leadership, as well as through the vagaries of coincidence and mistake. This book seeks to undermine many of these assumptions.

Arguments about the existence of secret treachery in the highest ranks of public and private leadership have rarely seemed so popular and pervasive as they seem today. The commercially successful film *JFK* is merely one example of the post-Watergate genre of conspiracy fiction (examples of which include the Mel Gibson/Julia Roberts film *Conspiracy Theory* and television shows such as *The X-Files* and *Dark Skies*). Uncovering the secrets of public and private power is also a staple of investigative journalism, political campaigns, and the everyday lives of citizens distributing and receiving information about personal, professional, economic, and political treachery. The discursive practices of journalism, rumors, and gossip, while not necessarily concerning conspiracy, often resemble the interpretive and narrative elements of conspiracy theory in their linkage of individual pieces of information into an explanatory framework that posits an affirmative effort by a clandestine force to consolidate power and subordinate others. Implicit in this circulation of populist narratives, investigations of official perfidy, and generalized suspicion is the notion that not only is there interest in — nay, a *demand* for — a comprehensive explanation for the failure of some political, social, and/or personal order, but that such an explanation may aptly describe reality.

On the one hand, conspiracy theory is often characterized as illegitimate, pathological, and a threat to political stability; on the other hand, it seems an entertaining narrative form, a populist expression of a democratic culture, that circulates deep skepticism about the truth of the current political order throughout contemporary culture.

This book is both an extended argument about the partiality of the first characterization and an attempt to grapple with the issues related to the second. Understanding and effectively reacting to conspiracy's role in contemporary political culture requires more than labeling it as pathological Other or mere ideology. Articulating a necessary distance between "the people" and "power," conspiracy theory draws on the most simplistic, disabling, and dangerous interpretations of political order, including fascism, totalitarianism, racism, and anti-Semitism — yet it also represents a populist possibility, a resistance to power that implicitly imagines a better, collective future. The song lyrics at the beginning of this chapter intermingle these competing descriptions of conspiracy theory in reference to a troubling historical event (the JFK assassination) that fuels debate and an "industry" of assassination studies — theories that then circulate in mainstream popular culture (as in the song's reference to a theater marquee advertising *JFK*). The song is deeply paranoid, warning of an elite of "the rich and the powerful"; analogizing this elite's amorphous power to a frightening image of a giant swatting the common folk like flies; describing the disciplinary apparatuses of high-technology surveillance and consumerism; and offering obscurity and "insignificance" — the conditions of the song's narrator and the contemporary political subject he invokes — as the only refuge from exposure and danger. Insignificance — both the ability to be invisible to power and the condition of political voicelessness — provides the context for conspiracy theory's emergence (as a pathology that arises from insignificance) and a "cover" for the political subject (as a tactical response of the insignificant).

This book suggests a further play on this notion of insignificance, arguing that populist conspiracy theory is the manifestation of a political life lived *in significance*: in reading the signs of the powerful, in finding and investigating conspiracy. Conspiracy theory arises when the political is interpreted within a specific, conspiratorial narrative frame by those for whom politics is inaccessible and its meaning is impenetrable or secret. It is in conspiracy theory's endless practices and proliferating texts of uncovering the conspiratorial plot that a populist imagination, a sort of populist political unconscious, stirs.[9] The analysis of conspiracy theory's signification within a sense of political insignificance requires a symptomatic critique of conspiracy theory as political ideology, and a cultural analysis of the signifying practices of its endless circulation through countless cultural texts such as films, television, popular songs, fanzines, and computer networks. If conspiracy theory is, in Christopher Hitchens's provocative terms, "the white noise which moves in to fill the vacuity of the official version,"[10] then it is necessary for an evocative, emancipatory politics to understand the noise of popular politics, and to appropriate its signifying practices for a truly progressive populism.

Above all, conspiracy theory is a theory of power. As such, it deserves attention for its understanding of the uneven distribution of resources and coercive power. Conspiracy theory perceives the power of the ruling individual, group, or coalition to be thoroughly instrumental, controlling virtually all aspects of social life, politics, and economics. The singularity of its instrumentalism is its belief that although power has real effects and creates traces that can be discovered by those aware of its existence, the "truth" of power — the identities and motivations of actors who actually wield power — remains hidden to the "naked" eye of those who dismiss or are ignorant of the conspiracy. Secrecy, in short, constitutes conspiracy's most egregious wrong.[11] Yet, unlike "vulgar" or "plain" Marxist instrumentalism, conspiracy theory does not claim that the state is used by "the ruling class for enforcing and guaranteeing the stability of the class structure itself."[12] Although economic control plays a role in many conspiracy theories (e.g., international bankers based in New York who control the Federal Reserve and who are often, but not exclusively, identified as Jewish), analysis of hierarchical structures based on economic class, race, and other antagonisms does not. Like the state and everything else under the dominance of the conspiracy, economic control is simply another instrument of the conspiracy. Conspiracy theories seek to explain the power of ethnic, social, or even supernatural elites over "the people" rather than focus on the systematic exploitation of the oppressed through control of the relations of production and ideological structures of domination.

Conspiracy theory thus seems a rather disabling theory of power. If the conspiracy is in complete control, and if those who are controlled are utterly unaware of the conspiracy's existence, then effective resistance is unlikely, or it at least requires the most desperate of measures. Indeed, conspiracy theorists spend most of their time collecting and interpreting information rather than in the traditional politics of movement building and forging alliances with other groups. At particular conjunctures, however, such as the tenuous association between the John Birch Society and parts of the Republican Party in the 1960s and the mobilization of the Christian Coalition on behalf of Republicans in the 1990s, conspiracy theories can have important effects on major political parties.[13] More typical types of conspiracy theorists' political activism, which often appear in conjunction with each other, are vanguardism, in which small groups attempt to bring about political change by leading the masses in a particular direction, and radical separatism. Both of these tendencies are at work in the rise of the diverse "militia movement," in which groups and individuals simultaneously attempt to separate themselves from what they see as a dangerous federal government encroaching on their rights and land, and to evangelize the unconverted about the reality of the current political situation. Yet, conspiracy theory has also had a remarkably productive role in American history in the development of a secular Enlightenment rationality that perceived power in the hands of humans rather than of a divine entity, among colonists in the years leading up to and during the American Revolution, and in the construction of an American national identity.[14] The notion that conspiracy theory is disabling therefore needs both further investigation and historical contextualization.

Let me declare my own position clearly: There *are* elements of secret treachery in the contemporary political and economic order. Foreign covert actions that employ economic exploitation of native populations, political assassinations, and subversion of democratic and revolutionary movements, as well as domestic policies of covert surveillance and "countersubversion" such as the FBI's COINTELPRO program, have played important roles in twentieth-century history. Secretive alliances between private individuals and groups with shared class interests *do* enjoy power over seats of public and private power that is greater than their numbers would allow them in a participatory democratic state. Yet, totalizing conspiracy theories suffer from a lack of substantive proof, dizzying leaps of logic, and oversimplification of the political and economic structures of power. Structural, institutionally based inequities in the distribution of power, capital, and resources do not constitute conspiracy; rather, they help to define capitalism. Thus, the existence of governmental secrecy neither proves the existence of all-encompassing conspiracies nor provides a rationale for them. Although conspiracy theories are certainly resistant to dominant political discourses, they rarely enable effective political engagement and often are related directly or indirectly to virulent forms of scapegoating, racism, and fascism.

The book contains eight chapters, divided into three parts with an Introduction and an Afterword. After the Introduction, Part I, "Conspiracy Theory as Political Ideology," describes and analyzes approaches to conspiracy theory as a political practice. Part II, "Uncovering the Plot of Conspiracy," develops a cultural analysis with two chapters on the interpretive and narrative practices of conspiracy theory. Part III, "Conspiracy in Everyday Life," consists of three chapters on different sets of conspiracy theorists and their specific engagement in contemporary politics and culture. The Afterword uses conspiracy theory and the extremes of populist discourse to suggest the strengths and limits of cultural analyses that celebrate the popular.

Chapter 1, "Richard Hofstadter and 'The Paranoid Style,' " is an extended exegesis and critique of the most prominent and influential account of conspiracy theory and populist "extremism." A prominent postwar American historian, Hofstadter, along with fellow liberal historians and political scientists of the 1950s and 1960s, developed the notion that American populist movements express a political pathology akin to "paranoia" that remains dangerous to the country's inclusive and pluralistic political party system, which works through the formation of broad "consensus." The chapter critiques both the political and epistemological assumptions of consensus, pluralism, and process, and their application in recognizing the seeming Other as a form of political sickness.

Chapter 2, "John Doe #2 Goes to Washington: Militias, Pathology, and Discipline," describes and critiques mainstream political approaches to the emergence and dangers of the militia movement. Although the chapter provides a brief account of the complex local and national strains of this far-right movement, its goal is to analyze the ways in which the Hofstadter political-pathology approach continues to inform the study of populist groups, and its resulting implications for the response to such movements. The discursive apparatus of "pathology," the chapter argues in its analysis of a prominent Senate subcommittee hearing on the militias in the wake of the Oklahoma City bombing and of two prominent books on the militias, limits political analysis to simplistic labeling and limits political response to calls for greater disciplinary surveillance and control.

Hofstadter's approach is not the only viable critique of American populism and conspiracy theory. Chapter 3, "Conspiracy Theory and Populism," examines how some progressives have attempted to retain a critique of the structural inequities of contemporary capitalism while condemning those "leftists" whose theories and analyses have been "seduced" and "infected" by the incorrect simplifications, misattributions of wrongdoing, and outright scapegoating of conspiracy theory. This approach works from a conception of "ideology" that condemns conspiracy theory by proving it wrong, questioning its logic, and associating it with fascism and the extreme right wing. Although the progressive critique is far more effective than that of Hofstadterian centrists who cling to an exclusive "consensus" politics, it does not fully confront the discursive practices of conspiracy and the cultural practices and meanings that circulate within those discourses. Without such an inquiry, conspiracy theory and populism are too easily dismissed as ideological, leading to an analytic closure and disabling any potential articulation of populism in a more grounded, liberatory direction.

Part II addresses this shortcoming by examining the politics of conspiracy as a signifying practice. Chapter 4, "The Clinton Chronicles: Conspiracy Theory as Interpretation," begins with the observation that conspiracy theory is an attempt to apprehend the past and the present by placing disparate events within a unifying interpretive frame. As an interpretive practice, conspiracy theory works as a form of hyperactive semiosis in which history and politics serve as reservoirs of signs that demand (over)interpretation, and that signify, for the interpreter, far more than their conventional meaning. The chapter discusses three distinct ways of conceiving of this interpretive practice: as paranoia, as desire, and as production. As with the notion of conspiracy theory as a form of political paranoia, understanding conspiracy theory as a paranoid form of interpretation is somewhat insightful: conspiracy theory does resemble the text-book definition of paranoia as a systematic and chronic delusion that is, para-doxically, logically sustained in the interpretation of perceived external stim-uli, but it displaces the cultural and specifically semiotic challenge posed by conspiracy theory's notion of signification and interpretation onto a relatively simplistic notion of pathology. Both desire and production, however, conceive of conspiracy theory as an active, indeed endless, process that continually seeks, but never fully arrives at, a final interpretation. Employing Slavoj Žižek's read-ing of Jacques Lacan and Gilles Deleuze and Félix Guattari's notion of the "regime of signs,"[15] this chapter analyzes the impossible, almost utopian drive of the theorist who continually fetishizes individual signs while placing them within vast interpretive structures that try to stop the signs' unlimited semio-sis. Conspiracy theory pays back more in meaning than the theorist's original investment by recognizing, depleting, building, and destroying new signs in the perpetual motion of interpretation, producing a surplus of interpretation and affective dividends.[16] It thus displaces the citizen's desire for political sig-nificance onto a signifying regime in which interpretation replaces political engagement.

Chapter 5, "*JFK, The X-Files,* and Beyond: Conspiracy Theory as Narra-tive," concerns the narrative framework within which this interpretive practice attempts to position the signs it seeks and so abundantly finds. The narrative frame and interpretive practices are mutually dependent elements of conspir-acy theory as practice. Interpretation cannot take place in an explanatory vac-uum, and so the conspiracy's progenitors and motives are required for signs to be understood; at the same time, in order for the secret political order to be re-vealed in a narrative, it must be found in signs that are read for deeper meanings. Moreover, because the interpretation of conspiracy is endless, the conspiracy narrative can have no final closure. Although "nonfictional" and fictional nar-ratives attempt to resolve seemingly all-powerful cabals through the work of the singular investigator, their closures cannot fully contain the secret worlds they divulge or the challenges that these worlds represent. Instead, they offer reformist and heroic solutions in which the truth is found and order is restored by characters working within or returning power to the political structures previously infiltrated by the evil conspiracy. The structural challenge posed by the conspiracy cannot be fully contained within this closure — except when the conspiracy narrative is articulated within the surreal and parodic, as in the novels of Richard Condon (and the cinematic adaptation of his *Winter Kills* [1979]) and Craig Baldwin's film *Tribulation 99* (1991). The conspiracy narrative is an emplotment of power, a mapping of an explicable power structure that both serves and undermines conspiracy theory's excessive interpretive practices.

Part III consists of three studies of the discursive practices of specific communities that engage in conspiracy theory. Chapter 6, "Millennialism and Christian Conspiracy Theory," analyzes one particular set of religious texts and practices that resemble and are closely tied to conspiracy theory: popular Christian apocalyptic, or eschatology, that attempts to provide an accessible, comprehensible, and all-encompassing narrative frame that can explain the imminent return of Christ to a mass audience. In addition to constructing a narrative, popular eschatology provides a call for believers to interpret current events in relation to Scripture in order to know and celebrate the rapture and Christ's return. Although overtly spiritual, popular eschatology is implicitly political in its strong linking of a coming millennium to conservative political dogma specifically opposed to a presumed "secular humanist conspiracy." It also offers ardent political support for Zionism and a strong Jewish state of Israel, while holding anti-Semitic spiritual beliefs that characterize Jews who refuse to convert to true Christianity as being doomed to the Antichrist's seductive powers and the tribulation's apocalypse. Thus, while distinct from more "secular" conspiracy theories — particularly in its perverse desire for the conspiracy's victory, in that such a victory would further ensure Christ's return — popular eschatology shares a number of interpretive practices and texts, and at times forms overt alliances, with secular theorists. Chapter 6 looks closely at three different types of popular eschatological texts: nonfiction books that introduce biblical prophecy to new readers, syndicated television "news" shows that describe and explain current events within the eschatological framework, and novels that represent eschatological beliefs within the conventions of the thriller genre. As a set of interpretive practices and a master narrative that overlaps with and is quite similar to that of "secular" conspiracy theory, popular eschatology demonstrates the struggle over the meanings of history, the relation of history to the present, and the meanings and possibilities of the apocalyptic future.

The next two chapters are related studies of the affective engagement and alliances among individuals involved in the pursuit of conspiracy theory. Chapter 7, "The Conspiracy 'Community,'" analyzes the problematic construction of a "conspiracy community," an aggregate of theorists, theories, and the media (including radio shows, magazine and book publishers, computer networks and bulletin boards, and mail-order catalogs) that circulate theories and provide a forum for their discussion. The conspiracy "community" is built on two crucial conflicts: First, although the groups who believe in differing theories sometimes build alliances and often share information based on mutual hatred of an assumed conspirator, these groups may be intensely competitive with one another as to which theory is correct, and their theories may be mutually exclusive (if, for example, the Rockefellers are the ultimate ruling power, then by definition the British royal family *cannot* be). Second, the basic unit of investigation in the discursive practices of conspiracy is the solitary individual who is distrustful of the collective. From spy novels and films to Kennedy assassination researchers, no one is as heroic or is granted as much agency as the singular investigator. These conflicts make imagining a collectivity based on conspiracy theory virtually impossible. Describing the "community" and the death and life of Danny Casolaro, one of the community's more recent tragic heroes, the chapter describes conspiracy theory's ultimate failure as a political enterprise. Almost by definition ineffectual as a collective, the conspiracy community can do little more than point helplessly to a future when closure will occur, interpretation can stop, and the political becomes transparent — a future that will never arrive. Only in that impossible moment can the "community" truly exist and the individual body of Danny Casolaro, the narrative agent of historical change, be successfully articulated within the collective; only then can the dead body of the lone investigator whose suspicious death reverberates among theorists and across individual events and theories fully reveal its secrets.

Chapter 8, "Conspiracy Theory as Play," concerns the knowing, bemused attachment with which one segment of conspiracy theory followers views the paranoia of "apocalypse culture."[17] In the books of Robert Anton Wilson, a science-fiction/fantasy author and New Age philosopher; in a card and role-playing game loosely based on *Illuminatus!,* Wilson's most famous work; and in a network of do-it-yourself fanzines and parodic "cults," conspiracy theory serves as a form of play, an interpretive practice that seeks to decipher events in a simultaneously paranoid and humorous way. Without accepting conspiracy theory as a necessarily correct interpretation of politics, this set of cultural forms and practices identifies and attempts to replicate the productive aspects of pursuing conspiracy as an aesthetic experience. Within these forms and practices, conspiracy theory is, literally, a thrill for a bored subculture, and can be produced in publications, at a weekend convention, and in a set of "roles" that can be assumed in an anarchic game that infuses the players' everyday lives. Chapter 8 discusses the rather complex intertwining in these practices of both a transgressive, carnivalesque revelry through paranoid reinterpretation of "accepted" history, and a deeply cynical embrace of an ideological practice that abandons activism, hope, and reality in favor of fantasy and the excitement of a manufactured sense of "paranoia."

The Afterword seeks to confront the populist vein that runs through much of the popularization of American cultural studies with the most regressive and dangerous tendencies of populist politics, exemplified by the novel that has become a central cultural artifact of the contemporary American neo-Nazi movement, *The Turner Diaries*. A penultimate example of "resistance," *The Turner Diaries* is a virulently fascist, racist, patriarchal, and anti-Semitic novel that presents a utopian future of white supremacy by misinterpreting and reimagining the past and the present. In order to theorize populism and articulate it in liberatory ways, one must confront and challenge the most virulent tendencies of populism's antagonism between "the people" and "the power bloc" without simply dismissing populism as *necessarily* racist and reactionary, and as lacking significance as a discursive formation that is symptomatic of a broader longing for a better, more significant position within a political and social order.

Some final words on what this book is *not*. It is not intended as an encyclopedia of conspiracy theories, or as a compendium of the most logical explanations of the plots on which conspiracy theorists obsess, or as a thorough account of the range of communities of conspiracy theorists.[18] Each of these would be an enormously valuable contribution to current political debates and the study of contemporary social movements, but they are quite different projects from the one I have chosen. This book is intended, rather, as an analysis of the role of conspiracy theory in contemporary populism that attempts to provide both a theoretical and a political take on the cultural present. It is intentionally partial and provocative, and is meant to spur debate about the role of interpretive and narrative practices in popular politics, as well as about the relationship between the political discourses of the marginal and extreme, and the mainstream and dominant.

Part I
Conspiracy Theory as Political Ideology

1. Richard Hofstadter and "The Paranoid Style"

The most extensive body of research and analysis on the politics and history of American conspiracy theory was developed in the 1950s and 1960s by American historians and political scientists, the former working within the somewhat broad, and at that time dominant, historiographic framework that has been identified as "consensus" or "counterprogressive" history, and the latter working within a similarly broad theory of "pluralism" in American political science. Much of the work on political extremism, mass movements, and other dangers to the prevailing "consensus" and "pluralism" demonstrated an interdisciplinary approach between the two disciplines. Richard Hofstadter, the consensus historian whose work largely established the consensus critique of conspiracy theory, shared with pluralists many of the same assumptions about the essential character of American democracy. What Hofstadter and others termed "political paranoia"—a pathology suffered by those existing outside of the pluralistic consensus who promoted fears of conspiracy—was merely one issue associated with the study of pluralism and consensus.[1] Nevertheless, because these historians' and political scientists' discussions of "the fear of subversion," "the fear of conspiracy," "antipolitics in America," and "the paranoid style in American politics" took place during the rise of the "New American Right" of McCarthyism and, later, Barry Goldwater, as well as during the surge in visibility of reactionary groups such as the John Birch Society, their work was widely disseminated within academia and among concerned intellectuals.

Their work remains influential in academic and popular conceptions of the politics of conspiracy theories. Senator Daniel Patrick Moynihan, for example, used it during the mid-1980s to condemn the extreme right-wing faction of the Republican Party, and sources as varied as the *Washington Post,* the *Wall Street Journal* editorial page, the *New Yorker,* and the conservative magazine *The National Interest* have employed the notion of a "paranoid style" and "paranoid" politics to explain Arab fears of the United States, Oliver Stone's film *JFK,* and the militias.[2] This chapter will focus on Hofstadter's work and the implications of its continuing influence, but I begin by briefly discussing the historical and intellectual context for "pluralism" and "consensus history," which is crucial in attempting to understand Hofstadter's significance for the contemporary conceptualization of conspiracy theory as politics.

Pluralism, Consensus, and the Fear of "Extremism"

The theory and advocacy of "democratic pluralism" in contemporary American political science have been the result of a confluence of a number of distinct traditions in social theory. Pluralists base their notion of governance and political practice on the assumption that a democracy is composed of a multiplicity of competing groups, themselves made up of individuals acting to advance their own interests. The modern notion of pluralism has relied on Max Weber's concern for a rational, impersonal society, as well as Émile Durkheim's interest in the role of social order in limiting the number and influence of individuals without strong attachments to groups. Moving from these assumptions, "pluralism" employs a market-based theory of political practice in which, according to William Kornhauser's 1959 work *The Politics of Mass Society,* "Democracy is essentially an institutional procedure for changing leadership by free competition for the popular vote."[3] In order to win the consent of their constituents, political parties and representatives "compete" for the votes of interested groups in the marketplace of politics. By trading their members' votes in exchange for the fulfillment of their own practical political interests, groups play a meaningful role in electing and constituting a genuinely pluralistic democracy. The fact that, as with owners of the means of production in a capitalist market economy, certain elites can manipulate and control the "political marketplace" does not negate the effectiveness of a pluralistic democracy for defenders of such a system. Political theorist John Dunn characterizes the assumptions of pluralists as follows:

America was the stablest of all democracies and the most pluralist of all democracies; and, if it turned out that it was also less *politically* egalitarian than had previously been suspected or at least claimed, then *this* meant that the findings of American political science (a notoriously value-free intellectual practice) were that stable and authentically pluralist democracy was somewhat more oligarchical than had previously been supposed. Even in its own dreary terms the democratic government offered in this theory seems a somewhat ineffective mechanism for protecting the interest of quite a number of governed.[4]

The Other to a pluralist democracy during the postwar period is a "mass society" marked by "large numbers of people who are not integrated into any broad social groupings," and elites who no longer had the autonomy and protection to rule and do what is best for society in an impersonal manner.[5] In a "mass society," atomized masses, no longer associated with or beholden to groups that can channel their needs and discontent into proper political and social behavior, place undue pressure on elites, thus inviting totalitarian rule by a "charismatic," as opposed to a rational and practical, leadership. If "pluralism" represents the goal of a democratic society, "mass society" represents democracy's inherent dangers. Fearful of the latter, proponents of pluralism warn of "extremists" on the left and the right who "must be deeply alienated from the complex of rules which keep the strivings for various values in restraint and balance.... [Extremists'] hostility is incompatible with that freedom from intense emotion which pluralistic politics needs for prosperity."[6] The "alienated mass man," estranged from his "unwanted or unknown self," often seeks "flight into activism" in these extremist groups, substituting a real knowledge and practice of politics for the pathological demagoguery of extremist ideology.[7] One element of such extremist ideology is a "paranoid" fear of conspiracy.

"Consensus" history shares many of the same assumptions concerning reasonable and irrational politics as theories of "pluralism." Within the discipline of history, "consensus" conceptions of the history of American politics were "counter" to (though not necessarily and at all times against) the "Progressive" school of Charles A. Beard, Frederick Jackson Turner, and other earlier twentieth-century historians, and thus in addition to being called "consensus" historians, they are also referred to as "counterprogressives." Consensus history critiqued the Progressives' celebration of liberal reform, as well as their narrative of American history as a series of conflicts between differing philosophies (e.g., between Alexander Hamilton and Thomas Jefferson) and between the rich and powerful and the poor and powerless. Beyond mere rejection of their predecessors, however, consensus historians also developed a distinct counternarrative to that of the Progressives that described what they saw as a uniquely American history, identity, and form of political philosophy and practice, produced through a particular historical experience. The distinctly American politics described by consensus historians was moderate and pragmatic; even the conflicts identified by Progressive historians and accepted by counterprogressives were perceived by the latter as practical linkages among conflicting political parties and interest groups rather than as intense ideological battles.[8] Consensus historians thus strongly echoed the mid-nineteenth-century observations of Alexis de Tocqueville — whose *Democracy in America* had been nearly forgotten during the Progressive era — of America as an organic, distinct whole.[9]

As the Cold War developed, predominantly mainstream liberal and neoconservative historians articulated a notion of consensus in their vision of the United States as an outpost of pragmatic rationality in a dangerous world of ideology, totalitarianism, and fascism. Fearful of the excesses of the left, epitomized for consensus historians by all forms of communism and particularly by Stalin, and of the fascist right of Hitler and Mussolini, counterprogressive/consensus historians prized moderation and unity as uniquely positive aspects of a peaceful, pluralistic American tradition (though some, such as Louis Hartz, were more critical of what they saw as America's stifling, anti-intellectual unity).[10] Much of their work described American consensus as a project that was still incomplete. For Richard Hofstadter, "consensus" worked best when conceptualized in historical writing as analogous to the role played by

> an appropriate frame . . . to a painting: *it sets the boundaries of the scene* and enables us to see where the picture breaks off and *the alien environment begins.* Consensus is, in other words, the limited field within and upon which any (thus lim-

ited) conflict takes place; it does not play the role of a general theory that functions outside of historical context and circumstance, but instead works best as a measure of the degree of legitimacy and acceptance a political system or specific issue achieves among "the politically active public."[11]

Consensus history was ascendent during the era of the liberal Cold War intellectual, a time in which, at least among members of the intelligentsia, such consensus was achieved and such a frame was successfully built. As C. Wright Mills asserted in *The Power Elite,* postwar American intellectuals had "abandoned criticism for the new American celebration."[12] Andrew Ross, employing Antonio Gramsci's conception of hegemony, has described this process of consensus building among intellectuals during the period as the formation of a "historic bloc" in which intellectuals served as "functionaries or cultural deputies of the dominant group, by lending their cultural authority to the process of eliciting 'spontaneous' or popular consent for the ideas and authority of this group."[13] In this sense, consensus historians, as part of an entire class of dominant intellectuals, played a central role in the process of legitimation of Cold War policy and ideology. Despite calls for and proclamations of "the end of ideology," the commonsensical assumptions of American "consensus" in the historic past and the political present assumed the status of "objectivity" in the way Gramscian notions of ideology describe.[14] In a sympathetic but detached analysis of consensus historians during the period of their dominance in American history, J. Rogers Hollingsworth describes this process well: "In a period when the American people have had an insatiable desire to develop an image of themselves and to explain their institutions to people of other nations, the consensus and continuity themes have helped to point out the distinctiveness of American history—thus permitting the American people to better understand what it means to be an American.[15] What Hollingsworth describes, however, is the role of intellectuals linked to ruling "historic blocs" in the winning of *consent* from the masses rather than consensus. As Gramsci wrote, "To the extent that ideologies are historically necessary they have a validity which is 'psychological'; they 'organize' human masses, and create the terrain on which men move, acquire consciousness of their position, struggle, etc."[16] "Consensus"—or, more precisely, consent—must be won and protected; the "painting's frame," in Hofstadter's terminology, must be tight, the "alien environment" seen as such, and measurement must constantly be taken of past and present and found or made reasonably secure.

In this context, it is not surprising that although they focused chiefly on right-wing extremists at the time, those consensus historians and political-science "pluralists" concerned with this political "paranoia" were suspicious of virtually any type of populism.[17] Their response to contemporary developments was not limited to populisms of the right; according to Hofstadter, McCarthyism "aroused in some intellectuals more distaste than they had ever thought they would feel for popular passions and anti-establishment demagogy. The populism of the right inspired a new skepticism about the older populism of the left."[18] This became particularly important during the years of student activism and the emergence of the New Left, contemporaneous with some of the later work of consensus historians on political "paranoia," when what were seen as the new populisms of the left became the object of many older historians' scorn and criticism. From its earliest moments, consensus history has used "extremism" as a convenient and versatile label for a variety of forms of dissent. Ultimately, the need to account for the rise in such extremism through explanatory frameworks and historical parallels consumed a sizable body of literature in the journals, essay collections, and books of American historians, particularly from the mid-1950s to 1970.[19]

This apprehension to the point of neurosis about the construction and maintenance of "consensus" and "pluralism" is an appropriate context with which to begin an analysis of Hofstadter's work on what he termed the "paranoid style in American politics," because of his emphasis on the social-psychological basis for conspiracy theory. The essays that constitute this work, written between the mid-1950s and early 1960s and collected in a 1966 book, are the most influential and widely cited on the subject of conspiracy theory and countersubversion.[20] Although his studies of political paranoia are but a small part of the corpus of his work, they fit within the general movement of his writings away from a leftist critique of the history of American political consensus in his 1948 work, *The American Political Tradition*. At that time, Hofstadter found the lack of distinction between "liberal" and "conservative" political traditions and practices in American politics to be dangerous in a new, postwar era. The early book's one phrase that most historiographers identify while discussing the development of consensus history—Hofstadter's appraisal of America's political tradition as one of "a democracy in cupidity rather than a democracy of fraternity"[21]—demonstrates a critical analysis early in his career of what he saw as both a central aspect of American politics and its main defect: the overwhelming dominance of political structures by elites.

As Hofstadter's work developed over the course of the 1950s and 1960s, however, he began to describe "consensus" in far more positive terms, privileging American substantive political moderation and its structures of political process as fortifications against extremism and insurgency. According to historiographer Peter Novick, Hofstadter's own political views moved increasingly toward those of mainstream liberalism throughout the 1950s, and he came to celebrate the New Deal as a triumph of rational politics over the decidedly mixed tradition of reform and progressivism that he had more critically examined in *The Age of Reform* (1955).[22] Similarly, he began to describe democracy in pragmatic and procedural terms rather than as a set of ideals or principles, moving toward a position quite similar to that of his pluralist contemporaries in political science.[23] Hofstadter came to privilege what he termed the "political" and "the political intelligence," which referred not simply to a process or realm but to pragmatic engagement with structures of power and consensus, and which was opposed to those groups and individuals unwilling to so engage:

> Whereas the distinctively political intelligence begins with the political world, and attempts to make an assessment of how far a given set of goals can in fact be realized in the face of a certain balance of forces, the secularized fundamentalist mind begins with a definition of that which is absolutely right, and looks upon politics as an arena in which that right must be realized.[24]

Although clearly more liberal than the equally prodigious work of Daniel Boorstin, a contemporary who was a more unabashed booster of American consensus, Hofstadter's writings took on a more conservative cast throughout the 1950s, particularly in his critical analyses of the dissension and opposition of groups such as the Populists, the Progressives, and the far right.[25] These studies, borrowing from social psychology and literary studies in their emphasis on symbols and notions of the personal and social unconscious, set many of the terms of the debate for the explosion of studies of the pathological style and causes of political "paranoia" that would follow.

Revolting in Style
The Style and Practices of Paranoid Politics

Hofstadter's work is not merely important because of its influence; the stress that he places on the rituals and symbols of popular political practice provides a crucial precedent for current cultural studies of conspiracy theory. Hofstadter makes his emphasis on the culture of popular politics quite clear, and explains in the introduction to his 1966 collection of essays on the topic: "[These essays] focus on the way large segments of the public respond to civic issues, make them their own, put them to work on national problems, and express their response to these problems in distinctive rhetorical styles."[26] For Hofstadter, politics as it is practiced and experienced on the popular level is not created from above and imposed on those below, nor does it concern merely policy issues, political parties, and the personalities and actions of great figures. Instead, popular politics exists in rituals and symbols. "The public," while it does not create civic issues, plays a role in appropriating, reshaping, and "working" on the political; indeed, "political life acts as a sounding board for identities, values, fears, and aspirations" (ix). An important starting point for understanding Hofstadter's notion of "political paranoia," then, is to note how it emphasizes the popular aspects of politics, as well as the complexity and competing interests involved in the political process. It is thus not surprising to note that when he surveyed consensus history, the historiographic narrative that he helped to construct, Hofstadter was proudest of its "rediscovery of the complexity in American history," and particularly of its recognition of the multiplicity of sociological, ethnic, and cultural forces at work in it.[27]

Although popular politics and the complex forces at work within it are integral to American history, Hofstadter argued that they are more to be feared than championed or even tolerated. For Hofstadter, the public's rhetoric — or at least a sector of the public significant enough to require documentation, analysis, and dread — lacks the rationality and wellness necessary for proper political discourse. Instead, popular, or perhaps more precisely, *mass* reaction to "striking symbolic acts or memorable statements, or...public figures who themselves have symbolic appeal" demonstrates "the nonrational side of politics" (ix). He declared at one point that what interested him in popular or mass political symbols and rhetoric was "the possibility of using political rhetoric to get at political pathology" (6). The term "political pathology," opposed to properly rational political action, describes an objectionable manifestation of aberrant practices expressed in specific forms of rhetoric and symbols. Rather than communicating through true, transparent statements of the interest politics that should dominate a representative democracy, "pathological" rhetoric communicates as a "style." He defined "style" as "above all, a way of seeing the world and of expressing oneself" (4) that is concerned with "the way in which ideas are believed and advocated rather than with the truth or falsity of their content" (5).

Hofstadter objected not merely to the form of "paranoid" political discourse, however, but also to its content. While allowing that "not all of the charges and fears [of those who engage in the paranoid style] need be dismissed as entirely without foundation," he separated the modicum of truth that conspiracy claims might have from "the apocalyptic and absolutist framework" in which they appear (17). In fact, conspiracy *does* exist, Hofstadter admitted: legitimate political "strategies" often require secrecy, and thus they demand some measure of conspiracy. Yet, such strategies are merely mechanisms to a properly political end and do not, in and of themselves, constitute historical forces with real-world effects. To think so is merely to fall into the paranoid style, to convert a singular incident into a larger framework, and to willfully misinterpret or misread evidence and misplace it into a "sick" explanatory framework.

Thus, Hofstadter implied a continuum between proper politics and pathology, as well as between justifiable, or at least understandable, prejudice and fear, and those expressions of prejudice and fear that are beyond the limits of legitimate politics. Some expressions of group fear, particularly of a threatening, distinct Other, are not necessarily forms of unjustifiable paranoia or instances of a paranoid style. For example, he argued that the desire among "Yankee" Protestants in the first half of the nineteenth century for ethnic and religious homogeneity need not be dismissed "out of hand" (i.e., categorically condemned as bigoted), except when anti-Catholic sentiments were expressed in a militant style, or suffered from "a large paranoid infusion" about Masonic rituals and secret plots (19). Thus, although "style" refers most directly to the forms that extremist political rhetoric assumes, it also clearly refers to the content within this form — a little fear (legitimate or otherwise), a little xenophobia, and even a touch of racism in the form of a fear of an Other are defensible within political discourse if phrased correctly and taken a reasonable spoonful at a time. A more substantial "infusion" of paranoia, however, does not simply alter the framework of the paranoid explanation; it also deeply affects the evidence that would seem to be poured into such a framework. The paranoid style, then, transforms both the terms and the specific substance of potentially legitimate issues into irrational rhetoric. As Daniel Bell had commented a few years earlier, "The tendency to convert concrete issues into ideological problems, to invest them with moral color and high emotional charge, is to invite conflicts which can only damage a society."[28] The calls of the "paranoid style" to morality and emotion, and the "damaging conflicts" that this style attempts to produce, emanate from the "ideology" on which the style is based rather than on the rationality and objectivity of a truly democratic political order.

Although Hofstadter did not define all forms of dissent as outside the norm, his notion of legitimate dissent and rational discourse was inextricably tied to that of establishment liberals and neoconservatives during the Cold War period in which his and others' discussion of political paranoia took place. In discussing Barry Goldwater and the 1964 Republican presidential primaries and general election, Hofstadter explicitly described the two-party system as demanding a "loyal opposition" that "accepts the ultimate good intentions of the other" and that includes a "certain sobriety born of experience" of compromise, consensus, and the realities of the "professional code" of political process (100–106). By contrast, Goldwater and his followers had "little in common with the temperate and compromising spirit of true conservatism in the classical sense of the word" (43–44). Hofstadter's example of an acceptable conservatism was Senator Robert A. Taft's reasonable Republican opposition to the New Deal, which recognized expediency and responsibility in the political process and shared at least some of the New Deal's basic assumptions (if not sympathy for or belief in the full program) concerning the need for some form of social and economic protection for the unfortunate dispossessed of capitalism (97). Similarly, a strong, rational anticommunism was acceptable, particularly in foreign policy; the problem with the "pseudoconservatism" of Goldwater was its inward-looking paranoia, which, rather than looking abroad, where realistic measures to strengthen anticommunist forces might be made, focused almost exclusively on the largely phantom threat of communist "infiltration" (46).[29] For Hofstadter's Cold War liberalism, these assumptions constituted the common ground and common sense from which any properly consensual political opposition must begin.

If Taft represented a reasonable conservatism that Goldwater exceeded, the emergent New Left represented for the older, more conservative Hofstadter a parallel example of extremism at the other end of the political spectrum. For example, he cited the "popular left-wing press" in a list of movements that fit within the paranoid style, a list that included abolitionists who suspected a slaveholders' conspiracy, anti-Masonic and anti-Catholic groups, nineteenth-century Populist Party fears of international bankers, and the contemporary American right wing (9). Although he spent far more space on McCarthy, Goldwater, and their followers, this is undoubtedly less because he saw, in the early to mid-1960s, any essential distinction between the far left and the far right, and more because of the prominence of the far right at the time in which he wrote. When Hofstadter asserted that "What most liberals now hope for is not to carry on with some ambitious new program, but simply to defend as much as possible of the old achievements and to try to keep traditional liberties of expression that are threatened" (43), his rhetorical flourish of "most liberals" assumes a common sense of Cold War liberalism that denies the legitimacy of all but the most loyal opposition. Again, extremes of right and left are defined both by the content of their positions (right-wing libertarian economic policy connected with a paranoid fear of domestic communist infiltration, social conservatism, and anti-intellectualism on the one hand; radical "new programs" influenced by socialism on the other) and the form of their rhetorical opposition.[30]

The necessary protection against such extremism for both Hofstadter's consensus politics and for "pluralistic" democratic theory was a functioning two-party political system. In *The Politics of Unreason* (1970), a work that followed the tradition that Hofstadter had established, leading political scientist Seymour Martin Lipset and coauthor Earl Raab argued that the two-party system, except in instances such as the 1964 election (an exception that would seem ultimately to prove the rule, given Goldwater's convincing defeat), works as a bulwark against development of extremist movements, because mainstream political parties "have not been ideological agents, but coalition parties, compromise parties, designed pragmatically for electoral victories."[31] Indeed, Hofstadter went so far as to say that in their deep distrust and hostile attacks on mainstream, establishment political leaders, Goldwater conservatives (and, by implication, far leftists) moved beyond simple personal attack and into radical critique by calling "into question the validity of the political system that keeps putting such [leaders] into office" (100).

In a sense, Hofstadter was absolutely right: particularly among leftists, fear of an economic and power elite (whether conspiratorial or not) is symptomatic of profound suspicions of not only the process but the structures of the American political system—a system in which, by this point in his career, Hofstadter found little of importance at fault. The distinction between process and structure, however, is one that Goldwater conservatives would make, arguing that the success of corrupt leaders and the electoral failures of their own candidate were not the fault of the structures of the American democratic system per se, but rather the fault of some aspect(s) of the political process, such as the Republican Party establishment, the media, or political dirty tricks by political opponents. In either case, given his and others' assumptions about the essential wellness of both the American democratic structure and its political and electoral process, Hofstadter again relied on a binary opposition between the "ideology" of those who would, in the "style" of their rhetoric and the content of their form, refuse to employ proper political discourse and positions, and a transparent, proper politics that would recognize and play fairly within the functioning system of "compromise," "consensus," and "pragmatism."

Status Symbols
Mass Society, Anxiety, Paranoia, and the Causes of the Paranoid Style

This opposition between "style" produced by "ideology" and proper, rational political discourse matches Hofstadter's at times contradictory struggle to define and explain the causes of the paranoid style. He found such explanations in the rise of a "mass society," in the anxiety and resentment among groups who felt their level of status threatened, and in the social psychology of group behavior. I want to begin by discussing the issue of "mass society," because this aspect of Hofstadter's argument most clearly distinguishes the "paranoid" style of the twentieth-century United States from that of preceding centuries.

Many American intellectuals throughout the 1950s and early 1960s participated in worried discussions of mass culture and society, discussions that had begun in Europe with the work of Émile Durkheim, Georg Simmel, and, later, the Frankfurt School. The postwar American version expressed typical Cold War loathing of American mass society by linking social, political, and cultural differences with disease, in which the body politic and the hallowed but fragile ground of culture (whether in terms of a distinctive "American culture" or an aristocratic "high culture") were perceived as existing under the continual threat of infection from outside forces. This was a period in which the "consensus" about the identity and distinction of American culture was never so clear and yet never seemed so threatened, in which "consensus" was built in and on fear of annihilation. Much of the discourse of the Cold War — a battle taking place at home and all over the world between the objective, rational, and moral democracy of the United States and the irrational, monolithic militarism of the Soviet Union — provides a frame of reference for consensus history's fear of extremism and pluralist political theory's fear of the rise of a "mass man."

In this context, intellectuals deeply dreaded and harshly criticized the pervasiveness of commodified mass and middlebrow culture, which was seen as a threat to the sacred domain, fully realized aesthetics, and reasoned public appreciation of the best of American culture. Of particular significance was the distinction between high and various levels of commodified culture, a distinction that was a subject of widespread intellectual debate throughout the postwar era. During this period, the act of defining categories of "taste," and specifically of defining those categories distinguished as aberrant and/or mass, was a critical practice of intellectual authority.[32] For Hofstadter, the production and consumption of the paranoid style paralleled the production and consumption of commodified mass culture and were an index of poor education into the values of politics: "A distorted style is, then, a possible signal that may alert us to a distorted judgment, just as in art an ugly style is a cue to fundamental defects of taste" (6). Similarly, the mass media, in deeply affecting American political culture, had changed the relationship between politics and the public:

> The growth of the mass media of communication and their
> use in politics have brought politics closer to the people than
> ever before and have made politics a form of entertainment
> in which the spectators feel themselves involved. Thus it has
> become, more than ever before, an arena in which private
> emotions and personal problems can be readily projected.
> Mass communications have made it possible to keep the
> mass man in an almost constant state of political mobiliza-
> tion. (63)[33]

The connection between an argument such as this, concerning politics, and those being made by intellectuals concerning taste and culture, is important. For example, in delineating the distinctions between high, middlebrow, and mass culture, Dwight Macdonald, constituting himself as both defender of the high and as sympathetic supporter of the masses who no longer produced their own "authentic" culture, perceived the greatest danger to high culture coming "not so much from mass cult as from a peculiar hybrid bred from the latter's unnatural intercourse with the former. A whole middle culture [which Macdonald defined as mass culture with a 'cultural figleaf'] has come into existence and it threatens to absorb both its parents."[34] Similarly, for Hofstadter, the problem posed by the paranoid style lay not so much with "the masses," whose passions had always been reasonably well absorbed and blunted within the structures of American politics, but in a new, emergent politics that threatened the older stability. In the context in which it was made, Hofstadter's argument concerning the effects of mass communications and mass culture on politics must be read as an expression of deep anxiety about the intrusion into politics of "entertainment," "spectators," "private emotions and personal problems," audience "projection," and the "political mobilization" of "mass man." These terms serve as clear, disruptive threats to the ideal order of proper politics.

Andreas Huyssen has identified the dominant binary in nineteenth-century culture as being between, on the one hand, "mass culture" and women, and, on the other, "authentic culture," the prerogative of men. Although this strong association made by modernist European artists and intellectuals was somewhat less pervasive in American postwar mass culture debates, it remains as a residual element in Hofstadter's argument. Huyssen writes, "The problem [for the modernist artist] is not the desire to differentiate between forms of high art and depraved forms of mass culture and its co-optations. The problem is rather the persistent gendering as feminine of that which is devalued."[35] Hofstadter's brand of modernist politics was based on a series of crucial divisions between the legitimate and the illegitimate, the rational and the emotional, and the political and the personal. Retaining that boundary was crucial, and his and many of his contemporaries' fears of McCarthyism, Goldwater, and any "extremist politics" or "irrational" political discourse were not merely that the extremist or irrational would prove victorious over the legitimate and rational (though such fears were certainly present), but that the border between order and its Other would disappear.

In this sense, Hofstadter's fear of the loss of a clear set of divisions included the fear of secure gendered boundaries as a structuring principle, just as the politics (not to mention the history and political science departments) of his era was based on the exclusion of women and the "qualities" with which they were presumed to enter the realms of the political and the historical. In implying that the political Other of extremism is Woman (personal, emotional, pathological), he thus reaffirmed patriarchal structures that further solidified the marginal status and repression of women. This implication fits within more general Cold War fears that the potential for the rise of extremism and paranoid fears of conspiracy should not only be focused abroad, against an expansionist Soviet Union under Stalin, but at home, in the rise of a mass society and mass culture that threatened political and patriarchal order. Whereas the "infiltration" of communism that McCarthy et al. feared was merely the projection of the pathological, the fear of the "mass man," and especially of his vulnerability to persuasion, could not be underestimated. The notion of a "paranoid" style of American politics to be feared and loathed made perfect sense — it seemed to describe a pathology that could be spread more easily through an unwitting public weakened by the breakdown and disintegration of "traditional" American cultural, social, and political structures.

Accordingly, one could perform a psychoanalytic reading of Hofstadter's fears parallel to the social psychology he performed on populist conspiracy theorists, seeing his notion of pathology in the terms described by Sander Gilman:

> Order and control are the antithesis of "pathology." "Pathology" is disorder and the loss of control, the giving over of

the self to the forces that lie beyond the self. It is because these forces actually lie within and are projected outside the self that the different is so readily defined as the pathological. Such definitions are an efficient way of displacing the consciousness that the self, as a biological entity subject to the inexorable rules of aging and decay, ultimately cannot be controlled.[36]

Afraid of the decay of American politics and culture by the onslaught of postwar technological and social changes, Hofstadter, his contemporaries, and his followers constituted a notion of the pathological political Other as that which lay beyond the pale of political discourse. Although I do not want to stretch this suggestive reading beyond its limits (which might lead one, in a stereotypically postmodern turn, to celebrate the "pathological" uncritically as necessarily leading to the liberation of social order from the chains of the dominant), I want both to stress the historical context in which the term "pathology" is associated with populist conspiracy theory and to note its unthinking assumptions about inherent health of the Political Self.

If the development of "mass culture" provides a specific historical context to the twentieth-century example of "the paranoid style," Hofstadter's social-psychological explanations provide a more universal frame of reference. The paranoid style, he argued, is at once "always present in some considerable minority of the population" (39) and only manifests itself in episodic waves. Hofstadter cited Norman Cohn's work on millennialism throughout medieval Europe in order to demonstrate the degree to which the paranoid style has appeared in different places over centuries of Western history.[37] In order to be activated, this "paranoid tendency" must be mobilized by "social conflicts that involve ultimate schemes of values and that bring fundamental fears and hatreds, rather than negotiable interests, into political action. Catastrophe or the fear of catastrophe is more likely to elicit the syndrome of paranoid rhetoric" (39).

Hofstadter's distinction between two types of political discourses and practices would seem to contradict this assertion, however. "Status" politics, "the clash of various projective rationalizations arising from status aspirations and other personal motives" and the general type of political discourse within which the "paranoid style" exists, tends to become dominant during periods of prosperity. During times of depression and economic crisis, on the other hand, a more constructive "interest" politics, based instead on "the clash of material aims and needs among various groups and blocs" and focused on passing legislation, must necessarily become dominant (53–54). Whereas "status politics" is based on emotion and ideology, "interest politics" concerns the more properly political struggle for jobs, economic security, and bargaining power.[38] Although Hofstadter did hedge this polarity to a degree in theory (in times of depression, "politics is more clearly a matter of interests, although of course status considerations are still present" [53]), he implicitly described the historical periods of interest and status as mutually exclusive.[39] Because status politics is difficult to reconcile within "the normal political processes of bargain and compromise" (39), and proponents of such politics, "being less concerned with the uses of power than with its alleged misuse, do not offer positive programs to solve social problems" (87–88), the paranoid style rises in importance when struggles over status that cannot be or refuse to be resolved through rational political discourse become most visible. The paranoid "style" and "tendency," then, are not so much universal as they are conjunctural, appearing at particular moments and requiring certain determinants.

The notion of "status politics" was an attempt, Hofstadter explained, to account for three separate but related aspects of American culture:

> First is the problem of American identity, as it is complicated by our immigrant origins and the problems of ethnic minorities; second, the problem of social status, defined as the capacity of various groups and occupations to command personal deference in society; and, finally, the effort of Americans of diverse cultural and moral persuasions to win reassurance that their values are respected by the community at large. (87)

Hofstadter rightly identified some of the most crucial strains for American political practice, and particularly for American cultural politics: the problems of constructing and maintaining "nationhood" and a "national identity" within a society of ethnic and racial (and, although not mentioned in this context by Hofstadter, class, gender, geographic, and sexual) diversity and conflict; and of competing groups and individuals, structured by those conflicts, attempting to classify their tastes and values and those of others within structures of economic, educational, and cultural capital. Yet, he perceived the central problem that status politics represents to be the problematic role that emotions and the psychological makeup of groups and individuals play in the attempt to resolve these strains through reasonable political means in a pluralistic democracy. He proceeded from the assumption that these problems can be and are resolved when "interest politics" dominates because these problems are historically specific and psychological rather than endemic to the American political system, which is fundamentally sound. But, as Michael Rogin has argued, the notion of "status anxiety" is flawed both as a concept and as it was and continues to be used. The irrationality inherent in the term labels as anxious and deviant whole groups of people seeking to redress wrongs and to participate — some for the first time — in political movements. In doing so, consensus historians construct an Other that posits dominant society as "normal" and labels as pathological those left outside dominant society by force or choice. Thus, anxiety becomes a useful method to bracket virtually any type of nonmainstream political discourse and movement, placing it outside the normative regime of politics as a form of political pathology.[40] Furthermore, defining the political as a pluralistic, rational, decision-driven debate over "interests" fails to recognize its contingent, social conditions, and instead assumes that "interests" are themselves prepolitical — formed at an authentic moment when the individual and the group fully recognize their own desires.[41]

But what precisely did Hofstadter mean by "paranoia" and "pathology"? He clearly wished to delineate his usage from its psychoanalytic and social-psychological origins:

> Although they both tend to be overheated, oversuspicious, overaggressive, grandiose, and apocalyptic in expression, the clinical paranoid sees the hostile and conspiratorial world directed specifically *against* him; whereas the spokesman of the paranoid style finds it directed against a nation, a culture, a way of life whose fate affects not himself alone but millions of others. (4; emphasis in original)

Hofstadter relied on many of what he assumed were the components of a psychoanalytic definition to analyze the "paranoid style," such as the degree to which the paranoid's enemy is a projection of the self, which is then imitated (as in, for example, the John Birch Society, a "secret" group formed to study and root out communists' secret infiltration of the United States, or in the tens of quasi-secretive militias of the 1990s), and the fact that the "paranoid [style's] mentality is far more coherent than the real world, since it leaves no room for mistakes, failures, or ambiguities" (32–36).[42]

Ultimately, however, Hofstadter applied a theory of individual pathology to a social phenomenon — an interesting, perhaps productive exercise for an analogy, but problematic if, as with Hofstadter, one is attempting to produce a concept that can be used across history to explain, for example, populist political dissent in the 1990s. As American historiographer John Higham argued in his 1959 critical analysis of consensus historians, Hofstadter and others who posited political conflict as psychological pathology "substitute[d] a schism in the soul for a schism in society," and either refused to see or trivialized conflict by describing it as "psychological adjustments to institutional change."[43] By labeling as pathological any challenge or resistance to "consensus," the notion of the "paranoid style" serves as an excuse for neglecting, equating, and even repressing political protest of all sorts. A symbolic, stylistic, and pathological anxiety represents little more than an irksome but temporary cry from the margins that must be either defused or incorporated within a pluralistic consensus. This condemnation of conspiracy theory is thus limited in its ability to analyze, challenge, and redirect the populism of conspiracy theory.

2. John Doe #2 Goes to Washington
Militias, Pathology, and Discipline

On 15 June 1995, less than two months after the explosion that demolished the Alfred P. Murrah Federal Building in Oklahoma City, the Senate subcommittee on Terrorism, Technology, and Government Information, a subcommittee of the powerful Senate Judiciary Committee, held a hearing on the increasingly visible national militia movement. The event took place at the height of media coverage of the militias, a loose conglomeration of right-wing populist groups operating throughout the United States. Such groups, which had been largely ignored only two months earlier, appeared during this period on a regular basis in national and local newspapers and broadcast news reports. Allegations that the bombing suspects had some affiliation to one of the largest and most prominent militia groups prompted this heightened coverage. News reports featuring information supplied by "watchdog" organizations that track far-right groups, as well as from sociologists, law enforcement, and occasionally militia members themselves, framed the militias as outsiders and extremists who displayed a singular irrational pathology in their political beliefs and paramilitary activities.[1] Aside from statements from President Bill Clinton and federal law-enforcement agencies investigating the Oklahoma City bombing, there had been no official response from the federal government prior to 15 June, and so the Senate hearing took on significance, if only as a first attempt by the recently elected conservative Republican majorities in the Congress to respond to this "grassroots" far-right movement emanating from the middle of the country.

According to subcommittee chair Arlen Specter (Republican, Pennsylvania), the hearing was convened in order to allow the "airing" and "ventilation" of the beliefs and activities of the militia movement.[2] These metaphors of exposure and release, which Specter used throughout the three-hour session, gave the impression that he viewed the hearing as the opening of a dark, forbidding closet out of which seeped an annoying odor — an odor that might signify some greater danger lurking deeper inside. He based his strategy of confrontation on assumptions about the inherent rationality of the American political process and "marketplace of ideas," both of which, he seemed certain, would provide the necessary air and light to avert the danger. For Specter, permitting the militias to speak in their own words before his distinguished fellow senators would allow the American people to "draw their [own] conclusions" as to the dangers of the militias (114). He told gathered militia members: "My own sense is that it's healthy and the American people will applaud letting you speak your piece, no matter how much we disagree with you" (ibid.).

Specter's elision of himself and the American people is significant not only in his attempt to construct himself as the paternal voice of the country, but also in his assumed position as spokesman for the American political process. In so doing, he operated within the discourses of consensus and pluralism, positing a fundamental conflict between the rational structures and procedures of the American political and legal process, of which he was not only a part but also a spokesman, and the fundamentally irrational militias, whose beliefs and practices are inherently pathological. Because of Specter's position as a lawmaker, however, he has more immediate and recognizable material effects than Hofstadter and his contemporaries, and this subcommittee hearing and other official government action ostensibly against the threat of the militias illustrates the discursive and material effects of the concept of "political paranoia" on the technologies and practices of disciplinary power. This approach limits both analysis of and response to radical populist movements to strategies of containment, legislative enactments, surveillance, and policing, eliminating the possibility of understanding the conditions of a populist movement's rise or rearticulating particular elements at work in populist discourse. Populism and the notion of "the people" it invokes are seen merely as a marginal movement to fear, an object requiring greater disciplinary control.

This chapter explores governmental and mainstream activists' response to the militia movement in the wake of the Oklahoma City bombing and the revelation of alleged connections between the suspected bombers and the militias.

The central purpose is to note the strong connections, whether intentional or not, between the Hofstadter-consensus-pluralist approach to "political paranoia" and the contemporary response to the militias, and to demonstrate the results of this response. Mainstream antimilitia activists on the one hand, and elected and appointed officials on the other, work within vastly different discourses, and the language and images that they employ — from the vivid, alarmed warnings of activists to the bureaucratic and technical terminology of government employees — are quite distinct. Yet each demonstrates the grave limitations of the "pathology" metaphor for analysis and formulation of a response not tied to the imposition of greater disciplinary controls and surveillance.

The chapter begins with a general introduction to the militias, followed by an examination of the confrontation between senators and militia leaders during the subcommittee hearing. It concludes with an extended critique of two prominent books by antimilitia activists on what they describe as the threat to democracy and society posed by the militias.

Militias, Patriots, and the Decentralized Far Right

A relatively small but well-armed "movement" that has caught the attention and imagination of the media, local militias and national militia-related organizations aspire to be leaders in a return to the "citizens' army" of the Revolutionary War. Militia members buy arms and train themselves in military technique and strategy in order to fight what many of their members see as the rise of a centralized "one-world" government that seeks to usurp traditional American sovereignty at the local, state, and national levels. In their belief in this conspiracy, militias are joined by the related "Patriot" groups, which collect, interpret, and disseminate political information and theories, but do not necessarily engage in paramilitary training. Patriots and militias foresee this "New World Order" as a multinational force run by a small elite, which will pacify the American public first through the confiscation of privately owned guns and then through the imposition of a global totalitarian state. The most important catalysts in the rise of the militias and Patriots were the FBI's fatal raids on the Branch Davidian compound in Waco, Texas, the shooting of members of the family of white separatist Randy Weaver in a standoff at Ruby Ridge in rural Idaho by federal law-enforcement agents, and the ban on some assault weapons (called the "Brady Bill") as part of the Omnibus Crime Bill of 1994. Individuals and groups associated with some militias have historical and organizational ties to the survivalist groups of the 1970s and 1980s, reflecting this heritage particularly in their desire to build a purified society protected by heavily armed forces in the hinterlands of middle America.[3] In addition, many militia members have former, or in some cases current, associations with the U.S. military as members of the armed forces, as well as through the purchase or theft of equipment from military bases.[4]

Militias and Patriots are not a singular national movement. There are quite important ideological, geographic, and religious distinctions among individuals and groups, and members differently engage in militias and the "movement" at national, regional, and local levels. Nationally, individual figures such as Bo Gritz and Linda Thompson have become nationally recognized "stars" through their reputation, speaking tours, and sheer force of will;[5] in addition, a few militias, such as the Michigan Militia (MM) and the Militia of Montana (MOM), have attained national prominence through size, media coverage, and self-marketing.[6] Regional alliances or contacts also exist among groups that meet at events such as gun shows. But it is at the local level that individual members tend to join a particular militia group and gather to converse about political and social issues, and, if the militia is so inclined, train in paramilitary techniques.[7]

Although virtually all Patriot and militia groups reject gun control and federal taxation, their views on other issues can vary. Most strongly oppose the legalization of abortion and other types of federal social legislation (e.g., most civil-rights protections), land-use regulation (e.g., environmental protections), educational programs (e.g., the federal Goals 2000 program, which was an important factor in the establishment of the Michigan Militia), and modern federal court decisions (e.g., *Roe v. Wade*).[8] Many, but not all, individuals and groups subscribe to various oppositional readings of the U.S. Constitution and legal system, including the declaration of "sovereign citizenship" and "freeman" status. Under these beliefs, militia members and Patriots respect only the authority of militia- and/or Patriot-run "common law courts" and assert that no constitutional amendments passed after the first ten are legal.[9] Some militia members and Patriots also are part of, or are sympathetic to, the county supremacy movement of the Posse Comitatus, which holds that government authority rests solely with the county and respects neither state nor federal laws and government. Members of the Posse engaged in violent acts against the federal government in the 1970s and 1980s.

Various types of religious apocalypticism play a central role in the way many, but not all, militia-related individuals and groups interpret contemporary political and social phenomena, although the precise articulation of this apocalypticism reflects different religious convictions.[10] The militias' religious diversity is further reflected in different geographic areas — the Mormons and Christian Identity members who are more likely to live in the Pacific Northwest and Intermountain West have different understandings of Scripture, not to mention different privileged biblical passages and distinct scriptures (such as the Book of Mormon), from Protestant fundamentalists living in the same region as well as those in the Midwest and Plains states. Some militias and groups may participate in survivalist stockpiling of weapons, supplies, and food. Finally, at the furthest end of the spectrum are individuals and groups who are overtly or covertly racist, anti-Semitic, and neo-Nazi.[11]

Sociologist James Aho provides a useful set of ideological and religious distinctions among far-right-wing groups. He separates their clusters of beliefs into three categories: the most radical are Identity Christians, who hold "Jews" (differently defined among groups of Identity believers, but most often understood simply as an ethnic category) responsible for all of America's problems; Christian Constitutionalists hold a less defined group of "insiders," "Bilderbergers," "Trilateralists," and the like responsible without reference to ethnicity or race; and Issue-oriented Patriots are concerned with specific social or political issues such as abortion and sex education, and are more likely to see themselves as fighting a relatively diffuse threat such as "secular humanism."[12] The divisions between groups are permeable, and groups and individuals can overlap or move back and forth between different categories. One could make even narrower distinctions within these three general rubrics, but Aho's categories are helpful in recognizing the important differences among groups and individuals who might seem from the outside to be virtually identical. For example, the John Birch Society, a long-lived group that would most likely fall within the Christian Constitutionalists category, has strongly distanced itself from violent and racist elements among Identity Christians. While supporting law-abiding militia groups, the official Birch monthly publication, the *New*

American, has asserted that the Ku Klux Klan's violent terrorism is not the proper method of fighting the conspiratorial elite that controls the federal government.[13] Membership in the Michigan Militia, which has been composed largely of Christian Constitutionalists from previously established political movements such as the religious right, Ross Perot supporters, and Libertarian Party members, dropped in the weeks following the media reports of connections between it and the alleged perpetrators of the Oklahoma City bombing.[14] As both a practical and a public-relations strategy, the organization turned to minority recruitment and educational and political action programs in order to distinguish itself from Identity Christian groups.[15]

Although the militias are decentralized and have limited membership and support, they have received implicit, and at times explicit, support from individual elected representatives and larger national lobbying groups. A few federal and state lawmakers, most notably U.S. Representative Helen Chenoweth (Republican, Idaho) and Republican state senator Charles Duke of Colorado, have sought support from militia and Patriot groups, often resulting in intra-party conflicts between far-right and more "moderately" conservative Republican members of Congress over the extent to which, for example, environmental regulations should be eviscerated or eradicated.[16] The National Rifle Association (NRA), the largest and most powerful lobbying organization devoted to political action for gun owners and against gun control, epitomizes this conflict between militias as extrapolitical paramilitary organizations and militias as American citizens attempting to change the country from within. To resolve the conflict, the NRA attempts to appropriate local and regional militia movements and their sympathizers without losing status in Washington as an institution that can approach and successfully persuade members of both the Republican and Democratic parties.[17] In this respect, the militias are not simply paramilitary extremists; they have become activists on the far right of an increasingly conservative Republican Party, and act as part of the political process and the ongoing struggle to define American right-wing politics.

Ultimately, although militia groups and individuals may share many political views, cultural and social backgrounds, and ideological convictions, there is no single militia movement. A number of generalizations can be made, however, about militias and Patriots. Most members are reactionary and subscribe to a theory of power that resembles conspiracy theory; most consider themselves to be politically active in some way — whether by studying or teaching about the "secret truths" of power, and fighting abortion or sex education in schools, or by lobbying local, state, and federal representatives; and most own guns and train themselves in their use.

With this snapshot of the militia movement, let us return to the Senate hearing room and Senator Specter's attempt to "ventilate" the militia movement on the country's behalf.

Greetings from Montana!
The Senator Takes on the Commander in the "Marketplace of Ideas"

The Senate subcommittee hearing on the militias was very odd, as the photograph on the front page of the next morning's *Washington Post* captured well. Here was Senator Specter, the senior lawmaker readying himself for a quixotic run as a tough but "moderate" candidate for the Republican presidential nomination, walking away from militia "Commander" Norman Olson after shaking hands. "Norm" had recently resigned his leadership position in the Michigan Militia after claiming that the Oklahoma City bombing might actually have been perpetrated by the Japanese government, as a response to what he alleged was the U.S. government's primary role in recent gas attacks in Tokyo's subway system. In the photo, each man is clothed in the costume that best suits his respective position: Specter wears the conventional dark suit of the veteran senator, whereas Olson wears a loose-fitting camouflage outfit that covers his large, well-disciplined military body from the top of his head to the tips of his black combat boots.

Whatever their differences, these serious, sincere men were both on hand to perform their jobs. Specter's duty was to warn the American public of the potential dangers that the extremist militias represent; Olson wished to warn the American public of the real dangers of the federal government and the secret powers behind it. Specter, the former prosecutor best remembered for devising the Warren Commission's "single-bullet theory" of the assassination of President John F. Kennedy and for his atrocious conduct during the Clarence Thomas–Anita Hill hearings, was trying to cast himself as the protector of the nation's laws and safety;[18] Olson, retired military man, gun-shop owner, Baptist minister, and national figure in the militia movement, was trying just as hard to present himself and his compatriots at the hearing as protectors of the nation's freedom.

If judged by who was able to give the best lines for the assembled television and print news media, Olson and his group probably won. Specter's expression in the *Post* photo, taken before the hearings, suggests why. Appearing either slightly amused or disgusted as he walked away from the more dignified, at ease Olson, Specter looks entirely unprepared for dealing with these folks from the hinterlands, who probably composed the most peculiar panel that his subcommittee had ever faced. Their theories are irrational, potentially dangerous, perhaps even a little funny — in short, they were not the kind of "experts" or constituents that a distinguished attorney and lawmaker who has argued before the U.S. Supreme Court and sat in judgment over numerous Supreme Court nominees is prepared to face, except perhaps as witnesses or suspects in a criminal trial that he may have prosecuted decades before.

Indeed, Specter and his subcommittee were criticized by antimilitia activists, who had been researching the militia movement and its predecessors for more than a decade, for their lack of preparation and for not including a panel with extensive knowledge of some of the shadier and more dangerous elements at work in some of the militias. Such a panel might have also included individuals and federal employees who had been harassed or assaulted by militia groups. Their testimony could have provided evidence that the militia movement is not the collection of innocent "neighborhood watch" and "community service" organizations that Olson and his fellow militia members claimed to be, and demonstrated that there are not only a few "bad apples" in militias, but that parts of the movement had been infiltrated by full-fledged white supremacists.[19]

Instead, the subcommittee's hearing was split into three panels, the first featuring two Democratic senators from the states with the most prominent militia groups, Montana and Michigan; the second composed of federal, state, and local law-enforcement officials; and the third, which drew the most attention in posthearing news coverage, made up of militia leaders themselves. The members of the subcommittee, however, did not seem nearly so interested in the hearing as the panelists, as the dais on which the senators sat remained mostly empty for the entire proceeding (there were rarely as many as four senators in attendance at any one time). Specter had informed panelists that congressional business was taking place at the same time on the Senate floor, and he made certain to end the meeting on time in order for the few senators left in the room to participate in a floor vote. Members' busy schedules, apathy, or strategic decisions not to attend may have caused the empty chairs, but whatever the reasons, this relatively poor attendance clearly undercut any significance the hearing might have had in terms of either official policy consideration or general information gathering. The evening network news shows generally ignored this fact, however, and used footage that focused on the few senators who were in attendance and their face-offs with the militia members, implying in their coverage that this hearing was indeed a momentous event with wide-ranging legislative ramifications.

Senators, Law Enforcement, and "Authority"

The first two panels focused on the dangers of the militias and possible strategies to contain them. They were not simply concerned with containment however. They also attempted to define, in very precise and celebratory ways, the acceptable forms of civic and political engagement; that is, their concern was not merely to condemn militias as dangerous, but to declare and renew the fundamental health of American democracy and justice. Senator Specter opened his remarks with a discussion of free speech and its limits. He and fellow subcommittee member Senator Herb Kohl (Democrat, Wisconsin) introduced the discussion with two of the great sound bites of twentieth-century constitutional law concerning freedom of expression: first, that the right to free speech can be limited only by a "clear and present danger"; and second, that these limits to free speech exist because, borrowing a phrase from a 1949 opinion by Supreme Court Justice Robert Jackson, the Constitution is not a "suicide pact" (2–3).[20] This is a civic lesson's survey on free speech, asserting a particular individual right while cautioning that this right may be abridged when it becomes necessary to balance it against the potential harm to the state or to other individuals that its exercise might cause. If the speech act is dangerous, then it cannot be protected as a right but is subject to censure and restraint. The liberties of classical liberalism's juridical notion of rights are thus coupled with, and indeed are dependent on, disciplinary controls delimiting proper and safe behavior.[21]

This was not the end of the subcommittee's exegesis of the law of speech acts, however. If the constitutional right to free speech is an integral part of the basic groundwork on which America's liberal democracy rests, Specter's other approach to the militias' speech compromises his notion of the social relations of civil society. For this, he supplemented "rights" to be protected and "threats" to be disciplined with assumptions about that amalgamation of classical liberalism and capitalism, associated with a famous dissent by Justice Oliver Wendell Holmes: the "marketplace of ideas."[22] In this "marketplace," everyone — even the militias — is allowed to speak his or her piece. Here, the right to speak becomes a right to be heard, to "sell" one's ideas in competition with those of others over the definition of "truth"; as Specter would tell the militia members facing him on their later panel, "What I want to do is I want to hear all your ideas because I want your ideas compared to mine and I want to let the American public judge whether you are right or I am right" (99). The state has no business in Specter's notion of the market, except perhaps to referee; in the marketplace, the most worthy and efficient will win out. The militias might be dangerous, but under the procedures and structures of a liberal capitalist regime, they can be part of the pluralist mix of opinion, so long as they obey the "rules" of the marketplace, as enunciated and adjudicated within the law.

The "market" is, of course, not free, just as the "right" to speak is not a transhistorical, absolute protection from limitations imposed by state prosecution, private property owners, and private and government-run media organizations. Subject to the disciplinary controls of capital and government, and the relations imposed by class, race, gender, and other social hierarchies, the "marketplace of ideas" depends on both "freedoms" of exchange and entrenched disciplinary controls. This is not to say that militias constitute an emancipatory challenge to such disciplinary controls, nor that they deserve an absolute right to speak; instead, what is significant in this context is that in the extensive liberties that Specter, as representative of the liberal democratic state, offered, the discourse and formal freedoms of rights and markets hide the powerful disciplinary controls that filter and channel a multiplicity of voices into a unified notion of responsible and legal speech acts within the pluralist consensus.

In his introductory remarks, Senator Kohl provided a more explicitly stern complement to Specter's seemingly magnanimous invitation to the Constitution and the marketplace. Kohl described a brief list of recent incidents in which highway patrol officers found large weapon stockpiles in militia members' cars, and more generally warned of the militias' "gospel of hate" (2–4). In the first panel, a few minutes later, Democratic Senators Carl Levin of Michigan and Max Baucus of Montana echoed Kohl's comments and warned of the militias' deep strain of anti-Semitism and racism. They also detailed further instances of alleged militia threats, violence, and stockpiling of weaponry (4–6, 44–46). The implication was clear: these dangerous people pose a threat to society, and law enforcement should not again be caught off guard — assuming that the Oklahoma City bomb was indeed perpetrated by militias — by gun nuts with secret arms caches. Specter's blithe introduction to liberal theories of democracy and capitalist theories of the marketplace was nice, these senators implied, but there are limits to the formal and procedural structure intended to protect individual rights and the social marketplace. Liberties, in short, must be policed in order to remain truly free. The senators thus established early on in the hearing that militias constitute an unknown, and perhaps unknowable, threat, and therefore require some form of surveillance and disciplinary control.

In concluding his introductory statement, Kohl invoked what he implied is the greatest, most sacred marketplace that America offers dissenters such as the militias: elections, those "tools of change" originally crafted by the Constitution's framers and embedded in that hallowed document (3–4). He cited as evidence the recent 1994 elections, in which his own party lost its long-standing majority in the House of Representatives, thereby leading to another in a succession of peaceful changes in the American governing party. Senator Levin would later explain that in addition to the ballot box, the other democratic instrument of change for dissenters is an independent judiciary, which is able to protect people from the dangers and excesses of government (45). These peaceful "tools" would be mentioned again in the law-enforcement panel, and represented, according to the first two panels, the best formal solution to the militias' pathologies. As with the abstract notions of "rights" and the "marketplace," the equally abstract ideal of the universal franchise in democratic elections provides both a rejoinder to the militias and a "healthy" outlet for their political passions. Whether the current structure of political parties and financing enables a truly democratic system and truly free exercise — the militias expend much of their energy asserting that it does not — was neither relevant nor contestable within the authoritative discourse of the Senate.

The four senators' opening of the hearing, then, established the following points: We do not know exactly what these militias are, but we think they are dangerous; the militias need to recognize that rational activism that works toward a moderate consensus through electoral processes is the correct path for a political movement; and although the militias have constitutional rights, they must face the stern hand of constitutional but necessary governmental action to enforce peaceful, law-abiding behavior. The central conflict is between clear, content-neutral forms, structures, and processes ("rights," "markets," "votes," "justice") that constitute American democracy and that protect the speech and acts of all Americans, and the opaque, threatening speech and acts of the militias.

The law-enforcement panel represented yet another aspect of the privileged American democracy: a disinterested, instrumental policing apparatus functioning under the orders of elected officials. The panel consisted of a number of federal, state, and local officials, yet although it is local law enforcement that has to deal with militias on a regular basis, the two representatives from federal agencies were the most important for three reasons. First, they were the only officials present whose performance the Congress has any authority to review directly, and thus their testimony was especially important for funding and policy purposes. Second, any new federal laws the Congress might pass to curtail the militias, such as stronger gun control or antiparamilitary regulations, would be enforced by these agencies. Third, these agencies had been heavily criticized by militias for their allegedly illegal actions in Waco and Ruby Ridge. Therefore, I will focus my attention on the testimony of the two federal agents, Robert M. Bryant, an assistant director in the National Security Division of the FBI, and James Brown of the Bureau of Alcohol, Tobacco and Firearms (BATF).

Both agents were striking in their apparent desire — presumably reflecting the desire of their agencies — to give the appearance of a cautious, restrained approach to policing the militias. Both men noted the attorney general's guidelines regulating "general crimes, racketeering enterprises, and domestic security/terrorism investigation," which require a "reasonable indication of criminal activity" before authorizing a federal agency's active response (49–50). Bryant stressed the guidelines' stipulation that the FBI needs an "objective, factual basis regarding criminal activity" before acting; although this protects the rights to privacy and free expression of those suspected of a crime, Bryant duly admitted that it made fighting "terrorism" a "difficult and complex endeavor" (50). Brown reiterated this with respect to the BATF, which, he asserted, does not initiate an investigation on any "belief" that unlawful activity is transpiring but on suspected and real violations of law (78). In the testimony of their agents, the FBI and the BATF seemed merely to be following the ground rules set by the post–Watergate-era Church and Pike Commissions, which exposed and called for limiting the excesses of both the FBI and the CIA. The impression that this testimony attempted to create was in direct opposition to the well-known images of federal agents storming the Branch Davidian compound in Waco, and especially to the same compound as it burned out of control less than two months later — the "jack-booted government thugs" that the National Rifle Association claimed the FBI and BATF to be.[23] Instead, the agencies were composed merely of responsible bureaucrats following the wishes and "tough" rules of elected representatives.

These spokesmen of two of the most powerful law-enforcement agencies in the country almost seemed to be competing with each other to proclaim their agencies' hesitancy to perform surveillance and police the militias. At least partially a response to criticism from the far right, this strategy was also an attempt to legitimate the agencies among opinion leaders and supporters who, while defending the FBI and BATF, had expressed reservations about the agencies' conduct in the recent tragedies. Further, the agencies were also attempting to preempt possible criticism from the Congress if either house should launch investigations and hearings on the two incidents (which the Senate Judiciary Committee did, later that summer). The agencies clearly wanted to establish that their work followed proper bureaucratic procedure. Unlike the violent, unknowable militias, the FBI and BATF followed reason and rules, and obeyed the chain of command of the governing structures of American lawmaking and law enforcement.

Whatever its purpose, the agents' testimony produced a response from the senators that was no doubt welcome at FBI and BATF headquarters, and further epitomized the odd qualities of this hearing. During the question-and-answer period, Senators Specter and Diane Feinstein (Democrat, California) repeatedly questioned all of the law-enforcement officers, but especially these two federal representatives, as to whether they had "sufficient authority" under current guidelines to conduct a thorough investigation in response to any specific or general threat a militia might pose (74–79). The senators' questions implied that the agencies faced too many limitations on their ability to perform surveillance and "proper" policing actions, and that for the good of the country the federal government should consider lifting these limits. Both Bryant and Brown avoided the question, but the prospect of greater authority for federal law enforcement had been put on the agenda despite — and perhaps even because of — the fact that the agencies themselves acted as though they did not want such authority. Ironically, these officers' description of their agencies' institutional restraint merely seemed to make the senators more determined to lift those restraints.

Because the senators had begun the hearing with reference to the disciplinary structures of the liberal democratic state, this exchange follows logically. Like the senators, the law-enforcement representatives had stressed formal bureaucratic rules and procedures, vowing to protect constitutional rights through responsible policing. Yet, as local and state law-enforcement officers reported, these militias were outside such a discursive construct: in Arizona, they were represented by a sixteen-year-old perpetrator of hate crimes; in Missouri, they killed innocent state troopers; in Montana, their violent threats paralyzed law enforcement. The only possible response to such pervasive threats within this discourse is through containment and "greater authority" for law enforcement — that is, through expanding the bureaucratic apparatus to allow it to perform surveillance against the militias, to inhibit or prohibit militia activities, and to provide the law-enforcement apparatus with enough authority and discretion to enforce the new laws. In short, the very discourse that required the law-enforcement officers to seem more restrained also required them to be given more authority.

It is not surprising, then, that the most important response from the federal government to the rise of the militias has been the Anti-Terrorism Act, originally introduced by President Clinton in 1995, shortly after the Oklahoma City bombing, and passed by both houses of Congress in April 1996.[24] Opposed by civil libertarian groups often associated with the left and gun owners' groups allied with the right, the bill widens federal law-enforcement power to authorize secretive "removal courts" to hear evidence in deportation proceedings, and to freeze the assets of anyone deemed to be an "agent" (which could include merely contributing money) of a group the government has designated a "foreign terrorist organization."[25] Further, it gives federal law enforcement greater discretion to initiate wiretaps and otherwise potentially invade the privacy of citizens suspected of engaging in "terrorist" activity. Although it was passed by Congress as a response to the Oklahoma City tragedy, most of the bill's provisions have little to do with the type of offense that the apprehended suspects of the crime allegedly perpetrated.[26] Nevertheless, it represents precisely the expansion of "authority" about which the senators seemed so eager to ask the federal law-enforcement agents during the militia hearing. Constructing the militia "movement" as an Other outside the legal and social apparatus of American society resulted in its members being labeled "terrorists" and subject to an expansion of disciplinary authority.

Militia Populism
"America" as "Conspiracy"

In terms of actual policy and lawmaking, the law-enforcement panel might have been the most significant in the hearing, but it was also the least telegenic, lacking the quasi-celebrity status of the senators on the subcommittee and, as would become apparent in the hearing itself and later on the evening news, lacking the sparks and sound bites of the militia leaders. The members of this third panel attempted to reclaim for themselves the very notion of America that the previous two panels had used to define the militias as an extremist Other. The militias' America, the panelists claimed, was also constructed on a foundation of abstract rights, social relationships, and normal and "healthy" behavior; and it was government and law-enforcement that represented the gravest threat to the nation and its citizens. At the same time, however, they attempted to challenge the limits of the bureaucratic discourse of authority presented by the senators and law-enforcement agents who had testified earlier. At different moments, then, the militia members would invoke certain inalienable rights (free speech, gun ownership) and claim that the corruption of political power (that is, elected representatives, the judiciary, and the police) had led to the illegal curtailment of those rights and threatened the safety and sanctity of the nation. In this effort to challenge both the official description of their activities and beliefs, and the previous panels' prescriptive remedies to stop them, the militia panelists attempted to rearticulate the American ideal of political practice to the practices of conspiracy theory.

There were five members on this panel: two associated with the Militia of Montana, two with the Michigan Militia, and James Johnson of the Ohio Unorganized Militia, the only African-American participant in the entire hearing.[27] First to speak was John Trochmann, the leader of the Militia of Montana, dressed in coat and tie and sporting the well-brushed, bushy beard that endeared him to news photographers and reporters as the stereotypical backwoods biblical patriarch. Trochmann quickly read a prepared statement that offered an image of the militias directly counter to that put forth by the other panels. Trochmann claimed that the militias are defensive, quasi-fraternal organizations dedicated to protecting Americans, a "giant neighborhood watch," representing a "cross-section of America," acting with a "singular, public mandate," following the dictates of the virtually sacred Declaration of Independence (83).

The spatial references that Trochmann used are especially interesting, given the militias' fetishization of the local as a sovereign entity under attack. Because the militias show great concern with national and international geopolitics (in their conspiracy theories, "international" bankers and the United Nations are all-powerful bugaboos), the "neighborhood" must refer not only to locality but also to the United States as a sovereign nation, thus defining the local in its relationship to powerful nonlocal forces. Hence the importance of the "cross-section" of America: In order to fight the current infringement of local sovereignty and even greater, future threats to personal freedom, militias must band together with other people in other localities. Once the corrupt federal government is finally cleansed, the local will thrive under the minimal authority of the nation. To "watch" this "neighborhood" requires more than simply sitting on one's front porch and confronting suspicious strangers; it requires gathering information and creating paramilitary/vigilante organizations to patrol, protect, and cleanse.

Trochmann then proceeded to list the reasons why the militias had formed and grown, and why the "neighborhood" needed watching. The list included allegations that under President Clinton, and specifically through his use of executive orders, the position of chief executive had assumed dictatorial, oppressive powers; state and local sovereignty is under threat from the federal government and the United Nations; federal taxation is unconstitutional and illegal; the country is actually run by a "banking elite" and not through democratically elected representatives; and so on (84). He, and other panelists who followed, thus provided the typical militia mixture of libertarian views and conspiracy theories about power (and Bob Fletcher of the Militia of Montana and Norm Olson would each later offer copious documents to prove similar allegations, including "six pounds of evidence of corruption in government"). Yet, Trochmann also displayed concern for the unemployed and homeless, as well as with the fate of constitutional protections for the right to bear arms (under the Second Amendment), protections against illegal search and seizure (under the Fourth Amendment), and rights of free speech and peaceful assembly (under the First Amendment).

Other than the expected militia invocation of the Second Amendment, these concerns for the poor and the Constitution have traditionally been associated with leftist civil libertarian and progressive causes. Discussion of them seemed out of place on the Capitol Hill of the 104th Congress, dominated as it was by representatives from both parties requesting federal agencies to be "tougher" on "terrorism," suspected criminals, regulations on industry and the economy, welfare "cheats," and the poor generally. Structural economic shifts, income disparity, abuses of law enforcement — such issues were not discussed in the two previous panels, which enabled Trochmann to position himself and the militias as sole champions of the downtrodden. Eschewing the bureaucratic discourse of law enforcement and governance, Trochmann attempted to speak to and for those who can gain no purchase within those discourses of power, for whom rules of engagement, the delicate balance between free speech and societal suicide, and the bureaucratic structure of the federal government and administrative agencies have little relevance.

This is not to say that either Trochmann or his fellow militia leaders are the least bit progressive, or even especially libertarian on any issues except gun control and certain types of federal regulations. Although Trochmann's ties to Christian Identity groups and the racist right are the subject of some debate, he has made visits to Identity compounds and associated with the group in the past.[28] At the very least, Trochmann is what James Aho terms a "Christian Constitutionalist" and a reactionary on most issues who endorses a patriarchal and heavily regulated social sphere alongside a radically decentralized government. Further, neither in his presentation at the Senate hearing nor in militia literature has he offered any proposal of a regulatory regime that he thinks would lessen the powers of the "banking elite" and multinational corporations. It seems safe to assume that any economic program that he and other militia members would endorse would at least resemble Patrick Buchanan's xenophobic protectionism. It is significant, nonetheless, that Trochmann was the only speaker at the hearing willing to articulate real social problems, even if he articulated them within a litany of unsubstantiated and unlikely claims about a looming totalitarian coup from within.

None of the other panel members' opening statements had quite the same impact as Trochmann's, except for that of James Johnson of Columbus, Ohio, who claimed affiliations with the Ohio Unorganized Militia and with his own organization, E Pluribus Unum. Although an anomaly, this African-American militia member is not unique; among militias in Arizona, for example, one reporter found a "small rainbow coalition" of blacks, Hispanics, and Jews.[29] As an African-American male, Johnson not only could claim to disprove by his very existence that the militias were racist, but he could also disprove to opponents that militia members are simply spoiled white males reacting irrationally to a loss of their position of privilege. When he complained along with his fellow panelists of "animosity" between citizens and their oppressive government and of suspicion of a mass media biased against him, he was much more difficult to refute than were John Trochmann and Norm Olson.

Later in the hearing, Johnson responded to a senator's question with a series of broadcast news-friendly slogans that referenced a wide range of recent events and protest movements from American history. The militia movement, Johnson said, is "the civil rights movement of the nineties. There are people sitting there with 'Don't tread on me' stamped on their foreheads. People drawing lines in the sand.... We're not baby killers, we're baby boomers. We're not terrorists, we're taxpayers." Ultimately, he said, the militia movement represents and is for "everybody," and is their "constitutional safety net" (103).

The references in this passage compose an astounding pastiche of American cultural and historical images pasted together in quick succession. The civil-rights reference at once resonates with the speaker's race and attempts to refute charges of racism. The notion of a "constitutional safety net" employs an image used to describe federal government "social" programs such as un-

employment insurance, Social Security, Medicare/Medicaid, and various welfare entitlements. Presumably, just as these programs would rescue individuals in economic distress, so the militias rescue individuals and the nation as a
whole from those forces seeking to abridge rights granted in the Constitution.
Johnson's set of dualities (baby killer/baby boomer, terrorist/taxpayer) makes
similar reference to precedent and politics. "Baby killers" refers most clearly
to the casualties in the Oklahoma City bombing, which included children in a
day-care center in the Alfred P. Murrah Federal Building; to contrast that image
with "baby boomers" is to transform militias into a lifestyle choice of a demographic group. The same is true for the next set of dualities, which literally attempts to transform the image of militias as "terrorists" — rare, extreme, dangerous — into the banal, a class ("taxpayers") into which virtually all American
adults fall. But the latter duality goes further, not simply rearticulating militias into the realm of the "normal," but rearticulating the "normal" into militias. Because one of the central tenets of Patriot and militia groups is resistance to "big government" and excessive taxes, Johnson invokes "taxpayer"
not only to mean "normal" but also to mean unhappy and resistant — we all
pay taxes, but we all hate paying taxes, and militias, by implication, are at the
forefront of those who are unhappy about paying taxes and are trying to do
something about it.

This subtle but crucial rearticulation of "baby boomers" and taxpayers in
general to the protests of militias is even clearer in the references to both the
earliest and the most recent American military victories. "Don't tread on me"
is a well-known slogan from the American Revolution, and the flag with which
it is associated, featuring a curled viper snake under the words, has become a
symbol for some militias.[30] The phrase "lines in the sand" also refers to an
American war, President George Bush's attempt to legitimate the Persian Gulf
War ("Desert Storm") by asserting that Iraqi leader Saddam Hussein had crossed
a hypothetical line in the desert, provoking war through an act of aggression.[31]
Ironically, many militia groups are at least skeptical about Bush's motives in
waging that war and consider it as simply a subterfuge in the larger consolida-
tion of global power by a secret elite. During a speech to a joint session of
Congress just prior to the war's beginning, Bush had outlined his vision of a
"New World Order" that most militia groups and individuals consider anathema,
and many conspiracy theories to which militias subscribe cite this speech as a

significant moment in the rise of a secret global power. As Mark ("Mark from Michigan") Koernke says in his widely circulated videotape *America in Peril,* "The primary mission of Operation Desert Dust, or what we call Desert Storm, was to see if the American people would eat the New World Order."

Of course, as with Trochmann's claim for the normalcy of the militias, Johnson's rhetoric is hollow and false. The civil-rights movement confronted and opposed the real, palpable oppression of segregation and racism, predominantly through nonviolent means, not by conducting paramilitary training. Further, the civil-rights movement called for and required the assistance of the federal government and judiciary in breaking local and state government institutions that legalized and enforced racism and segregation. In this sense, the basis of the militia movement's political beliefs — that the powers of the federal government and judiciary must be extremely limited, and that states and especially municipal and county governments should hold basic, but also limited, governing authority — is diametrically opposed to that of the civil-rights movement of the 1960s. Similarly, federal programs that make up the "safety net" for the poor (under attack by Republicans and most Democrats) would probably be eradicated in militias' vision of a limited government. This strained relationship between the militias and past and current American political movements and programs infuses all of the images Johnson attempted to appropriate. Although militia memberships undoubtedly include "baby boomers" and taxpayers (except, of course, for those such as the Freemen who refuse to pay their taxes), militias' beliefs and behavior in no way define such larger categories. "Don't tread on me" is a sentiment that many Americans undoubtedly share, but most would be unwilling to have it stamped on their foreheads.[32]

At the end of the testimony, Ken Adams of the Michigan Militia adopted Senator Specter's initial comments concerning the hearing's role as augmenting the "marketplace of ideas" and enabling the militia threat to be ventilated and dissipate, but instead implied that the hearing's result was to elevate the militias to a status equal to that of the Congress. "You have heard a lot of allegations from people here today," Adams said. "Maybe they're real, maybe they're not. If they're real, then let's expose them. If they are not, then let's expose them, and that is why I think this is a healthy forum that we have here today because we have started some communication" (106). To the extent that the militia members could challenge prevailing governmental, law-enforcement, and media depictions of their movement as inherently pathological, the militia panel was successful in their attempt to present themselves as "normal"; however, to the extent that they continued to appear a bit nutty (claims of "six pounds" of evidence of such treachery and danger as Russian tanks running wild on American soil; allegations of conspiracy made both to and about the relatively normal-looking senators sitting before them; conflicts between claims of historical connections to the civil-rights movement and the desire for a minimalist federal government), the militia members merely demonstrated the deep contradictions and limitations of their political protest. The senators, speaking from within the discourses of classical liberalism and pluralist consensus, could neither communicate with nor suggest more than disciplinary solutions to the challenge of the militia movement, but the militias themselves were able at least to attempt to rearticulate liberalism and consensus within a politics based on conspiracy theory.

Weathering the Imminent Storm
Mainstream Activists Take on the Militias

Although covering the militias has become, at least in the wake of Waco, Ruby Ridge, and Oklahoma City, something of a growth industry, a number of activists and organizations have been tracking the militias and their far-right predecessors for years. Two well-publicized books that are the product of such work are Kenneth Stern's *A Force upon the Plains* and Morris Dees's *The Gathering Storm*,[33] both of which warn of the imminent danger of the militias to American citizens and American democracy. Given their respective positions—Dees is chief trial counsel for the Southern Poverty Law Center (SPLC) and is best known for his successful civil suits against the Ku Klux Klan;[34] Stern is the American Jewish Committee's (AJC) expert on hate and hate groups—and their important role in describing militias to the mainstream media, policymakers, and potential donors to the charitable institutions for which they work, these books are significant attempts to put forth a working explanation of the phenomenon.

Their authorial voices are quite different from the scholarly tone of Richard Hofstadter's work: they not merely discuss—in Stern's case at some length and with extensive documentation — the development of what they perceive to be a very alarming social movement, but they prophesy a violent political apocalypse that requires immediate and forceful response, and they provide specific policy initiatives and community responses that can help the country avert the approaching peril. Their work is neither academic nor bound by the disciplinary conventions of political science and history, although both authors share many of the same assumptions about the pathological dangers of the margins to the militia movement that were developed in those disciplines, even though their work is more activist in its approach and aims.

The two books share a structuring narrative, beginning with the Alfred P. Murrah Federal Building bombing in Oklahoma City, moving backwards at least to the radical racist right of the 1980s (with brief stops in the history of the Klan and similar organizations), through the events of Ruby Ridge, Waco, and the Brady Bill, to the current, post–Oklahoma City period, and folding out toward a hazy and troubling future. It is a powerful narrative, evoking people and incidents that dominated the media for short but intense periods of time. Importantly, each author places himself within the story, not only describing where he was when he heard news of the fertilizer bomb, but demonstrating his special position with respect to the narrative's development: Dees as a successful activist lawyer with strong community ties and informed sources that led him to recognize, long before April 1995, that there was a "gathering storm"; and Stern, an activist researcher who had first heard of the militias in 1994 and who had been collecting information on them ever since. Indeed, both repeatedly quote from documents they had written warning of the probability of a militia-related terrorist attack before the bomb exploded: Dees wrote a letter to Attorney General Janet Reno in October 1994 (which he mentions five times throughout his book);[35] Stern notes in his book's Foreword that an AJC report he published in early April 1995, *Militias: A Growing Danger,* had predicted that "people connected with militias were posed to attack government officials, possibly on April 19, 1995, the second anniversary of the fiery end of the Branch Davidian compound in Waco."[36] As experts with personal histories and stakes in the militias, then, Dees and Stern present themselves as uniquely qualified to decipher the militias' actions, belief systems, and dangers.

The two books' titles and dust jackets clearly establish a shared framework for understanding the militias. These elements, which constitute the clearest evidence of how books are conceived of and marketed by their major publishing houses, organize potential buyers' and reviewers' first impressions of these timely accounts of major recent news events.[37] The very metaphors at work in their titles suggest a superhuman power, emanating either from nature (a storm) or from some unknown source (a force), that threatens the very structure of nation, community, and home. The hardcover dust jackets show truncated pictures of threatening white men: for Dees's book a masked, assault weapon-wielding figure in the foreground with a similar paramilitary figure wearing a gas mask in the background; for Stern's book, a blurry close-up of part of a white man's face whose mouth is open in a shout.

Reflecting the more explicit threat captured in its cover photo, Dees's account is the more straightforward and uncomplicated explanation of the militia danger. Written in a breathtaking style, citing far fewer sources and statistics than Stern's book, and focusing narrowly on the movement's alleged leaders, *The Gathering Storm* is simple in much the way that conspiracies are "simple," describing the militias as largely the product of the shadowy, sinister forces of violent white supremacists. The very first scene is an account of what Dees asserts is the origin of the militias, a meeting in Colorado presided over by Texas Klan leader Louis Beam. Beam is best known for his advocacy of "leaderless cells," small, autonomous groups of warriors striking out on their own and who, if caught, would be unable to provide information about group structures or leaders. Dees asserts that at this conference, attended by 150 white supremacists, "plans were laid for a citizens' militia movement like none this country has known."[38] The event's significance is that afterward,

> the movement changed from a disparate, fragmented group of pesky — and at times dangerous — gadflies to a serious, armed political challenge to the state itself.... During that weekend in the Rockies, a network of militant anti-government zealots was created. Alliances were formed from diverse factions: Identity, Posse Comitatus, the Klan, Aryan Nations, reconstructionists and other fundamentalist Christians, Neo-Nazis tax resisters, Second Amendment advocates, and anti-abortion extremists.[39]

Since that time, although "not every individual militia unit established had racist ties," and although many who joined may have been wishing to express their sincere frustration and patriotism, the militias have been controlled by these shadowy, murdering racists. The simile Dees uses to describe this relationship is illustrative of his homespun, commonsensical, explanatory tone: "Much like a tick buried in the thick hair on a dog's neck, [Louis] Beam, [Christian Identity leader Pete] Peters, and the others had embedded themselves into the militia movement and had helped set its agenda."[40] Yet, his account of this relationship is not altogether persuasive; the only evidence of the extreme racist right's hidden power over the militias that he cites as support, which comes from his own organization, is that of the 441 militia and 368 Patriot groups that existed between 1994 and 1996, 137 had ties to the racist right — less than 17 percent of all of these groups, even if one accepts Dees's figures.[41]

Dees considers individual militia members to be in thrall to these shadowy leaders. In one of the most interesting passages of the book, he outlines a possible defense strategy for Timothy McVeigh that illustrates this well. Dees suggests that the alleged bomber's legal team admit their client's guilt and focus on presenting mitigating circumstances that might avert the death penalty. These mitigating circumstances would be precisely the theory of the militias that Dees espouses: that a few shadowy figures, most notably white supremacist William Pierce (author of *The Turner Diaries,* a violent, apocalyptic adventure novel about a near-future race war), are the real perpetrators of the bombing because of their creation of McVeigh's twisted sense of patriotism. Like so many of his fellow patriots and militia members, McVeigh had been hypnotized into the sick world of race war. For Dees, the high-profile McVeigh trial could best expose these secret forces and enable the American public to understand the power that the gathering storm has over the vulnerable populace. (In June 1997, McVeigh was found guilty of planting the Oklahoma City bomb and was sentenced to die.)

Similarly, Stern begins his book by describing the militias as pathological contagion, summarizing his pre–Oklahoma City bombing report for the AJC in this way:

> If an individual went into a psychiatrist's office saying that
> he believed in black helicopters, that evil forces were chang-
> ing the weather to harass him, that foreign troops were com-

ing to take him away to a concentration camp, the doctor would diagnose the patient as clinically paranoid and prescribe treatment. The report warned that Americans could not ignore this same disease in the body politic: It was contagious, and those infected were well-armed.[42]

Unlike Dees's simpler conception of a shadowy, gathering storm, however, Stern presents this "infection" as a multistep process that does not necessarily lead all militia members to become the equivalent of Klan members. Instead, throughout the book, Stern organizes his discussion of the relationship between supremacists and militias around the metaphor of a funnel: First, the militias draw people in by using real political issues that concern those vulnerable to the militias' siren song, such as gun control and the environment. From there, a smaller number of the new recruits are moved toward what Stern terms a particular "ideology," opposition to what militias view as the "oppressive" federal government. The next step, to which fewer will be susceptible, is indoctrination into a belief system based on understanding power and world events as a global, possibly satanic conspiracy. Stern argues that it is simply a small jump from conspiracy theory to virulent anti-Semitism—the real basis for the militias' antigovernment sentiments, which simply recasts and hides the Protocols of the Elders of Zion within secular politics.[43] Finally, at the "narrowest end of the funnel, [the militias have] drawn in the hard core, where you get someone like Timothy McVeigh popping out.... The bigger the front end of the funnel is, the bigger the number that get to the core."[44] The indoctrination that moves recruits through the funnel takes place through the sharing and selling of massive "documentation," including books and videotapes, which makes a novice militia member reconsider and question all that s/he knows about power and politics—a step that constitutes "the first leap of faith toward political delusion."[45] Stern suggests that, like a tornado moving across Middle America, this funnel sucks in the innocent, turning them into part of a growing, violent, almost inhuman force.

Both books end with strong suggestions about how to curb this movement, focusing on efforts to stop the funnel/gathering storm. As in the Senate subcommittee hearing, Dees and Stern point to electoral politics as one of the most important solutions; Dees, for example, explicitly endorses the ballot box as the key to political change, asserting that "true patriots are in voting lines, not militia columns, doing their part to ensure the continuation of our democratic way of life."[46] On the one hand is a body politic dangerously vulnerable to infection and the slippery slope of fascism or "anarchy"; on the other is a robust body politic able to make ethical and pragmatic choices and affect change through the "marketplace" of electoral politics. Both authors, however, describe significant sectors of the American electorate as being so much a part of or vulnerable to the infection of extremism that this solution seems dubious at best. If the militias, and therefore white supremacists and other violent extremists, are having such success at recruiting eligible voters, then the militias as Stern and Dees describe them might be expected either to have great success in electoral politics or to have enough paramilitary might to render electoral politics moot. Either way, the "storm" takes over, the "force" sweeps over and beyond the plains, and Commander Doe ends up in charge.

This conflict between the rational politics of electoral, representative democracy and the irrational politics of the militias is especially difficult for Stern to resolve. He describes the crisis situation as analogous to Germany between the world wars, the American South during the heights of Klan violence and lynchings, and warlord-torn Somalia. Militia-related political goals such as states' rights and county supremacy are not about honest, rational politics, but are a cover for bigotry and a movement toward fifty lawless, warring individual states that do not protect basic human rights equally and for all. He uses this stark vision to describe the general tendency in "grassroots America," where the militias threaten, intimidate, and find support.[47]

In order to combat this crisis, Stern seems confident that those politicians who either explicitly or implicitly support the militias and political extremism will have bloodstained hands, when the militias become increasingly violent, and face angry constituents who vote them out of office.[48] Yet Stern, like Dees, is not entirely pleased with the results of electoral politics. Dees is more critical of Speaker of the House of Representatives Newt Gingrich and the Republican majority of the 104th Congress, whose success he traces back to and equates with George Wallace's 1968 presidential campaign and whom he condemns for helping to create "a climate and culture in which invective and irresponsible rhetoric is [sic] routinely used to demonize an opponent, legitimize insensitive stereotypes, and promote prejudice,"[49] whereas Stern condemns politicians in general and conservative Republicans in particular for "weighing political considerations" over condemning or holding hearings on militias after the Oklahoma City bombing.[50] Further, Stern spends an entire chapter on those elected politicians who serve as "poster children" for the militias, such as U.S. Representatives Helen Chenoweth (Idaho) and Steve Stockman (Texas), and Charles Duke, state senator from Colorado.[51] In the case of these elected representatives, the electoral process has not worked as a neutral, rational procedure that blunts the effects of the extremist margins; it is the very process by which the margins have come to the centers of power. Electoral politics may prove to be as vulnerable to the powerful forces driving the rise of the militias as the electorate that has been so easily conned into the funnel.

In addition to the ballot box, a second type of solution these authors propose focuses on the criminalization of paramilitary activity and heightened surveillance and policing actions against the militias. Both books include in appendices model statutes outlawing the kinds of military exercises for which the militias are best known. Further, both encourage granting the FBI increased authority to infiltrate groups (provided there is "a reasonable suspicion that the targets are violating or are about to violate federal law"), to gather intelligence on the Internet, and to open files and collect public information on militias who are obeying all applicable laws.[52] Dees and Stern both call for state and federal legislators and law enforcement to declare a low-intensity war on the militias through the enforcement of existing laws and the passing of new, militia-specific statutes.[53]

In particular, Dees endorses what became the Anti-Terrorism Act, although he is hesitant to call for a "complete overhaul" of the attorney general's "Guidelines concerning Domestic Security/Terrorist Activities" because of possible infringement of First Amendment rights to free speech and peaceable assembly.[54] Stern does not deal with specific legislation, though he does argue at length for more empowered federal agencies to fight the militias, asserting that even if increased surveillance, capture, and prosecution of paramilitary militias produce some violence and tragic consequences, "to do nothing would be worse."[55] By portraying the militias as a grave threat and a powerful force, both authors can conclude that only the most vigorous response by the federal government can neutralize them. In balancing possible civil-liberties infringe-ment with the need to counter this superhuman force, civil liberties may have to be sacrificed to some degree; as Dees notes in an insipid analogy borrowed from President Clinton, people were initially opposed to the small nuisance of metal detectors at airports, and now accept them as minor inconveniences for the greater good of safety.[56]

Stern calls for an academic response to the militias and the hate groups with whom he equates the militias. He wants a new discipline, "an overarch-ing intellectual framework" for "a field of study of hate" that would bring to-gether the strands of political science, literature, sociology, history, anthropol-ogy, and other disciplines that have dealt with issues related to "hate." This field would develop "theories and a vocabulary and case studies to show what increases or diminishes hate inside and outside of politics, and why."[57] Although admirable, Stern's benign, utilitarian vision of and confidence in the social sciences as the path to a cure for what he sees as a functional "outbreak" of "hate" seems misguided at best, and again implicitly relies on Hofstadter's and pluralism's notion of the pathologies of "extremist" politics. Stern as-sumes that "hate" and irrational politics are merely pathological responses to certain conditions that can be treated or contained through changed condi-tions and appeals to logic.

Dees and Stern present, in only slightly different ways, the center's fear of a violent, irrational margin. Yet these are practical, accessible books that at-tempt to provide some tools — "rational" electoral politics within the two-party system, passage and enforcement of the Anti-Terrorism Act, and a new field of social-scientific experts — for containing an extremist threat to American society. If these are the proposed solutions to the presumed irrational and su-perhuman force of the militias, then they seem flawed and desperate at best, given the degree of the American electorate's discontent with the two major parties, the dismaying provisions and misdirected nature of the Anti-Terror-ism Act, and the long history of failed instrumental attempts in the United States to solve social problems through the work of social scientists. Stern and Dees present the militia threat as so basic, pervasive, and dangerous that these measures seem feeble by comparison. From this perspective, their por-trait of the militia "storm" or "force" begins to take on the characteristics of the "paranoia" of the margins, and the hard-won consent of a previous era seems vulnerable to its inability to contain its Other.

The disciplinary authorities represented in the Senate hearing and the written accounts of the activist researchers share many of the same assumptions about why and how conspiracy theories are created, circulated, and affect the behavior of militia members. In addition to this overlap in description of the militia threat, they also share a firm belief in the remedy: stronger legislation and stricter law enforcement. Central to their analyses is the presupposition not only that there is something wrong with these militias—that they are ideological at best and composed of hypnotized victims at worst, for instance, or that their beliefs stem from resentment at economic displacement—but that there is something inherently pathological about them, and that because of the danger they embody, they require disciplinary surveillance and suppression as well as the curtailment of their otherwise inalienable "rights" to speak and engage in social relations.

I do not argue that this approach is inherently wrong, or that these rights are or should be inalienable and absolute, or that militias do not threaten anyone. Instead, my argument is that this discourse structures communication and relations in such a way that the farce of the Senate hearing and the tragedy of Waco are equally likely results of interactions between a self-described "healthy" disciplinary apparatus and a "pathological" ideological challenge posed by armed conspiracy theorists. Works on the disciplinary response of law enforcement to confrontations against MOVE in Philadelphia and the Branch Davidians in Waco have cogently argued that when confronting a group recognized only as a pathological Other, federal, state, and municipal officials are predisposed to formulate strategies that seek to impose (often martial) order. Robin Wagner-Pacifici argues, for example, that when faced with a "discursive breakdown" in which discourse "reaches some limit (acknowledged or unacknowledged) in appropriating the world representationally," such strategies lead both sides either to silence or increasingly belligerent and uncommunicative contact—which in turn can lead more easily to complete withdrawal and violence.[58] The Senate hearings and some antimilitia activists, in tying the pathology metaphor and the assumptions it makes about the political self and the extremist Other to formal legal doctrines and bureaucratic order, fail to conceptualize adequately the complex populist challenge of militias. Their arguments may lead merely to the militarization of confrontation between a more empowered state disciplinary machinery and marginal, well-armed groups whose very fears would thereby be realized.

3. Conspiracy Theory and Populism

Richard Hofstadter's notion of conspiracy theory as pathological politics remains not merely influential but dominant both in mainstream discourse and as an element in progressive political approaches to contemporary populism. As noted earlier, Hofstadter assumes a "consensus" among the public as to the "common sense" of political process and substance, and a "pluralist" politics of free elections between two national parties that represent the competing interests of the voting public; he would dismiss as pathological any radical challenge (from conspiracy theories to the New Left) asserting that elections are not "free," that consensus is neither broad nor publicly created, and that American politics is not open to wide sectors of the American plurality. This is not to say that Hofstadter was entirely wrong, nor that the analysis of conspiracy theory can only advance by "purging" elements of "pathology" from our conceptualization. Instead, this chapter will assert that recognizing the limitations and results of an approach that employs simplistic social-psychological frameworks within the assumptions of pluralism and consensus history enables a theoretical and political project that can better confront, and possibly rearticulate elements of, a populist discourse such as conspiracy theory as a political and cultural practice.

The chapter begins with a discussion of contemporary progressive approaches to conspiracy theory to the left of that represented by Dees and Stern, and takes that discussion as a starting point for considering what a more complex, radical approach to contemporary populism would entail. The progressive critique described differs in important ways from Hofstadter, especially in its oppositional stance to the American "consensus" that Hofstadter seeks to uphold. Yet progressives typically retain Hofstadter's problematic assumptions about the political pathology of populism.

Before turning to the progressive approach, I want to situate my analysis within a framework initially developed by Michael Rogin for conceptualizing historical accounts of "political demonology." Rogin contrasts what he calls a "symbolist" approach to populism, exemplified by Hofstadter's notion of "political paranoia," with a more politicized "realist" approach.[1] The "realist" considers the labeling and creation of fear about conspiratorial demons to be a purposive, instrumental tool of power; "realism," in this sense, refers to the historian's analysis of the manifest content and motives of the countersubversive. Rogin includes within this term critical and leftist historians ranging from progressives such as Charles A. Beard to New Leftists who focused their analysis on empirical evidence of manipulation by elite groups attempting to use fears in order to achieve their political goals.[2] For example, a realist analysis of Cold War anticommunist movements would study their effects and would focus on the expanded powers of the state to "fight" and, in reality, repress real and imagined communists and leftist movements of all types. The FBI's COINTELPRO, a program that carried out surveillance and disruption of antiwar, civil rights, and New Left groups during the 1960s and early 1970s, is one of the best-documented examples that realists would identify of the destructive and antidemocratic work of countersubversives.[3]

In emphasizing the rational basis of fears of conspiracy, realists consider those groups or individuals that seek to "expose" the secret machinations of subversive groups to be motivated by a desire to gain power and prestige through the very public process of exposition. For realists, countersubversives seek to impose or defend the imposition of repression through reference to external or internal threats, and do so, ultimately, to serve the purposes of capitalism, the state, powerful institutions, and/or ruling classes. Such countersubversion is created at the center of power, in political and economic elites, and is imposed on groups on the periphery, such as racial and ethnic minorities and the working class. Realists' implicit and explicit theories of the uses of conspiracy assume an instrumental politics in which political "paranoia" serves as an ideological mechanism with which certain groups knowingly repress others. The threatening imagery employed by countersubversive groups—of secret foreigners and hidden, seditious forces that threaten an innocent culture and society—

thus has both a purpose (political repression) and a referent (group to be repressed). A realist analysis ends with the identification and explanation of purpose and referent, and has little interest in the use and significance of specific types of symbols in popular political discourse.

The "symbolist" approach, epitomized by Hofstadter's work, characterizes the same phenomena of countersubversive expressions and activities as symptoms, in mythological and symbolic form, of the pathologies of peripheral groups. Indeed, the very term that Rogin uses to describe this approach — "symbolist" — denotes the practice by "symbolist" historians and analysts of "deeper" readings of the cultural and psychological causes for conspiracy theories. For example, Hofstadter's analysis of McCarthyism, while strongly critical of most of the Wisconsin senator's methods and assertions, is less concerned with virulent anticommunism's effects than with its "root causes" in the social psychology of the masses and in the expressive fight for status between the nativist provinces and the cosmopolitan, rational, and enlightened centers of power. Symbolists argue, then, that neither purpose nor referent is what it seems, and the mere identification of a singular purpose and presumably clear referent of conspiracy theory ignores the telling use of certain types of symbols as well as the pathological anxiety from which these symbols arise.

This contrast between symbolists and realists is in part based on the very different types of groups and individuals that the symbolists recognize and study as countersubversives. Symbolists' studies are of peripheral groups attacking the center: dispossessed classes in decline, groups and individuals fearing the erosion of status, power, and money, and rising classes and groups seeking to secure or improve their status. All of these groups share a common desire to mobilize "outsiders" and "extremists" against the state through their use of symptomatically demonological symbols and rhetoric. Rather than the realists' more "simplistic" concern with how things "appear," symbolists are interested in the "deeper" historical significance of "appearances"; rather than finding and rebuking instruments of power and political repression, in other words, they seek social and psychological symptoms and causes of "paranoia" and resentment.

There are, then, two central distinctions between realists and symbolists. First, they identify different types of countersubversion: for symbolists, countersubversives are largely populist movements against the center; for realists, they are representative of the repression of the periphery by powerful centers of power through the manipulation of fear and prejudice. Second, they focus on distinct domains and employ different methods of analysis: realists attempt to detect the instrumental motives of the centers of power, while symbolists diagnose cultural and psychological symptoms of illness. In addition, these two very different ways of viewing the significance and evidence of counter-subversion and fears of conspiracy have their basis in very different political commitments: realists tend to be activist, and, particularly in their contemporary leftist articulation, radical, while symbolists tend to be more supportive of dominant, mainstream political structures and policies, and are more likely to represent relatively centrist affiliations and an avowedly "apolitical" approach.

Contemporary Realists and the "Seduction" of Conspiracy

The Progressive Critique

An important, vibrant "realist" critique and fear of conspiracy theory has been articulated from the contemporary progressive left. Similar in some ways to Hofstadter's symbolist approach, this analysis fears the seduction of the left, and of the public in general, by simplistic and potentially dangerous pursuits that would distract progressives and potential sympathizers from more substantive investigations and condemnations of dominant American political and economic power. This critique has arisen at least in part because some elements of the left either dabble in conspiracy theory or find themselves labeled conspiracy theorists by the mainstream media. An instance of the latter was the description within conservative and some mainstream periodicals of Oliver Stone's "solution" to the Kennedy assassination mystery in his film *JFK*—that an alliance of the political, intelligence, military, and corporate elite combined to kill Kennedy—as an example of leftist conspiracy theory, largely because the perpetrators that the film identified were individuals and institutions that the antiwar movement, the New Left, and radical movements have vigorously critiqued in the years since Kennedy's death.[4] As to leftists becoming involved in the search for hidden elites, some individuals and groups that have been identified with the anti-Vietnam War and later protest movements since the rise of the New Left have publicly espoused beliefs in a "secret team" and/or other entities that control political events. Such conspiracism, progres-

sive critics of conspiracy theory argue, works only to harm the greater progressive cause, by blaming illusory groups for structural problems and legitimating conservative and mainstream dismissals of the left as paranoid kooks.
Worse, it leaves the left vulnerable both to the manipulation of right-wing and
fascist elements that compose much of the "conspiracy theory" network and
to the fascist scapegoating — exemplified in anti-Semitism and racism — that
is the inevitable result of such paranoia.[5]

The progressive critic who has most often and vehemently criticized conspiracy theories is Chip Berlet, an investigative journalist and political activist
whose monograph *Right Woos Left* forcefully asserts that vulnerable individuals and groups on the left are being seduced and used by right-wing populists
through conspiracy theories. Documenting practitioners on both sides of the
political spectrum, Berlet warns that this seduction comes at the price of the
demagoguery and racism that are characteristics of fascism. He notes several
incidents in which this seduction has occurred: in the Alaska Green Party, which
some extreme conservatives attempted to infiltrate; in the protest movement
against the Persian Gulf War, which perennial presidential candidate Lyndon
LaRouche's organization tried to use to recruit members; and among some investigative journalists, who either naively or unscrupulously accept aid and information from individuals with ties to right-wing and fascist organizations.[6]

In a 1992 article in the *Progressive* that was a synopsis of this longer monograph, Berlet argued that the left was particularly susceptible to such infiltration and manipulation after more than fifteen years of conservative ascendancy.
Out of power, the left has been more committed to critique than progressive
prescription, and leftists have become increasingly open to alliances with
those who might share their dislike of the dominant political order, even if
those with whom they would ally work from a radically different perspective.[7]
The title of the *Progressive* article, "Friendly Fascists," epitomizes a theme
that pervades Berlet's approach: that conspiracy theory operates via seduction, as right-wing extremists who seem to share leftists' antielitism and fear
of centralized power and wish to exchange intelligence and analysis infiltrate
and pervert left-wing groups and politics. Like Hofstadter, Berlet conceptualizes conspiracy theory as a form of infection that results from this seduction;
unlike Hofstadter, however, he does not worry about the health of an Ameri-

can consensus, but is instead concerned with the degree to which conspiracy theory afflicts progressive groups and thought through contact.

Berlet does not deny the historical evidence or future possibility of governmental malfeasance and covert operations. Indeed, Berlet and other leftists who have publicly rebuked conspiracy theory, such as Noam Chomsky and Michael Albert, have undertaken critical investigative work seeking to uncover otherwise hidden truths of American and capitalist power.[8] Instead, their emphasis is on drawing distinctions between conspiracy theory and what they see as proper progressive inquiry along three axes: the analysis of power, the gathering of information about covert power, and properly progressive political activism.

First, these leftist critics distinguish between the correct analytic approach to the causes of political events, which focuses on institutional, systemic, or structural (terms that are used virtually interchangeably) phenomena, and the analysis provided by conspiracy theories, which focus on the secretive machinations of one individual or a small, elite group. Albert, writing in *Z Magazine,* argues that conspiracy theory's emphasis on an individual or a particular group's rogue and secretive evil acts fails to recognize how "the normal operations of some institutions generate the behaviors and motivations" that lead to events such as political assassinations.[9] Berlet describes proper, as opposed to conspiracist, analysis of power similarly: "It's not an individual view of history; it's a structural view. It's a view that looks historically. What we've allowed ourselves to be suckered into is a historical misunderstanding. We now view history as a cabal of individuals secretly plotting."[10]

In a more systematic way, Chomsky's book-length study of the Kennedy administration's foreign-policy record rejects simplistic conspiracy theories connecting Kennedy's murder with an escalation of the Vietnam War. Using publicly available governmental records as well as secondary historical sources, Chomsky attacks the notion that the assassination took place because of Kennedy's desire to pull the American military out of Vietnam, and that Kennedy's death led directly to the escalation of the Vietnam War: "The available facts, as usual, lead us to seek the institutional sources of policy decisions and their stability. ... People who wish to understand and change the world will do well, in my opinion, to pay attention to it, not to engage in groundless speculation as to what one or another leader might have done."[11] For Chomsky, not only is this key aspect of many conspiracy theories about the Kennedy assassination based on incorrect assumptions concerning the structural causes of American international relations, but the Kennedy foreign-policy record demonstrates continuity with American Cold War militarism before and after his aborted presidency.

The second distinction that such critics make is epistemological, involving the pursuit, gathering, and analysis of information concerning the causes and meanings of political events. Leftist critics argue that conspiracy theories are often based on wrong or incomplete data from questionable origins. Dependent on unnamed sources, untraceable data, and anecdotal evidence, lacking adequate documentation for the evidence it does present, and drawing illogical, unfounded conclusions, conspiracy theory makes broad claims about power while remaining purely speculative. Conspiracy theories, these critics often argue persuasively, draw attention away from more mundane but better documented histories of the roles played by institutional structures in political, economic, and environmental exploitation. Berlet especially criticizes investigative reporters who fall prey to unreliable sources from the "murky netherworld of ex-intelligence agents, retired military officers, and self-anointed investigators" (as in, for example, the "October Surprise" story) for both amplifying conspiracy theories and draining the limited resources of progressive political organizations and media toward unverifiable speculation.[12]

Finally, left critics argue that proper political analysis leads directly to effective political activity. Identifying both the general and historically specific economic and political structures that dominate enables activists to organize protests strategically and to build collective, alternative institutions in order to effect real social change. Conspiracy theory, on the other hand, either misattributes dominance to individuals, or simplistically places the blame for the ills of the world on individuals rather than on underlying, structural causes. As a result, it cannot lead to effective political activity; rather, it leads to harmful scapegoating, or it misleads activists into thinking that merely removing an individual or a secret group will transform society. Further, Berlet asserts that conspiracy theory leads directly to fascism: "If [conspiracy theorists] dominate [political] debate, then political discourse in the U.S. will soon echo the themes of the fascist era in Europe where hysteria and holocaust, blood and bounty, blind patriotism and deaf obedience became synonymous with the national spirit."[13]

A Realist and Cultural Critique
The Limits of the Progressive Approach

Notwithstanding Berlet's occasional tendency to hyperbole, his is an important and generally worthy critique of the politics of conspiracy theory, particularly as it assumes — unlike Hofstadter's establishment liberalism — a properly critical, activist politics. Berlet's hyperbole is not unimportant, however, and he is not without his critics in both conspiracy-fearing and progressive circles. Daniel Brandt, who created and runs NameBase, an important electronic database of information on American covert intelligence and military personnel and operations culled from public sources, and who is more willing to work with right-wing conspiracy theorists than Berlet, has accused the latter of practicing a form of "politically correct purity" in which the work of researchers who trade information or associate with a non-leftist group (such as the bizarre LaRouche and racist Liberty Lobby organizations) is irrevocably tainted. For Brandt, the information gathered is more important than its source, so long as its source is "open and acknowledged" and its "quality and reliability" are checked.[14] Brandt charges, furthermore, that Berlet not only challenges conspiracy theory in print, but has gone so far as to participate in planning a public campaign against Lyndon LaRouche alongside intelligence operatives and mainstream media organizations.[15]

More damning, however, are charges made by Alexander Cockburn that Berlet overemphasizes the threat of small, marginal groups, and minimizes real centers of power and the abuses they perpetrate. In his long-running column in the *Nation,* Cockburn accused Berlet of serving as an apologist for the Anti-Defamation League of Bnai Brith (ADL), which in 1993 was indicted for collecting and distributing illegally obtained information and for running a private spy ring covertly associated with police departments that infiltrated and carried out surveillance on private, legal organizations opposed to or merely critical of Israel. Berlet, Cockburn alleged, had assumed the ADL's "old trick of conflating anti-Zionism with anti-Semitism," and, during the reaction against the ADL following the disclosures of its intelligence operation, Berlet's apologetic criticism "edge[d] any uncompromising criticism of the A.D.L. into the *verboten* zone of kookdom." Ultimately, Cockburn asserted that Berlet has "made a career out of anathematizing the New Alliance Party and LaRouche, whose deeds are entirely insignificant beside the deeds of Israel."[16] Ironically, Cockburn has accused Berlet of the same crime for which Berlet condemns conspiracy theory: misidentifying the enemies of the democracy in general and the left in particular, and paying too much attention to individuals and groups that are far less important in the struggle to achieve positive social change. Cockburn's argument is valid, especially given Berlet's implicit, and at times explicit, overstatement of the comparative threat posed by marginal and marginalized groups. This is not to say that Berlet's and others' leftist critique of conspiracy theory is unnecessary; rather, such a critique must recognize conspiracy theory's position within contemporary American politics and structures of domination.

More important for this work, however, are the absences in Berlet et al.'s work. Their critique conceptualizes conspiracy theory almost exclusively as a form of political knowledge and behavior that becomes increasingly popular as a result of the pressure of external forces. It thus relies on the same functionalist, simplistically psychological explanation outlined by Hofstadter in his discussion of "status" anxiety and political "pathologies," wherein popular politics is a pathological stimulus response to threatened status. For example, Berlet writes: "Typically, proponents of conspiratorial theories remain an isolated minority except in times of economic or social stress, when demagogic appeals tend to attract a larger following."[17] Another passage could have been lifted directly from Hofstadter: Conspiracy theorists "take advantage of situations in the historical moment where there's great economic and social stress, a change in relationships in terms of a country's status in the world. What they do is pick up on the anxiety that is produced during those periods and come up with a very simple, comforting scapegoat for these complex situations."[18] Based on an approach to contemporary power more critical than Hofstadter's, this is a *critical* functionalism, noting that the "production of anxiety" occurs when "the electorate has lost faith with the government and there are economic hard times."[19] But the critique simplistically assumes that political beliefs and behaviors are largely the result of crisis and manipulation, and "the people" believe or disbelieve in conspiracy theory based on the level of anxiety produced by their political and economic situation. It depends on seeing the belief in conspiracy as singular (all who believe in conspiracy are equally seduced victims of ideology), pathological, and unwarranted, and as a wholly political product of largely marginal demagogues.

In addition, this ideological critique remains almost entirely at the level of political content, without any interest in the form of symbolic expression, besides Hofstadter's undertheorized and simplistic notion of "paranoia."[20] It hardly describes or discusses the relationship between political and popular culture — from films, novels, and television, to the numerous and varied groups that produce and distribute conspiracy-related material, to the paranoia of everyday life in contemporary bureaucracies and capitalism — which circulate, in often complex and contradictory ways, the larger narratives and smaller details of conspiracy theory. Nor is it interested in the specific forms that these narrative and interpretive practices take, the specific drives at work in the production of "conspiracy" — practices that, in their circulation in mainstream cultural and political discourses and in their relationship to populist assumptions about power, require more than mere labeling and dismissal.[21] Nor, finally, is there a complex theory of political subjectivity: one is either pathological, and so vulnerable to the seductive powers of conspiracy theory, or one is not. Instead, this is a welcome ideological critique whose analysis is strong in its "debunking" of conspiracy theory but whose conceptualization of the social and cultural context of conspiracy theory is limited, assuming the most basic definition of ideology as determinant in the production of a singular "conspiracism."

The strength of Berlet et al.'s conceptualization, their critique of conspiracy theory as ideological practice, might lead one wrongly to assume that conspiracy theory's misrepresentation of social forces exhausts the significance of conspiracy theory. In this regard, Hofstadter's analysis, despite its ideological privileging of a "rational" Cold War center and fear of popular sentiment among the nonelite on the periphery, suggests an important component for the conceptualization of conspiracy theory by focusing on the culture and mythology of populism. Hofstadter's work demonstrates that situating conspiracy theory and political "mythology" in general within the historical, social, and cultural context in which they emerge is a crucial complement to denouncing conspiracy theory and proving its ideological base. Linking a progressive critique that recognizes the structural inequities of economic, political, and cultural power to a focus on cultural practices makes possible an analysis that recognizes the political and cultural role of conspiracy theory in popular conceptions of power, noting both their ideological misrepresentations and their nascent desire for a politics in which "the people" can affectively and effectively engage.

Populism and the Conditions of Possibility for Conspiracy Theory

Conspiracy Theory as Ideology

Such a recognition must necessarily begin with a discussion of the real role of power in contemporary political structures. The ability of a class, class fraction, or alliance of classes to influence and, at times, control the state demonstrates the degree to which certain corporate and private nongovernmental institutions constitute a measure of great — and, if not absolutely secret, neither public nor consensual — power. Examples of institutions with an inordinate ability to pursue and enact their individual and collective interests include large transnational corporations, financial institutions such as private banks and quasi-public financial organizations such as the International Monetary Fund (IMF) and the World Bank, and policy organizations and private foundations such as the Business Roundtable, the Council on Foreign Relations (CFR), the Trilateral Commission, and the Heritage Foundation. The fact that conspiracy theorists tremble in fear before the illusion of an omnipotent CFR and Trilateral Commission does not negate the fact that these groups often wield tremendous command over important aspects of American foreign and domestic policy, as well as over the decision-making process of public and private institutions around the world.[22] Similarly, the fact that "bankers" are perceived by some conspiracy theorists (often, but not always, as a cover for anti-Semitism) to be a secret, omnipotent group should not lead one to ignore the historically important role that finance capital, based in financial institutions and investment banks, has played in state and corporate structures, thus having great significance locally, nationally, and globally;[23] and simply because conspiracy theorists, and especially militias, fear a variety of agencies and arms of the federal government — from the Federal Bureau of Investigation and the Central Intelligence Agency to the Internal Revenue Service and the Bureau of Alcohol, Tobacco and Firearms — should not lead one to ignore such agencies' covert, and at times overt, role in repressing individual rights and political dissent in favor of corporate and imperialist interests in the United States and abroad.

One need not, in other words, assume that the state is the direct instrument of a hidden, transhistorical ruling class or elite to recognize the degree to which economic and political power are concentrated in the hands of a tiny sector of the national and international population. The efficacy of this control fluctuates over time, however, and it may be rife with the conflicts, contradictions, and inter- and intraclass struggles that define the winning and maintaining of hegemony. Political power and economic power are neither complete, static, nor wholly secretive; indeed, as Gramsci and contemporary Gramscian political and social theorists have argued, modern democracies must continually and publicly work to win the consent of the ruled, and to incorporate or contain — and at times crush — resistance. Although conspiracy as a totalizing, instrumental entity might not exist, then, relatively secretive, and at times quite open, concentrations of power, built through economic and social connections among elite groups, do. Conspiracy theory is thus ideological in that it substitutes the populist discourse of an antagonism between the people and powerful elites for the analysis of specific structures of power and the processes of struggle, particularly, though not exclusively, concerning class. It is ideological, in Stuart Hall's useful definition of the term, as a form of fetishism and metonymy precisely because conspiracy theory substitutes instrumental power, one part of the historical process, for the whole.[24]

Conspiracy Theory as Populist Discourse

Defining the specific ideological characteristics of conspiracy theory does not exhaust its significance, however. Ernesto Laclau's important theoretical work on populism, central to his book *Politics and Ideology in Marxist Theory,* proves quite helpful in this regard.[25] The assumption with which I begin this discussion of theories of populism is that conspiracy theory is a nonnecessary element of populist movements, but is itself necessarily populist in its evocation of an unwitting and unwilling populace in thrall to the secretive machinations of power. According to Laclau, populism is a set of "popular traditions" that constitutes "the complex of interpellations which express the 'people'/power bloc contradiction as distinct from a class contradiction" (167). The popular subject position interpellated within populist discourse is based on a division of the political into two camps that recognizes one side as a polar opposition that is "purely and simply [a] negation of the other."[26] An extreme example of this is a millenarian movement that splits the world into two distinct parts, recognizing itself as the embodiment of good and others as the absolute of evil; every element (beliefs, ways of life, etc.) linked to the movement is made equivalent and necessary and is part of that which is good, while every element linked to the Other is equivalent and evil. Thus, the discourse that produces the popular subject position operates in a logic of equivalence, whereby individual elements are linked to each other, forming a unity.[27] This notion of the linking of elements into a unity is central to conspiracy theory's interpretive and narrative practices (discussed in Part II).

For Laclau, populism represents a particular inflection of popular interpellations, and is an abstract, unstable domain that can be present in a variety of classes and can itself be articulated in different directions — toward, for example, fascist and anti-Semitic movements that link the elements of self and Other in a clearly delineated manner (i.e., "the people" versus the Jew).[28] The meaning and articulation of elements of populism change over time, overdetermined by and often linked to the state of economic, political, and ideological crises (175). The contradiction that populism assumes between "the people" and "power" is not entirely a misrepresentation of a real antagonism, in that the very impreciseness of the term "the people" enables it, at times, also to be used in liberation movements (165, 194–95). Thus, its ideological misrecognition does not disqualify it as a potential step toward real social change:

> It is precisely because "the people" can never be totally absorbed by any class discourse, because there is always a certain openness in the ideological domain, whose structuring principle is never complete, that the class struggle can also occur as ideological struggle. . . . Classes only exist as hegemonic forces to the extent that they can articulate popular interpellations to their own discourse. (195)

Laclau argues that populism is critical for both analysis and activism, because "classes cannot assert their hegemony without articulating the people in their discourse; and the specific form of this articulation in the case of a class which seeks to confront the power bloc as a whole, in order to assert its hegemony, will be populism" (196). In linking various individual movements opposing a dominant hegemonic formation through a logic of equivalence, a counterhegemonic struggle can enable a nonreductive political alliance that interpellates "the people" in a nonexclusive, yet still oppositional, way.

Ultimately, populism is best conceived of as an assemblage of often contradictory elements and interpellations of "the people" that are neutralized, articulated in specific directions, or infused with varying degrees of significance at particular conjunctures. These elements and interpellations are aspects of what Bonnie Honig, in her book *Political Theory and the Displacement of Politics,* has termed "remainders," resistances that "are engendered by every settlement, even by those that are relatively enabling or empowering," excesses left over from attempts to bring social and political order to human activity.[29] Honig especially criticizes liberal and communitarian political theorists who ignore remainders and neglect political struggle in favor of an illusory politics confined "to the juridical, administrative, or regulative tasks of stabilizing moral and political subjects, building consensus, maintaining agreements, or consolidating communities and identities" (2). This theoretical tendency displaces the disruption and conflict of political struggle in favor of an impossibly stable, ordered, and closed community and set of rational, just institutions. Populism is an element of what Honig recognizes as the politics of "perpetual contest, even within an ordered setting," the fight over resistances to institutional processes of political and social order (15). In Hofstadter's — and, at times, Berlet's — conceptualization of populism, the excess or remainder of consensus is a pathological refusal of normalcy and the result of economic, political, and cultural crises. For Honig, however, remainders are not by definition a troubling, sick exception to the democratic ideal but a production of the political itself, an aspect of the "perpetual contest." Of course, remainders and resistances are by no means solely progressive or liberatory; numerous conservative political movements (Honig identifies antiabortion activists as one example) have refused to be incorporated within dominant political structures and practices and have waged constant, often violent struggle for their cause. Indeed, one of the strengths of Laclau's theory of populism is its recognition that the remainders of political order such as populism can be articulated in different directions—toward, for example, patriarchal domination or liberatory struggle. Populism is both important and a recurring phenomenon precisely because it represents the inability of political and social order to incorporate fully all resistance and excess.

The most extensive use of Laclau's conception of populism has been the work of Stuart Hall and others on the rise of Thatcherism in Britain in the late 1970s and throughout the 1980s. Hall described Thatcherism as a successful articulation of "authoritarian populism," in which popular consent was constructed by a historic bloc in order "to harness to its support some popular discontents, neutralize the opposing forces, disaggregate the opposition and really incorporate some strategic elements of popular opinion into its own hegemonic project." A seeming paradox, the term "authoritarian populism" referred to Thatcherism's simultaneous oppressive form of class politics and its containment and mobilization of populist disaffection within a statist, concentrated form of political rule.[30] Thatcher used fears of immigrants, crime, bureaucracy, and cultural elites not only to secure electoral victories and exploit the forces of production for capital, but also to define "the people" in the most limited and repressive way, thereby absorbing "part of the ideological and political discourses of the dominated classes."[31] Ronald Reagan's nearly concurrent success in the United States—arising, as Lawrence Grossberg notes, in a different economic and political context[32]—was the culmination of a similar winning of popular consent through the articulation of certain populist elements (especially in Reaganism's description of the struggles between the "individual" and the federal bureaucracy and between the authentic American "people" and an "evil empire") to a powerful, militaristic state and deregulated economy. Again, Reagan's and Thatcher's success does not mean that "authoritarian populism" is the only possible mode of populist discourse; radical, popular democratic movements can be opposed to the authoritarian populist regime, working instead through an articulation of class antagonism and the liberatory elements of populist traditions.

Conspiracy theory, based on the perceived secret elite domination over and manipulation of the entirety of economic, political, and social relations, has played a role of varied importance in many, but by no means all, populist movements. It remains an element with a long tradition in American politics and culture that has been articulated in vastly different directions; hence, Berlet's findings concerning the recent "seduction" of the left by right-wing theories are not especially surprising. Conspiracy theory is a particularly unstable element in populism based on such profound suspicion and fear that its successful incorporation within a large populist movement would most likely occur in authoritarian or fascist regimes in which such fears of an omnipotent other could play a central role in defining "the people" through repression and ideological conformity. This is not a necessary result of conspiracy theory, however; it can also be merely one nonnecessary, marginal element within populist movements. For example, assumed and at times explicit anti-Semitism has existed as a trace and, often, as a central element in some nineteenth- and twentieth-century populist rants against "European bankers." During the latter part of his career as a prominent radio minister and political spokesman, Father Charles Coughlin associated "Jews" with bankers as a secret, omnipotent group, as did a minority of the late nineteenth-century American Populist movement.[33] By no means, however, does this provide a universal description of populist groups, and this tendency should lead one neither to equate populism with conspiracy theory nor to assume that all conspiracy theories, even those focusing especially on banking, are anti-Semitic; and, importantly, it should not lead one to consider all criticism of the role of finance capital in contemporary capitalism to be conspiracy theory.

Conspiracy theory as a theory of power, then, is an ideological misrecognition of power relations, articulated to but neither defining nor defined by populism, interpellating believers as "the people" opposed to a relatively secret, elite "power bloc." Yet, such a definition does not exhaust conspiracy theory's significance in contemporary politics and culture; as with populism, the interpellation of "the people" opposed to the "power bloc" plays a crucial role in any movement for social change. Moreover, as I have argued, just because overarching conspiracy theories are wrong does not mean that they are not on to something. Specifically, they ideologically address real structural inequities, and constitute a response to a withering civil society and the concentration of the ownership of the means of production, which together leave the political subject without the ability to be recognized or to signify in the public realm. In order to understand the explanatory power of the discourse of conspiracy theory and its ability to interpellate a popular subject position, it is necessary to sketch out the conditions of its possibility by looking specifically at the present economic, political, and ideological context.[34]

Conspiracy Theory and the
Contemporary American Political Subject

In the context of the explanatory power of conspiracy theory, the most important trend in the class structures of contemporary America has been what Michael Hardt and Antonio Negri describe as the subsumption of civil society by the neoliberal state. By this they refer to the degree to which the intermediate institutions that formerly played a central role in the relationship between citizen, capital, and state in the corporatist social-democratic model — such as labor unions, political parties, and local and federal governments — have been stripped of their social, economic, and political ability to represent the interests of political subjects and to be recognized as such. This has not only lessened the ability of individuals to engage politically and socially with one another, but has diminished their capacity to imagine a shared, collective future. It has thus affected interpersonal and group relations, as well as the relations between the individual and the state, and between labor and capital. Hardt and Negri focus on the decline in the rights and protections of labor as negotiated by institutional labor unions. Whereas unions formerly played a legitimating and disciplinary role in representing workers to capital and the state, they and the working class they claimed to represent are no longer necessary to an increasingly mobile financial and industrial capital in which productive labor, as earlier defined in twentieth-century Western capitalist democracies, has virtually disappeared.[35] Furthermore, as international trade agreements such as the General Agreement on Tariffs and Trade (GATT) and the North American Free Trade Agreement (NAFTA) have made clear, the increasingly global realm of trade and finance leaves remaining local and even national organizations of workers and citizens without adequate voices in decisions that affect their economic livelihoods.

If the diminishing rights and economic opportunities of the worker constitute a specifically economic withering of civil society, what Mike Davis has called the "destruction of social space" represents an important aspect of civil society's social decay. Davis has described the construction of "fortress L.A.," in which the emergent "public" spaces of urban and suburban America — the shopping mall, the office building, the secure suburban development, underclass housing projects, and other planned architectural spaces that increasingly constitute "public" gathering places — are designed to keep in certain classes and keep out others.[36] At the same time, an increasingly socially conservative and libertarian Congress and like-minded state and local officials are restructuring the priorities of governmental budgets away from public expenditures (education, welfare, mass transit) and toward policing and prison building. The privileged exist within safe, secure boundaries; the poor, whose ranks are disproportionately composed of people of color, are left within decaying cities and rural areas; and those in the middle are increasingly vulnerable to the vicissitudes of the economy and labor market. Within the economic and technological restructuring of the global economy, the local community, whether within an urban, suburban, or rural area, is an insecure though by no means impossible space for political and social action.[37]

Furthermore, the seemingly public space of mass communications leaves little room, in either print or broadcast media, for citizen ownership or expression, except within the structured interactivity of letters to the editor, talk radio, and opinion polls. Individual and corporate media moguls such as Rupert Murdoch, Gannett, Disney, and Time Warner control an overwhelming proportion of major media outlets, leaving "public expression" the site of a relatively controlled production and circulation of information.[38] Small-scale print media such as newsletters and independent magazines, small-run newspapers, "fanzines," and computer networks (most prominently the Internet and the World Wide Web) are alternative sources of information and interactive communication, but are less publicly prominent and are accessible to few other than those with disposable income and technological sophistication.

The tendency toward excluding real social antagonisms and debate from the public sphere, and the logic of control that has come to permeate the decaying institutions, structures, and spaces that compose what remains of civil society, leave little opportunity for the "citizen" to effectively or affectively engage with the state. Such engagement is displaced to the privatized realm of consumption, which has emerged as a model for political, social, and cultural activity as individual "choice" in the marketplace serves as an increasingly pervasive notion of "freedom." This is especially clear in the way that the terms "consumer" and "taxpayer" have come to represent the subject of democracy rather than "citizen," and in the ways that media coverage of elections concentrates on "handicapping" candidates' chances of winning and providing a "consumer guide" of possible choices in the marketplace of the ballot box.[39] With a marginalized and shrinking sphere of collective public action and interaction, a politics modeled on consumption leaves little room for individuals to act except by "exit" (e.g., the majority of adults choosing not to vote, and not even paying much attention to politics) or by "voice," allying with like-minded individuals (typically through established interest groups) in order to exert pressure in the political two-party "marketplace." Because the worthiness of one's "voice" and role as a "consumer" of political products is vastly asymmetrical because of inequities in access to political parties and candidates through the private funding of elections, however, those who have no "voice" and no capital with which to "consume" candidates and political parties exit the political sphere willingly (via silent satisfaction, apathy, and cynicism), by exclusion, or by force.[40] What is left of civil society and the political arena—the remnants of the democratic promise, the tightly structured and mediated "consensus"—is not a space where the voiceless can signify.

The lack of a vibrant civil society reduces political discourse to what Lawrence Grossberg has called the "mood politics" that commands what remains of public debate. Within such discourse, "scandal replaces debates, and emotional confessions become the dominant form of political self-definition. . . . [Scandal] becomes a strategy whereby a depoliticized politics becomes the site of a postmodern passion [and] . . . politics is relocated from the realm of social conditions to that of the affective and the scandalous."[41] This is not to say that a politics of affect is inherently ideological—indeed, any effective political movement must connect with members at an affective level. But it must, at the same time, work within and restructure economic and social conditions. In a politics of scandal, however, political debate and action focus on and equate real or imagined, meaningless or horrifying political scandals, stripping them of context. Scandal becomes the issue around which candidates, political parties, and the political system itself are identified. Watergate, as Jean Baudrillard has argued, served (and continues to serve) as the political scandal par excellence, "an extraordinary operation of [discursive] intoxication" that concealed and thus furthered underlying economic and political structures through an infusion of political "morality."[42] "Nixon" continues to represent the base of all corrupt politicians who have followed him, while "Watergate" serves as the symbolic (and, as in "Contragate" and "Whitewatergate," etymological) origin of many "scandals" since, thus limiting public discussions of power to notions of scandalous corruption, and limiting conceptions of resistance and change to impeachment, special prosecutors, and term limits.

In the "mood politics" of scandal, in which "change" can only be imagined as the removal of one politician or party for another, the politics of trust and certainty shape the affective connection between the public and the political. The production and manipulation of trust are among the most crucial practices of contemporary politics, as the perceived trustworthiness of candidates, Zygmunt Bauman argues, serves as the ultimate guarantor of political choice. If "scandal" is the limit of contemporary politics, "trust" serves as the most valuable commodity of politics. "Negative" campaigning attempts to raise doubt in the minds of a fearful electorate: Can we trust this one to lead the military? To pilot the economy? To restore law and order? A barrage of such campaigns every electoral season, combined with the production of "scandal" in public discourse, provides a context for the cynicism that arises from a weariness of scandal and a lack of trust in either individual candidates or the political system that nominates them. Once "scandal" is less an event than a structure of feeling, legitimacy can no longer be produced through normal channels, and political subjects are left with what Bauman terms a "functionality of dissatisfaction" in which political "moods" and allegiances within and across groups and beliefs are inherently unstable.[43]

This is also a condition of possibility for the circulation and growth of conspiratorial fear, a more extreme form of political cynicism in which dissatisfaction is stabilized within a narrative that provides an all-encompassing scandal as its center. The certainty of conspiracy theory, its eminent trustworthiness, lies in its utter lack of trust: the only thing of which one can truly be certain is the deception with which rulers rule. Paradoxically, the conspiracy theorist only "trusts" politics to be corrupt, or, more to the point, to be defined by secret plans for a global takeover. It is the extreme — indeed, ultimate — skepticism of the political sphere by a sector of the population that feels excluded. In addition, conspiracy theory requires a belief in a form of hypnotic ideology that requires one to assume that dominant explanations of motive, cause, and effect are pure deception. Brian Massumi places such profound skepticism within the "everyday fear" of contemporary capitalism, wherein the formerly distinctive domains of production, reproduction, and consumption have converged, and the never-ending flow of mass-mediated images and decontextualizing practices brings about an end to the acceptance of, and even the notion of, linear causality. He writes, "If the contemporary condition of possibility of being human is disequilibrium, continuity and balance are no longer relevant concepts."[44]

Indeed, if scandal and trust are the measure of politics, and fear of the loss of employment, personal control, and identity in a continually transforming economy and shrinking civil society saturates the everyday lives of a considerable portion of the public, then conspiracy theory constitutes a profoundly satisfying politics. It not only explains the victory of seemingly demonological forces and the emptiness and inaccessibility of politics, but it also establishes a particular logic based on the interpretation of phenomena within an explanatory narrative form that is profoundly skeptical of dominant discourse. Continuity and balance, increasingly unsustainable at the personal level, reemerge in the theory and practice of following conspiracy.

If this very general discussion describes the larger conditions of possibility for conspiracy theory, the more specific structures and antagonisms of race and gender are also integral in the tendency of engaging in conspiracy theory among certain populations that are or consider themselves to be subjected to an external power. Rumors of conspiracy concerning ongoing attempts by federal and corporate elites to perpetrate racial genocide against people of color often circulate within what Regina Austin has termed the "black public sphere" of African-American controlled institutions.[45] Such rumors focus especially on threats to the African-American body; for example, the products of Church's Fried Chicken franchises (which, according to these rumors, are owned by the Ku Klux Klan) purportedly induce sterility in black males, and the federal government and the military have created and used the human immunodeficiency virus (HIV) as a way to eradicate unwanted populations, including blacks.[46] These fears are explicitly political as well, concerning such events as the assassinations of Malcolm X and Martin Luther King Jr., which many blacks (as well as whites) view not as singular deeds by individual perpetrators but as part of the systematic harassment and murder of African-American leaders.[47] There is no way to understand such fears — whether, in the case of the Church's rumor, they are outlandish and unsubstantiated, or in the cases of the King and Malcolm X assassinations, they are quite reasonable given the abundant evidence of surveillance and provocative actions of state and federal agencies against these leaders — except in relation to the enslavement and economic oppression of blacks in the United States, which provides a historical context for their belief in conspiracies against African-Americans.[48]

At the same time, the white male "crises" of the post–Vietnam era — most clearly visible in feminist and nonwhite challenges to the economic and political domination of Anglo-American patriarchy — played crucial roles in the emergence in the 1980s of what James William Gibson has called the "New War" culture. This paramilitary cultural movement includes popular images and narratives (the Rambo films and countless genre novels, gun advertisements, *Soldier of Fortune* magazine, etc.), sites and practices such as "Paintball" war games and shooting ranges, and, more seriously, the rise of militias and survivalist groups. Its champion is the warrior hero, the fiercely patriarchal destructive force so powerful that he cannot be fully integrated into society; its evil Other is a powerful, clandestine, depraved, and feminized political force (which Gibson calls the "New Order") that subjugates individual rights and the "natural" patriarchal order.[49] The politics of the New War reinvigorate older narratives about conspiracy within a militaristic framework, positing "manly" strength and resolve as the only method of white male resistance to the onslaught of the New Order.

This articulation of paramilitary masculinity to conspiracy theory is not, however, to say that women do not engage in and with conspiracy theory. Women leaders on the religious far right, for example, often invoke perceived conspiratorial threats to patriarchal order and "feminize" moral political movements in the image of what Linda Kintz has called the "Pure Mother" of patriarchy.[50] Some radical proponents of feminism at times invoke notions of a conspiratorial patriarchy that succeeds through politics, law, and culture in maintaining the subjugation of women.[51] Yet, in its tendency toward both a fetishistic conception of reason and rationality through quasi-scientific practices of historical investigation, and a masculinist fantasy of a looming, necessary, and violent apocalypse between the people and the secretive and evil elite, conspiracy theory assumes differences between "real," virile knowledge and resistance, and feminized, imprecise thought and equivocation.[52]

Thus the more general conditions of the late twentieth-century American political subject, interpellated in a process that includes negotiation with the secret Other of bureaucracy and only publicly enacted in the unsatisfactory moments in which the citizenry's consumer choice is tallied, is also determined by a specific class, racial, and gender context.[53] In this regard, a critique of the political demands a critique of everyday life, and vice versa; to conceptualize the political context and practices that lead to conspiracy theory, one must also confront the cultural and social context of which "politics" plays a crucial role. To affect these contexts requires not simply an appeal to an ideal rationality that exists beyond ideology, but a structural change in the relationship between politics and everyday life. The implications of this are two-fold: first, as this chapter has argued, conspiracy theory is symptomatic of the structural problems of a specific political, economic, and social context and thus should not be dismissed and analyzed simply as a pathology; and second, conspiracy theory and the contemporary practices of populist politics require a cultural analysis that can complement an ideological and empirical "debunking." In short, neither a realist nor a symbolist approach to the political populism and demonology of conspiracy theory can provide an adequate description and analysis by itself. At stake is not merely a better framework for conceptualizing conspiracy theory in all of its complexity, but the formulation of a response that can best de- and rearticulate conspiracy theory's populist protest and yearnings.

Part II
Uncovering the Plot of Conspiracy

4. The Clinton Chronicles
Conspiracy Theory as Interpretation

In early 1994, when asked by CNN's Larry King about rumors of foul play in the suicide of his friend and deputy White House counsel Vincent Foster, President Bill Clinton responded by saying, "I don't think we know any more than in the beginning because I just really don't believe there is anything more to know."[1] On the surface, Clinton's statement demonstrates his desire to shut off the innuendos and accusations that had been circulating among some Clinton opponents. Various theories, circulated on radio talk shows and in partisan political periodicals, the editorial section of the *Wall Street Journal,* conspiracy-oriented publications, and computer networks, purported to link Foster with shady financial transactions made by the Clintons and associated with the emerging Whitewater land development scandal, while other theories linked Foster sexually with Hillary Clinton. These rumors were false and there was nothing more to know, Clinton argued, so there was no reason to look for anything more to know.

But Clinton's statement also demonstrates the profound trouble that dominant discourses have when confronted by the politics, interpretive practices, and narrative constructions of conspiracy theory. In particular, the statement "I just really don't believe there is anything more to know" makes no sense within the hermeneutics of conspiracy because the statement assumes limits of interpretation — an assumption that can gain no purchase within a system that respects no limits in its assumptions about the secret treachery of true political power. Conspiracy theory demands continual interpretation in which there is *always* something more to know about an alleged conspiracy, the evidence of which is subjected to an investigative machine that depends on the perpetual motion of signification. Further, the very attempt to shut interpretation down is itself a suspicious act that requires interpretation. Thus, Clinton's declaration of a limit to interpretation itself signifies excessively: for a conspiracy theorist, when the president says that there is nothing more to know, he is simultaneously circulating a profound error (there is *always* something more to know) and presenting another statement, linked to previous ones that he and his associates have made, that demonstrates the devious and conspiratorial nature of the Clinton presidency (*we* know that he knows more). Clinton is trapped in a circular, endless game in which every declaration of innocence and every piece of evidence put forward in order to exonerate him becomes interpreted as further proof of his guilt.

At still another level, however, Clinton's statement *does* speak for the conspiracy theorist. There really *is* nothing more to know, as each detail or sign links with another in an endless chain of details within a singular narrative frame. One can and must continually collect and interpret evidence, but the explanation of that evidence is always already formed. Interpretation may be endless, but it is contained within the explication of the conspiracy. For a conspiracy theorist focused on the Clinton presidency, there are undoubtedly numerous scandals awaiting disclosure, as well as details that require further investigation and interpretation about those scandals already known; however, the larger explanation behind these individual scandals — a popular one is that Clinton is an agent of a "New World Order" seeking to impose a totalitarian regime — has already been developed and merely requires further proof of Clinton's inherent insidiousness. The links are contingent: competing theories utilize the same detail in different ways, while even the same theory may move in alternate directions as it develops. That which is already known — the full disclosure that Clinton claims already to have made and that the theorist has already uncovered — is itself subject to new knowledge and new interpretations.

This chapter concerns these intensely active interpretive practices of conspiracy theory. Conspiracy theory works as a form of hyperactive semiosis in which history and politics serve as reservoirs of signs that demand (over)interpretation, and that signify, for the interpreter, far more than their conventional meaning. Again, Hofstadter's powerful notion of the "paranoid style" of conspiracy theory is attractive as a framework for analysis. As noted ear-

lier, Hofstadter did not assert that conspiracy theorists were necessarily paranoid but that their way of interpreting the world was like that of the paranoid.
His most important claim in this respect was that conspiracy theorists view
current and historical events as a series of plots to undermine a rightful order
by an enemy on whom they project their own anxieties and desires.[2]

Although understanding conspiracy theory as a paranoid form of interpretation provides some insight, it displaces the cultural and specifically semiotic
challenge posed by conspiracy theory's interpretive practices onto a relatively
simplistic notion of pathology. Hofstadter's work can best be used analogi-
cally. The paradoxes of paranoia, for example, provide a useful way of thinking through conspiracy theory's role as an interpretive framework.[3] As with
clinical paranoia, the interpretive practices of conspiracy theory are in many
instances delusional, but are structured in a manner that is internally consistent and logical, engaging in a logic that is at once tautological and Procrustean:
associating disparate individual events and figures, drawing firm conclusions
based on scant or nonexistent evidence, and asserting either too simplistic or
too complicated explanations to account for historical or present-day events.
As a kind of residual or regressive practice within a presumably "postmodern" era that marks the end of master narratives, conspiracy theorists posit
highly and imaginatively integrative analyses of individual pieces of evidence
that do not provide direct proof of a conspiracy into an all-encompassing framework that can describe the breadth of modern (and, in some theories, premod-
ern and ancient) history and politics.[4] Such integration is both admirably secure at a time when even dominant, "consensual" historical explanations are
increasingly contested, and representative of a popular desire to reconstruct
the master narrative as a mode of expression — thus serving as an excessively
integrative interpretive practice that moves beyond the norms of inference.
Yet, these interpretive practices are not per se pathological, and an approach
that would label them as such is both politically and analytically limited in its
ability to explain and respond to the specifically hermeneutical aspects of conspiracy theory.[5]

This chapter discusses two ways of conceiving of this interpretive practice,
as desire and as production. Both desire and production conceive of conspiracy theory as active, indeed endless, processes that continually seek, but never

fully arrive at, a final interpretation. They do not begin analysis by labeling conspiracy theory pathological, but take conspiracy theory's marginality and hyperactivity as starting points to examine its explanatory power and attraction in contemporary popular politics. They enable a cultural analysis of conspiracy theory's ideological, circular, and endless desire for a totalizing method of mapping and understanding an order where power seems always elsewhere, and of conspiracy theory as a practice that produces the circular desire to desire in meaningful and intense effects and an incessant chain of interpretation. Thus, as an interpretive practice, conspiracy theory represents an impossible, almost utopian drive to seize and fetishize individual signs in order to place them within vast interpretive structures that unsuccessfully attempt to stop the signs' unlimited semiosis. Conspiracy theory displaces the citizen's desire for political significance onto a signifying regime in which interpretation and a narrative of conspiracy replace meaningful political engagement.

In order to ground what will at times become a rather abstract, theoretical discussion, this chapter utilizes some of the conspiracies concerning President Clinton as examples. Accordingly, I begin with some details of two such theories before describing and explicating these two approaches to conspiracy theory's interpretive practices.

The Clinton Chronicles

In an August 1994 article titled "Whatever It Is, Bill Clinton Likely Did It," *U.S. News and World Report* chronicled what it termed a "weird era" marked by "intense, fecund and often bizarre charges" leveled against the president.[6] In the article, White House counsel Lloyd Cutler complained about "a level of invective and viciousness that is unparalleled. . . . There are a great many people who would like to bring President Clinton down who will stop at practically nothing."[7] In fact, as the editor of one of the most widely circulated conspiracy fanzines, *Steamshovel Press,* had noted in a column in the *Washington Post* earlier that year, while some of the Clinton era conspiracy theories have been produced and circulated by such noted conservatives as Rush Limbaugh and the Reverend Jerry Falwell, many of the conspiracies to which Clinton has been linked were initially identified with previous presidents and politicians, and particularly with his most recent predecessors — both Republicans.[8] In other words, Cutler was justified in complaining about the fact that Clinton had been the target of an abundance of conspiracy theories, but for many theorists, the attacks were neither partisan nor personal. As a group, conspiracy theorists' distrust and fears of power and secret plans are not necessarily connected to any one individual or political party (indeed, George Bush's call for a "New World Order" in a 1991 speech and his membership in Yale's infamous secret Skull and Bones society made him just as much a target of conspiracy theories as Clinton) but instead exceed the particularities of established political conflicts (most clearly Republican versus Democrat) for more global and historical explanations of events.

The *Washington Post* column by fanzine editor Kenn Thomas discusses a number of theories, including two that I will describe here: the Vincent Foster suicide and Clinton's connection to the deceased Georgetown University Professor Carroll Quigley. At the time of his death, Foster was deputy White House counsel, and he had been a longtime Arkansas friend of the president and former associate of the first lady in the prominent Rose law firm in Little Rock. His demise was identified almost immediately as suspicious by the ever-incredulous conspiracy community, and by the time of the 1995 Senate Whitewater hearings, a *Time*/CNN poll found that only 35 percent of the one thousand adults surveyed believed that Foster had committed suicide, despite the well-circulated conclusions of the U.S. Park Police (in whose jurisdiction Foster's body had been found), as well as of the FBI and an independent counsel.[9] The office of the White House counsel even issued an internal memorandum (that was later leaked) alleging that Republican congressional staff members collected and disseminated information from the Internet on theories of a Foster murder and on Whitewater in general.[10] From the circumstances of Foster's death — including his body's location in a relatively remote Washington park, shrouded details about the position of the body, and the antique gun supposedly found near it — to the files that were alleged to be missing from his office after it had been thoroughly searched by White House lead counsel Bernard Nussbaum, Foster's death has reeked of signs that give reason for the suspicious at least to doubt the simple explanation of suicide. A videotape titled *The Clinton Chronicles,* produced by a California organization called Citizens

Bill Clinton's Body Count
The Dead can no longer testify!

Dead:

Vince Foster

Vince Foster's 20 July 1993 death was initially ruled a suicide.
- Vince Foster's death is currently under investigation by Special Prosecutor Kenneth Starr.
- There are still a lot of unanswered questions concerning Foster's death and its connection to Bill and Hillary Clinton.

Luther "Jerry" Parks

Murdered in Little Rock on 26 September 1993, Jerry Parks' company provided security for Clinton's presidential campaign and transition headquarters.
- Parks was ambushed and killed by at least three bullets fired at close range from a 9mm semi-automatic pistol as he was driving home.
- Now the dead man's son, Gary Parks, charges that his father, who ran American Contract Services Inc., was killed "to save Bill Clinton's political career."
- Interviewed in the "London Telegraph," the younger Parks said "my dad was working on Clinton's infidelities for about six years, starting in the campaign around 1983," and had compiled name-and-photo-filled files on Mr. Clinton that he kept hidden in his bedroom.
- Shortly before he was killed, Mr. Parks' Little Rock home was broken into. Not only were the phone lines severed and security system dismantled, but Jane Parks, Mr. Parks' widow, says the pair of Clinton files turned up missing and "must have been stolen." – "25 March 1994, Washington Times"

Kathy Ferguson

Kathy Ferguson, former wife of the Arkansas state trooper that is being sued along with President Clinton for sexual harassment by Paula Jones.
- Kathy Ferguson died from a gunshot wound to the right temple early Thursday, 12 May 1994.
- It is currently being investigated as an apparent suicide. She was apparently moving out of her boyfriend's home, as her bags were packed. – "Associated Press"

Reprinted directly from "Clinton Death List" Web site at
http://www.av.qnet.com/~jlund/bodies.htm.

- Though Kathy was already divorced at the time of the 1991 sexual harassment incident, she may have been aware of details of her husband's activities at that time, or she may have known of other earlier incidents.

Bill Shelton

Bill Shelton was an Arkansas Police Officer.
- Bill Shelton was found on the grave of Kathy Ferguson 12 June 1994 with a suicide note next to the body. A bullet had entered behind his right ear. – "The Economist"

Suzanne Coleman

Suzanne had an affair with Clinton when he was Attorney General in Arkansas.
- On 15 February 1977, Suzanne Coleman "committed suicide" with a gunshot to the back of the head.
- No autopsy was performed, and she was seven-and-a-half months pregnant with Clinton's child.

Herschel Firday

Hershel Firday was a member of Clinton's campaign finance committee and head of an Arkansas law firm.
- On 1 March 1994, he died in a small plane crash. He was landing in a drizzle at dusk at his own airfield.

Dr. Ronald Rogers

On 3 March 1994, Arkansas Dentist Ronald Rogers, was about to meet with a British journalist.
- Dr. Rogers reportedly had ties to the Clintons.
- Rogers died in another small plane crash as he flew from Dallas to Denver. The plane reported electrical problems at 22:30 near the Texas-Oklahoma border. It crashed in clear weather 40 miles south of where it dropped off radar.

Jon Walker

On 15 August 1993, Jon Walker died when he "mysteriously" fell from the top of the Lincoln Towers building in Arlington, VA.
- He had been an investigator for the Resolution Trust Corporation (RTC).
- In that capacity in March of 1992, he had contacted the Kansas RTC regional office for information concerning ties between Whitewater, Madison Guaranty, and the Clintons. – "The Economist"

Stanley Huggins
   On 23 June 1994, he was found dead in Delaware, "reportedly" from viral
   pneumonia.
   • He had headed a 1987 examination into Madison Guaranty's loan practices
     and produced a large report which has not been released. – "The Economist"

C. Victor Riser III
   The national finance co-chairman of the Clinton for President campaign.
   • C. Victor Riser III, another Clinton associate, was "killed" in a plane crash in
     July 1992.

Paul Tully
   Mr. Tully was Democratic National Committee political director.
   • Paul Tully, died from unknown causes in his hotel room in Little Rock in
     September 1992.
   • No autopsy was performed.

Danny Casolaro
   Danny Casolaro was investigating the Justice Department's stealing of
   PROMIS from when he was murdered on 9 August 1991 [*sic*].
   • Theories have the two connected through BCCI and the Contra drug
     smuggling operation out of Mena, Arkansas.

Calvin Walraven
   Calvin Walraven, a police informant, testified against former Surgeon General
   Jocelyn Elder's son in a cocaine trafficking trial.
   • Calvin died of a shotgun wound to the head 10 days after the trial. It was
     ruled a "suicide."

for Honest Government and heavily promoted by the Reverend Jerry Falwell
and other far rightists, clearly implies that Foster was murdered to cover up a
number of the first couple's misdeeds, particularly the corrupt dealings surrounding the Whitewater scandal.[11] The story has remained in circulation at
least partially through the efforts of right-wing organizations such as the Western Journalism Center, an organization largely funded by conservative philan-
thropist Richard Mellon Scaife.[12] In one of the wilder theories, purported by
Chicago conspiracy theorist Sherman Skolnick, Foster was murdered for trying
to stop a CIA-aided assassination of Saddam Hussein. Skolnick has charged
that Saddam's killing would have led the Iraqi dictator's half brother to release bank records linking Clinton (and George Bush) to the Italian state bank

Banco Nazionale del Lavoro, which helped to fund the arming of Iraq and which has also played a role in a number of other real and alleged scandals.[13] Foster has also become merely one name in the "Clinton Death List," a roster of deceased individuals linked directly or remotely to Clinton whose deaths have been even the least bit "suspicious." The "death list" has been circulated among far-right-wing groups and all over the Internet via electronic mail, World Wide Web pages, and USENET bulletin boards.[14]

Carroll Quigley is best known among conspiracy theorists for his book *Tragedy and Hope,* a relatively fawning, "insider's" account of the plans of an Anglo-American political elite to oversee global geopolitics and economic development. Originally published in 1966 by Macmillan, the book became quite popular with the John Birch Society and other far-right-wing groups for its description of the relationship between the British Round Table groups, originally funded by the (Cecil) Rhodes Trust and composed of financial and political elites in England and its colonies, and its American counterpart, the "Eastern establishment."[15] Ironically, Clinton connected himself to Quigley before a national television audience in his speech accepting the 1992 Democratic presidential nomination, when he cited Quigley's class at Georgetown for teaching him of the greatness of America and the moral responsibility to contribute to its improvement.[16] Clinton's reference resonated with the John Birch Society, which has had a longtime fixation on Quigley's work (it sells two of his books, including *Tragedy and Hope*); John Edlam, the organization's research director, told the *Washington Times,* "[Quigley] is one of the few insiders who came out and exposed the Eastern establishment plan for world government. He detailed the plan, he'd seen the documents, he wanted it to work."[17] By citing Quigley, then, Clinton signaled to the "Eastern establishment" of financiers, industrialists, and journalists — as well as to the John Birch Society — that he was planning on working with this secret conspiracy to promote their designs for domination and a "new world order." At the same time, a different organization, A-albionic Research of Ferndale, Michigan, saw Clinton as signaling his allegiance to a "Jesuit/Vatican conspiracy for the Old World Order" with strong ties to Georgetown, the Jesuit university in the nation's capital.[18]

Suspicions and accusations concerning Vince Foster's death and Clinton's connection to Quigley are examples of specific instances or events tying the president to larger theories of conspiracies. I turn now to theoretical concerns with the interpretive practice of conspiracy theories, using these instances as examples.

Conspiracy Theory as Desire

Conspiracy theory resembles a drive in its prodigious commitment to learn and know the presumed secrets of power and domination. In their endless striving for more information, conspiracy theorists clearly *want something* — the "truth," as they would understand it, and either the return to or the formation of a truly transparent state of relations with others as well as with the greater Other of power. This desire constitutes neither a basic need nor a clear demand: although some who search for evidence of a conspiracy are impoverished, their search does not promise the fulfillment of their basic needs; and although some conspiracy theorists actively make political demands individually and collectively, their search seems only tangentially related to the fulfillment of specific demands concerning government programs and laws. It is in this sense that I want to explore the interpretive practices of conspiracy theory, and the degree to which they present a demand that is split from need.[19] Interpreting conspiracy is repetitive, endlessly reproduced, and continually frustrated, and holds a complex relationship to its seeming object of desire: the structure, order, and solution represented by conspiracy.

Interpretive Desire in Practice

A critical component of the conspiracy theorist's work is interpreting individual phenomena such that each detail that signifies "conspiracy" is linked within a larger interpretive frame. Each kernel of information or empirical detail thus becomes evidence of the existence of a conspiracy. Conspiracy theory is intensely captivating and energizing, requiring enormous attention to the particularities of the distant and recent past, as well as to the present historical moment. Like Gnostics, conspiracy theorists interpret for individual and small-group enlightenment, finding significance in the mundane and wonderment in the apparently explicable. The act of interpretation is itself part of the larger project of locating the final order of determination behind the conspiracy — reflecting the theorist's basic assumption that each act by the conspiracy is itself part of a larger conspiratorial project whose purpose stretches the limits of the conspiratorial imagination. By this I mean that the *existence* of the conspiracy—the thing that must be located by interpretation—is more discoverable than its ultimate *motive,* which is often quite vaguely understood and defined (typically as some general wish for power or the wish to achieve some great degree of evil).

Because everything—the economy, political power, culture, and so on—connects in some way, the theorist develops a kind of reflex of seeking other orders behind the visible. Like the central characters in Thomas Pynchon's novels, such as Oedipa Maas in *The Crying of Lot 49* (1966) and *V*'s Herbert Stencil (1963), conspiracy theorists' seemingly paranoid instinct is not any more pathological than the world in which they perceive themselves to be operating, which constantly places before them connections and other orders that they must try to understand and to which they must respond.[20] In making connections, theorists place links along an interpretive chain; as connections are the epiphenomena of a base, hidden truth, they use the connective chain to approach the presumed final layer.

The interpretive practices of conspiracy theory are paradoxical, both an inherently active practice that is cultivated as a response to a specific historical, political, and social context, and deeply limited by a powerful logic and marked by broad structural similarities across time and social groups. They are a type of reflex—confronted with phenomena (the death of a politician, a scandal, an unexplained natural or human occurrence), the individual theorist immediately employs a certain type of interpretive framework—but result in the production of connections, even if such connections already "exist" in coded form in the phenomena themselves. Events may already have been produced by members of the secret group, but they must be identified as such by those who seek and discover the real, deeper meaning of power. Although connections require the work of the interpreter, however, the interpretive practices of conspiracy are neither free nor especially creative. The framework of conspiracy focuses and even determines interpretation: the conspiracy theorist does not arrive alone at a conclusion concerning a specific piece of evidence of a conspiracy; the conclusion comes with the theorist to the evidence, arriving at the instant of interpretation. But again, the specific path of the interpretive chain is never fully determined, as the numerous mutations of conspiracy theory demonstrate.

And so: Bill Clinton had already been a student of Carroll Quigley long before the presidential nominee stepped to the podium at Madison Square Garden. The fact that Clinton cited the dead Georgetown professor in his speech accepting the Democratic nomination for president was not, in and of itself, a significant fact; countless Americans doubtless ignored the rising politician's praise for an obscure mentor buried in the midst of an otherwise generic—if important within the context of the presidential campaign—political speech. For those already aware of Quigley's work and its relation to "conspiracy," and who had already developed the interpretive framework that seeks to understand and place the rise of a political candidate within a framework of conspiracy, however, the initial interpretation of this citation by connecting Clinton with Quigley was part of a simple "reflex." Yet, the interpretive process did not end at this initial connection. Instead, Quigley became one link in an interpretive chain that sought the unmasking of the "real" meaning of Clinton—first, in his performative role as presidential candidate (what does he *mean*?) and then, more urgently, as an epiphenomenon of a broader conspiracy (what does *he* mean?). Of course, the framework within which such interpretive acts take place is fairly secure, as demonstrated by the distinct, but of course quite similar, theories of the Quigley connection described earlier. Similarly, one can imagine an identical process occurring as President Bush described the "New World Order" that would emerge from the Persian Gulf War—here is George Herbert Walker Bush, former director of Central Intelligence and member of Skull and Bones, signaling his plans for the one-world government for all the world to see! The connections are available for those who seek to make connections; the order of the Other is there for those who know of such orders.

Conspiracy Theory's Desire in Time
The Past Arrives, but the Future Never Comes

Making connections and seeking orders assumes an important temporal sequence. Superficially, the practice seems simple. In the past, conspiratorial acts have taken place; these acts have produced the present, when such acts continue to take place; past and the present acts leave traces that the active, properly interpretive mind can identify. The past produces the present, and the interpreter must scour the past and the present for the "answer" that can best explain this relationship. In understanding the past and the present, the interpreter draws conclusions that can affect the future, under the assumption that once the final connection is made, the ultimate secret order will finally be uncovered. The history of twentieth-century conspiracy theories, however, demonstrates that the interpretive practice does not in fact end but continues to engage in the search for more connections in the present and the past. Totalizing conspiracy theories notoriously "fail"; they do not, and cannot, adequately find a final order. The future, when the secret will be revealed, never arrives.

Interpretation, then, is not merely active, it is *endlessly* active in finding and linking details to the larger conspiracy. Unfortunately, if the chain is endless, so the layers of deception are infinite, and if the connections are never completed, then the base truth remains out of reach (as in the final moment of *The Crying of Lot 49,* when both Oedipa Maas and the reader are left in suspended animation awaiting some answer to the novel's central mystery). *The Clinton Chronicles* and the "Clinton Death List," for instance, are infinitely expansive, built on a conception of the president's unfolding and lethal perfidy and the inevitability of the single requirement for those who are added to the "death list." New revelations merely add to an existing framework, and the act of finding those new revelations is repetitive over the course of Clinton's significance as an epiphenomenon of the broader conspiracy that the theorist seeks to uncover. Based on a circular drive to find the "truth"—a kind of epistemophilia—such interpretation becomes akin to the Lacanian notion of desire, which requires, at its core, that its ultimate fulfillment be continually deferred.

Given this ongoing deferral of satisfaction, the demand of this desire is not simply to expose the secret. The conspiracy is an enormous structure always on the horizon of interpretation and the cause of everything, always the point toward which interpretation moves but which it never fully reaches.[21] If satisfaction is defined as the proof and public recognition of the "truth" of conspiracy and the efficacious remedy of the crisis, then conspiracy theory desires *dis*satisfaction.[22] It is, after all, a speculative approach that assumes its own marginality — conspiracy theory by definition perceives itself to be continually dominated and manipulated by its more powerful conspiratorial adversary even if, at certain conjunctions, conspiracy theorists have amassed enormous resources and power. Thus, in government regimes based on the fear of a secret group, such as the Third Reich and Congress in the throes of McCarthyism, the fear of a Jewish conspiracy and/or a communist conspiracy was based on the fear of a group considered more powerful than the nation in peril. By contrast, in contemporary liberal democracies, individual conspiracies may be exposed and condemned by society on a regular basis, but conspiracy as a totalizing phenomenon, as a whole way of life, is a practice that seems continually to be frustrated in its inability to persuade and affect political order. Ultimately, the conspiracy theorist's interpretive practice of seeking connections and a deeper order represents a desire to seek further connections and deeper orders. There is, however, no final connection, no deepest order. The interpretive search must continue.

For a conspiracy theorist, an end to the conspiracy is thinkable — indeed, even predicted. After all, the defeat of Clinton and his ilk (however defined) is the prescriptive end of *The Clinton Chronicles,* and that is always possible. Someday, *he will be exposed* — or at least, parts of him may be uncovered. The end of the practice of interpreting conspiracy, however, is unthinkable — indeed, the practice is based on the impossibility of its own completion. There can be only two explanations for the lifting of the final veil of deception. First, the conspiracy may have become so prevalent that it no longer requires secrecy — clearly an unhappy result in which the threatened apocalypse has come to pass. Second, the conspiracy may have proven too inept to avoid full detection — in which case it was not much of a conspiracy to begin with. The latter is a different, but similarly feared, kind of end, in which an enthralling practice reaches a final closure.[23] Although the accomplishment of this "goal" of conspiracy would be disappointing by definition, it is impossible. Slavoj Žižek describes this impossibility well: "When we encounter in reality an object which has all the properties of the fantasized object of desire, we are nevertheless necessarily somewhat disappointed; we experience a certain 'this is not it'; it becomes evident that the finally found real object is not the reference of desire even though it possesses all the required properties."[24] The desire that manifests itself in interpreting conspiracy cannot simply end; should it approach such an end, the interpretive framework would be reconstructed with new details. Closure, the satisfaction of this desire, cannot be reached. There is always another conspiracy to track, and the new political and social order that replaces conspiracy would by definition constitute a new relation of power, which would by definition require the deepest of suspicions. The "Clinton Death List" grows, or changes name, or changes shape to include new, different events and figures. There is always another Clinton, just as, before him, there was always another Bush.

Documenting Desire in Detail

In *The Clinton Chronicles* and the "Clinton Death List," and especially in speculations about Vince Foster's suicide, the individual detail plays an enormously important role as an object produced by interpretive desire. "Clinton" is constructed from a multiplicity of details strung together: Quigley, Foster's body, and the like. The detail articulated as "conspiracy" does not exist except as it is produced by the interpretation that "finds" it. The detail is, to borrow from Lacan the notion of the *objet petit a,* the "object cause of desire: an object that is, in a way, posited by desire itself."[25] The detail cannot be seen by the "naked eye," by someone unfamiliar with the evidence and the implications of it; and, for critics of such theories, the "significant" detail (such as the antique gun and the amount of blood found in Fort Marcy Park with Foster's corpse) is merely insignificant: unimportant, unable to signify anything beyond itself. To locate evidence of a conspiracy, in other words, is to see evidence that is invisible for those who do not believe in the conspiracy; the object, seen and cherished by the one who desires it, does not exist for the person whose desire does not produce it.

In naming the object evidence of a conspiracy, the theorist performs an act that retroactively constitutes the referent: the meaning of the object that is named is radically contingent on that act of naming.[26] Clinton's reference to Quigley was merely one part of a longer speech, itself the culmination of an extended presidential primary campaign and political career. "Quigley" gains significance only after its identification and labeling "conspiracy" by the theorist. "Conspiracy" arrives from the future, constructed retroactively through the analysis of the speech's details within an interpretive frame that gives "Clinton" its name and meaning: conspiracy. Clinton cites Quigley; magically, Clinton becomes retroactively linked to an entire historical chain ("New World Order") that is fully connected yet never complete.

The detail is the object desired, produced by desire; as such, it signifies a singular meaning "conspiracy" and, in the degree of control that the interpretive desire wields in linking the detail within a larger framework, it is generic, devoid of specificity.[27] Lacan writes, "man thinks with his object," as in the game that Freud observed his grandson playing in absence of the child's mother, *fort-da,* an endlessly repetitive sequence in which the reel itself, the ball that the boy threw and the string by which he drew the ball back, serves as the object produced by the child's desire.[28] Like the child's reel, the single detail and the succession of details linked within an interpretive frame are sites of interpretive control for the conspiracy theorists. This is most clearly the case in the incredible attention to detail of the Kennedy assassination literature, where the physics of bullet trajectory and the traces of evidence ("accepted" or controversial) become the objects of fetishization. The same is true of the Foster "suicide," in which details (the gun, the body, the "suicide note," and so on) must be found, investigated, and massaged to produce their meanings. Each new detail leads to the need for more details. In describing the process of interpretation among believers in UFOs, Keith Thompson describes a process of "masking, unmasking, displaying, concealing, always in the context of *getting closer to the hidden truth*" in which each step toward revelation signifies a new mask, a new disguise to reveal.[29] Paradoxically, although the detail is produced by the conspiracy theorist's interpretive desire, desire also makes the detail disappear. Once "unmasked," the detail becomes merely part of "conspiracy." Once Vince Foster is a "suicide," the individual details enabling that conclusion lose texture and focus, becoming objects only suitable for occasional debate with nonbelievers. Vince Foster's antique gun becomes an object of desire once it is named as a lie; the theorist is able to see its significance only when s/he does not see it, when it becomes a layer of meaning that must be peeled away in search of another, better one.

Within this interpretive practice, conspiracy serves as the point within the text, the organizing principle, that is able to explain everything. At "conspiracy," all interpretation, details, causal explanations, and narrative representations of the "truth" behind the past and the present meet and end. Vince Foster, his gun, the leaves in the park, the "suicide note," the papers stolen from the office, and so on, are explained through and arrive at Clinton's secret treachery and the broader but even more secretive cabal of those behind him. More than simply an interpretive or internal textual thing, however, "conspiracy" is transcendent in the interpretive operation. It explains everything, past, present, and likely future, and exists outside of the details being interpreted, the interpretive act, and the larger frame organizing the conspiracy theorist's work.[30] What began as a textual effect, the way in which a single detail's significance is understood, has become a transcendent stopping point; what began as that which is presumptively searched for, the traces of conspiracy, becomes that transcendent thing which drives the search itself. Interpretation may be endless, but it is organized—indeed, controlled—by the very particular logic of conspiracy.

The endless, circular search (the connections) and the thing that never arrives (the final order that is never revealed) represent a popular, albeit "ideological," desire to find, understand, and represent the totality of social relations. Conspiracy theory clearly wants something: it is a never-ending practice that combs the past and the present for evidence of some transcendent, all-explanatory thing. Denying an unknowable past and present based on complexity and contingency, conspiracy theory wants to enjoy the pleasure of control, of finding the correct answer to the riddle of power, of mastering its desire of political order.[31] The problem with a purely psychoanalytic approach is that it would posit this desire as simply symptomatic of some greater individual trauma: the subject does not know what it wants, but the cause of this ignorance and the resulting pathologies can be found by the analyst and theorist.

Even cultural critics and theorists who do not succumb to simplistic notions of political paranoia often posit a notion of conspiracy theory as symptom. Carl Freedman, for example, argues that interpretive and narrative paranoia, exemplified by the work of Philip K. Dick, is "the normative subjectivity of capitalist society"; he identifies commodity fetishism, which is based on an ongoing overinterpretation of the surplus value of objects, and monopoly capitalism, which must continue to hide itself behind seemingly fair and open political and economic structures, as ideological apparatuses that interpellate us as paranoid subjects. In other words, paranoiac desire, rather than a pathological disposition toward seeing things that are not there, is a "normal" desire within the highly structured economic and cultural regime of capitalism.[32] Fredric Jameson further characterizes this "normal" desire as a utopian—albeit ideological—drive to undertake a "cognitive mapping" of totality, an interpretive practice that can represent the articulation of local experience to the global system of "late" capitalism. Cinematic conspiracy narratives such as *The Parallax View* and *All the President's Men* are an "unconscious, collective effort at trying to figure out where we are and what landscapes and forces confront us in a late twentieth century whose abominations are heightened by their concealment and their bureaucratic impersonality."[33] Similarly, the "inexhaustible production" of political conspiracy theories (the Kennedy assassination, the secret power of Jewish bankers, etc.) is "the poor person's cognitive mapping in the postmodern age; it is a degraded figure of the total logic of late capitalism, a desperate attempt to represent the latter's system, whose failure is marked by its slippage into sheer theme and content."[34] Jameson and Freedman would invert the order assumed by Hofstadter and others by asserting that the seemingly "pathological" is in fact a structured, "normal" response to bureaucratic and capitalist order, and a conspiratorial framework represents a subject's ideological, but utopian, desire to understand and place itself within a vast and destructive system.

Conspiracy theory does fetishize and totalize, but these are only parts of its interpretive practices, aspects of its desire to find the evidence and meaning of the conspiracy it tracks. Žižek writes that "Fantasy is a means for an ideology to take its own failure into account in advance."[35] In a similar way, conspiracy theory masks the impossible ideals of representative, participatory democracy within a capitalist economy. Displacing the fears of this impossibility onto fears of conspiracy, condensing these fears into notions of murderous, licentious presidents and secretive cabals, the conspiracy theorist enjoys her/his symptom, indulging in its practice, reveling in its excess, never fully reaching the fulfillment of desire lest s/he be confronted with the realization that the notion of a willful, secretive conspiracy by an elite cabal is not quite right.

Yet, domination, manipulation, and corruption are integral to the history of capital, and in simply dismissing fears of conspiracy as pathological and paranoid, one erases the human, economic, and environmental disasters that go unrecognized and unremembered. The goal should be not to label the symptom a pathology but to articulate it in emancipatory directions by recognizing and identifying the utopian desires bound within it and, in relation to conspiracy theory's role as an interpretive practice, "targeting semiosic discovery toward the public good."[36] Vilifying Clinton as a monster or as the public representative of an elite cabal masks his role within global structures of dominance and capital that are the grounds for real, not fantastic, struggle. Only by recognizing the semiotic excess and lack of political significance represented in conspiracy theory can we begin to understand its implications.

Conspiracy Theory as Production

Conspiracy theory's interpretive desire is only partially defined by signification. Conspiracy theory is a *practice* of desire that *moves*—back in time, around and through events, collecting details, surrounding the conspiracy and encrusting the conspiracy's shadow with a long and growing signifying chain. It may not know what it ultimately wants, but it knows what it wants for the moment: to keep moving, to keep desiring. This movement—ideological and symptomatic though it may be—is *productive,* producing not only a circular, seemingly endless desire and a proliferation of conspiracy-related texts, but also affective intensities and flows, self-generating and forever flying through space and time. An analysis of conspiracy theory requires a description of conspiracy theory's intensity and amplification of affect—what one observer has called the "conspiracy rush," the affective engagement of sensing conspiracy that is intimately bound to conspiracy theory as interpretive practice. The production and proliferation of conspiracy-focused texts and practices are effects of the specificities of conspiracy theory, and particularly of the affective and interpretive aspects of the specific mode of production of conspiracy theory's regime of signs. The theories discussed in previous chapters exhaust their interest in conspiracy theory at the level of texts and practices by relating effect (political behavior) to cause (political pathology). Neither Hofstadter nor the progressive approach seeks to describe or explore the specificities of conspiracy theory's effects, and especially that which makes it affectively engaging and immensely productive. This section concerns the specificities of conspiracy theory's interpretation in terms of affect, and its effects in terms of production.

To distinguish this discussion from that of the previous section, I rely on Lawrence Grossberg's helpful distinction between affect and desire: "Libidinal affect (or desire in psychoanalytic terms) is always focused on an object (whether real or imaginary), while nonlibidinal affect (affect for short) is always dispersed into the entire context of daily life. Desire can be satisfied, if only temporarily and mistakenly, while affect can only be realized."[37] The realization of conspiracy theory's affect occurs in the assemblage of ideas, elements, and practices. Clinton is more than simply a president to chronicle; he is a part of daily life, of the affective chronicle of the conspiracy theorist who finds "Clinton" everywhere. As such, "Clinton" is both producer of and produced in a multiplicity of texts and practices; he does not simply *cause* conspiracies through his actions, coupled with political disagreement or pathological fear—he is an effect of conspiracy theory. Ultimately, "Clinton" is not only the author of the "death list" through his alleged murder of its victims, he is created by it, an effect of each name and dead body. Dispersed throughout everyday life, conspiracy theory operates as a machine in its assemblage of information into lists, chronicles, narratives, and file cabinets.

Gilles Deleuze and Félix Guattari's notion of desire, more akin to this conception of affect than Lacan's, is useful here. They employ the concept of the "regime of signs" to conceptualize machinelike systems of signifying practices. Their description of the despot-god regime of signs would seem to describe not only the endlessness and circularity of the conspiracy theorist's process of interpretation but that which this interpretation produces.[38] The regime is marked by its endlessly productive qualities of signification and interpretation, in which

> [a]ll signs are signs of signs. The question is not yet what a
> given sign signifies but to which other signs it refers, or which
> signs add themselves to it to form a network without begin-
> ning or end that projects its shadow onto an amorphous at-

mospheric continuum. It is this amorphous continuum that
for the moment plays the role of the "signified," but it continually glides beneath the signifier, for which it serves only
as a medium or wall: the specific forms of all contents dis-
solve in it.[39]

Conspiracy theory is not free of constraint; as Deleuze and Guattari write,
"mighty is the signifier that constitutes the chain," and in their concept of the
paranoid despotic regime, the "superpower of the signifier" masters the network of signs.[40] Tearing signs away from the seemingly secure chains of dominant historical and news accounts, conspiracy theory rechains them to a new
signifier. Professor Quigley of Georgetown becomes "Quigley," court scribe
of the conspiracy. The reduction and inhibition of the network of signs, although a limit on the possibilities of signification and interpretation — and
thus on what Brian Massumi has called the "incipience" of intensity and affect in responding to the resonation of outside events and stimuli[41] — do not
inhibit the productivity of the regime. Conspiracy theory may be a limit to interpretation, enabling certain types of assemblages and not others, but in its
might the regime requires engagement, to tear the sign from its chain, to move,
to produce new chains. It decodes pluralist/consensus accounts of power, only
to recode "power" within the superpower of conspiracy.[42]

A central metaphor that Deleuze and Guattari use to describe the despot-
god regime of signs is usury and debt: "Nothing is ever over and done with in
a regime of this kind. It's made for that, it's the tragic regime of infinite debt,
to which one is simultaneously debtor and creditor."[43] The signifying regime
within which the conspiracy theorist operates requires constant attention for
signification, and pays back more in meaning than the original investment.
"Clinton" and the forces he represents produce an embarrassment of riches;
they are the impossible cause of so many things, as is true with the conspiracy
that drives any such theory. In this way, conspiracy theory is a productive signifying system, like capital, identifying new and depleting old resources (what
happened to Bush, anyway?), destroying and building new signs and chains in
an endless process of interpretation.[44]

Deleuze and Guattari link the despot-god regime of signs to their distinctive
notion of desire. Being opposed to psychoanalytic theory (Freudian as well as

Lacanian), Deleuze and Guattari refuse to limit desire by assuming that the fantasized object of desire is produced in order to cover an unfillable or essential lack.[45] Instead, they describe desire as a machine, a "desiring-production," an immanent factory of flows and intensities. In interpreting, the conspiracy theorist produces the desire for more interpretation, for the further connection of more connections; like the *briocleur,* showing "an indifference toward the act of producing and toward the product, toward the set of instruments to be used and toward the over-all result to be achieved," but with a drive toward "continually producing production."[46] As Elizabeth Grosz writes, "desire is an actualization, a series of practices, bringing things together and separating them, making machines, making reality."[47] Lloyd Cutler was right to be concerned about the conspiracy industry surrounding Clinton — which is slightly more "legitimate" (backed by such well-circulated media outlets as Rush Limbaugh, the *Washington Times,* and the editorial page of the *Wall Street Journal*) and better funded than theories concerning Bush — as it shows no sign of abating (and among some will never abate), and spins new theories and revelations almost daily.[48] Conspiracy theories begin to approximate an unlimited semiosis not unlike a perpetual-motion machine, a regime that constantly processes signs for interpretation, producing more theories and more signs in the process.

Umberto Eco's novel *Foucault's Pendulum* is a wonderful representation of the effects of conspiracy theory's affective engagement and interpretation, which Eco in his semiotic work before and after the novel's publication has called "overinterpretation." *Foucault's Pendulum* relates the story of three friends in present-day Milan who create a metaphysical conspiracy concerning a mélange of "secret societies" (including Rosicrucians, Knights Templar, and the Freemasons), which is in turn believed and made true by a secret group of occultists ("the diabolicals"). What begins as a clever intellectual game of using analogies, similarities, and fictional associations between historical figures in order to make "paranoid" connections — but making them "knowingly," deliberately misreading details in creating the transcendent "truth" of spiritual secrets and powerful hidden orders — becomes a fully assembled "plan" that exceeds its creators, that becomes something more than a game.[49]

Here, conspiracy theory has real effects, not only in terms of the "fun" of cleverly devising texts open and suggestive enough to be interpreted in particular ways, but in the very real violence perpetrated by the "diabolicals" as a result of these games. Interpretation is dangerous: as the narrator Casaubon declares, "Now I have come to believe that the whole world is an enigma, a harmless enigma that is made terrible by our own mad attempt to interpret it as though it had an underlying truth" (81). Like the Tristero postal conspiracy that seems ready to consume Oedipa Maas at the end of *The Crying of Lot 49,* the interpretive effects of *Foucault's Pendulum* are at once humorous and frightening, enervating and deadly. Casaubon and friends create the terms and conditions of their own "paranoia," which seems ready, as the novel closes, to claim them all as victims.

Constructing the "Plan" — or, more generally, interpreting conspiracy — is, as C. W. Spinks argues, an example of what Charles Sanders Peirce called "abduction," or "hypothesis":[50]

> Hypothesis substitutes, for a complicated tangle of predicates attached to one subject, a single conception. Now, there is a particular sensation belonging to the act of thinking that each of these predicates inheres in the subject. In hypothetic inference this complicated feeling so produced is replaced by a single feeling of greater intensity, that belonging to the act of thinking the hypothetic conclusion. . . . Thus, the various sounds made by the instruments of an orchestra strike upon the ear, and the result is a peculiar musical emotion, quite distinct from the sounds themselves.[51]

Reducing the complex to a singularity creates a new text ("a single conception" different from "the sounds themselves") and affective sensations ("a single feeling of greater intensity," "a peculiar musical emotion") from a set of physical stimuli (the "various sounds" that "strike upon the ear"). In response to this excerpt from Peirce, Eco writes, in *A Theory of Semiotics,* that the significance of abduction is "the idea that the hearer, hearing music, grasps something more than the single 'meaning' of each sound. . . . The hypothetical movement is fulfilled when a new sense (a new combinational quality) is assigned to every sound, inasmuch as they compose the new contextual meaning of the musical piece."[52] Abduction is the process of interpreting unexplained events or results by figuring out a law that can explain them, a process of "figuring out" that often, in the case of great scientific discoveries, requires imaginative or analogical steps. In the process of abduction, the text to be interpreted contains a "secret code" of the law but requires an inventive or at least quite dynamic and productive interpretive act to identify and decipher the explanatory law.[53]

On first glance, the production of "conspiracy" from a set of speculations about the connections between historical facts and current events is a form of abduction: the assemblage of fragments of signs into a new piece, a semiotic process producing a feeling of "greater intensity" in its discovery of meaning. Yet, conspiracy theory would seem to differ from these definitions and descriptions, if not in kind, then in degree. Casaubon et al.'s "Plan" is a production of disparate elements elegantly and intelligently articulated to compose a "new sense," but it is more a literal abduction or kidnapping of a series of historical signs and relatively open texts than the more polite "borrowing" for analogical purposes or "finding" of a law that Peirce describes.[54] This more closely resembles the Hermetic tradition of interpretation, where, Eco writes elsewhere, "As long as some kind of relationship can be established, the criterion does not matter. Once the mechanism of analogy has been set in motion there is no guarantee it will stop."[55] Overwhelmed by an "excess of wonder,"[56] the Hermetic tradition is

> based on the principles of universal analogy and sympathy, according to which every item of the furniture of the world is linked to every other element (or to many) of this sublunar world and to every element (or to many) of the superior world by means of similitudes or resemblances. It is through similitudes that the otherwise occult parenthood between things is manifested and every sublunar body bears the traces of that parenthood impressed on it as a *signature*.[57]

In place of the worldly or "sublunar," the conspiracy theorist ponders the seemingly superficial or semantic meaning of and connections between everyday news accounts; in place of the "superior" world, the conspiracy of power places its signature on these everyday events, and the interpretive work of the conspiracy theorist is to unmask these meanings and connections.

Thus, the "Clinton Death List," composed from thorough scourings of obituaries (reported and unreported), articulates a "new" recognition of the object conspiracy, tearing away and kidnapping individual pieces into a new, star-tlingly full composition. The conspiracy grows, it expands, it is transformed from a list into a complex diagram, a monstrous, multilayered being threaten-ing to devour the nation. The "superior" threatens to overcome the "sublunar," to eradicate its identity in a perverse reversal of the basis of the Hermetic in-terpretive drive.

In addition to this, however, I want to focus on the sheer pleasure of read-ing *Foucault's Pendulum* and the reader's recognition of both the intense and dangerous attachment of the diabolicals to this hermeneutical practice and the great fun of Casaubon and his friends in "creating" the analogies and myster-ies on which the diabolicals obsess. I will return to this in chapter 8's discus-sion of conspiracy theory as play, but it is crucial to recognize the gamelike quality to this engagement. As opposed to a mystery that would gradually pare down the list of suspects and motives as it progresses, *Foucault's Pendulum* and the "Plan" engage in vast proliferations of ideas and connections that them-selves produce more ideas and connections. The process of abduction is at once frightening to the conspiracy theorist (something must be done!) and a source of enjoyment (there is much to do!), a practice that constantly requires attention and effort while providing rewards in provisional and incomplete answers and excitement. In Georg Simmel's lovely phrase, the fascination of the secret works "to intensify the unknown through imagination," to provide one who seeks the secret's unveiling a sense of exception and privilege en-hanced at those moments when especially revelatory information is interpreted.[58] This regime of signs offers a great deal to its subjects.

A Property Right in Conspiracy's Products?

If it is such a great deal, what is it that the subject of conspiracy's interpretive practices gets? If recent events are any indication, it gets a very limited prop-erty right in not only the products of one's theorizing, but in the status of the-orist itself.

Consider, for instance, the rereleased book *Report from Iron Mountain,* whose current status seems to resemble nothing less than the "Plan" come to life.[59] Originally conceived by a small group of leftists in the 1960s as a satire of the dreary reports of establishment, Vietnam War–era think tanks and government commissions, the "report" purported to be a secret document by a "Special Study Group" that argued that war was a necessary part of modern societies and must be continued no matter the possibility of establishing peace. Accordingly, the report asserted, the maintenance of American and international order required continual military engagement, an aggressive, global police force, and the possible substitution of false threats such as pollution and extraterrestrials during occasional lulls in conflict. Although a hoax, the document was published by Dial Press in 1967 without the name of its author, Leonard C. Lewin. Its initial release was quite successful, aided by a pseudonymous book review in the *Washington Post* by economist John Kenneth Galbraith, who knew of the report's actual origins.

As numerous news reports and book reviews noted upon the book's 1996 rerelease, Patriots and militia members as well as less aligned conspiracy theorists had seized the book as evidence of the emergence of the New World Order.[60] The book's rerelease had in fact been prompted by its wide dissemination on the Internet, where the assumption that it was an actual government document that had for some reason been released led to the mistaken belief that it was in the public domain. Stripped of its historical context and physical anchoring on the page, it had been distributed via E-mail and was available on the World Wide Web to any curious party; stripped of its status as property, it became part of and available within the domain of a particular "public." The report was no longer an implausible hoax intended to send up insipid and immoral bureaucratic discourse; it had instead become evidence and an element of numerous assemblages of conspiracy theory, thus productive of new texts and practices. In an attempt to stop this process, Lewin imposed both authorship and ownership by telling the world of the document's origins, and allowing Simon and Schuster to publish the book and stop all unauthorized distribution of it. As Lewin told the *New York Times,* "The nutties out there are told by their leaders — who claim to have special knowledge — that this is a real government document because it fits how they view the Government: wicked.... What this is is a copyright violation."[61]

Of course, as this chapter has argued, the status of the property right in political information is precisely what is at stake in conspiracy theory. The details that Lewin and his coauthors "created" were precisely the details that conspiracy theorists seek and fetishize, and on which their interpretive frameworks depend. Lewin objects to the transformation of his fictional, satirical text into a nonfictional, serious one that signifies in ways that he was intending to mock. What conspiracy theorists have done is to "steal" these fictional signs of power and place them in the new contexts of their interpretive chains, to rewrite Lewin's fiction into fact, to reposition his details into the broader conspiracy narratives that they construct.

Consider as well first lady Hillary Clinton's charges that Whitewater independent counsel Kenneth Starr's investigation into President Clinton's then-alleged relationship and dealings with former White House intern Monica Lewinsky was part of a "vast right-wing conspiracy" intended to destroy her husband's presidency.[62] The conspiracy theorists demonizing the president, in other words, were themselves part of a vast conspiracy, their status as marginal conspiracy theorists and thus operators of the vast interpretive machinery of conspiracy made vulnerable by the fact that they themselves are part of a conspiracy. Mrs. Clinton's exchange with an interviewer for the broadcast network morning news show is illustrative in this regard:

> Q. You have said, I understand, to some close friends, that this is the last great battle and that one side or the other is going down here.
> A. Well, I don't know if I've been that dramatic. That would sound like a good line from a movie. But I do believe that this is a battle.
> I mean, look at the very people who are involved in this. They have popped up in other settings.... The great story here for anybody willing to find it and write about it and explain it is this vast right-wing conspiracy that has been conspiring against my husband.[63]

The first lady calls for investigation and interpretation, finding the details of collaboration and uncovering the plot, turning the investigation around from the "Clinton Chronicles" to the chronicles of the individuals and groups producing them. If *Iron Mountain* demonstrates the tenuous property right in the detail, then Mrs. Clinton's argument demonstrates the equally tenuous right in the status of conspiracy theorist. In this regime of political signs, the status of interpreter and interpreted is never secure. Mrs. Clinton also invokes nicely the fact that interpreting conspiracy is inextricably bound to narrative, to the dramatic and cinematic that the specter of a vast conspiracy seems to conjure and that is the subject of the next chapter.

5. *JFK, The X-Files,* and Beyond
Conspiracy Theory as Narrative

Mr. Stone defended himself on grounds of narrative efficiency and
dramatic coherence.

> —from a *New York Times* report of a public panel
> discussion of the film *JFK*[1]

Few recent films have faced the voluminous and vituperative criticism that
met the release of Oliver Stone's *JFK* in 1991. If a conspiracy theory concerning
the assassination of an American president can become a top-grossing film
produced by a major Hollywood studio, many film reviewers, op-ed columnists,
and former and current government officials often explicitly asked, what trou-
bled future lies ahead for the political education and beliefs of American citizens? The crux of their concern, however, seemed to lie beyond the political
and social implications of the film's commercial success, and seem based on
issues fundamental to contemporary cultural crises over representation and the
real. For some commentators, *JFK*'s popular appeal was the fault of the contemporary news industry, which, by virtue of these same critics' misplaced
nostalgia for a mythical "golden age" of the American press, had lately become too little attached to truth and too much attached to commerce;[2] for others, the film's success was the fault of the "video age," wherein people, and
particularly children and adolescents, "believe uncritically what they see" (as
opposed, presumably, to other ages, other technologies, and the enhanced critical faculties of other senses).[3] Common to all of the criticism was the assertion that fault lay squarely in the hands of Stone, the technically talented au-
teur with the politics and historical sense of a drug-addled 1960s throwback.
It was Stone, after all, who had the Hollywood reputation and financial back-
ing to get such a film made, and it was Stone who could shape the shaggy-dog
tale of New Orleans District Attorney Jim Garrison's investigation into a stir-
ring Capraesque story that tapped into public cynicism and doubts about the
conclusions of the Warren Commission.[4]

This latter point, concerning Stone's self-proclaimed "efficient" and seemingly "coherent" narrative, not merely helps to explain *JFK*'s success and perceived threat to American political stability and cultural sanity, but also represents a central aspect of conspiracy theory's place in contemporary American culture. All of *JFK*'s re-creations, fancy editing techniques, leaps of faith, and conjectures presented as accepted facts would have been meaningless (and, indeed, are common fare in the virtually countless written and visual texts that constitute the corpus of assassination literature) had the film not presented a gripping, dramatic story. The gripping, dramatic story is, ultimately, at the heart of conspiracy theory, whether the narrative appears in mainstream Hollywood films such as *JFK,* the novels of latter-day pulp novelists such as Robert Ludlum, or the putatively nonfiction accounts of conspiracy theorists describing "real" conspiracies.

The conspiracy narrative is compelling in its rapid, global movement, its focus on the actions of the perpetrators of the evil conspiracy and of the defender of the moral order, and its attempt to explain a wide range of seemingly disparate, past and present events and structures within a relatively coherent framework. "Conspiracy" is not a convention of Hollywood film production because of filmmakers' antiestablishment bias or commercial cynicism, for which *New York Times* columnist A. M. Rosenthal condemned both *JFK* and Tim Robbins's fictional political biography *Bob Roberts* (1992);[5] rather, it is a narrative with a particular dynamic and trajectory that is at once a generic shorthand and a culturally and politically compelling narrative framework for filmmakers, conspiracy theorists, and audiences alike.[6]

The conspiracy narrative circulates in contemporary culture as both historical and fictional narrative. Numerous novels, feature films, and television series include in their fictional conspiracy thrillers real people, places, and events, whereas the explicitly "historical" work of conspiracy theorists typically conjures up unproven, often quite fanciful narratives to explain historical developments. *JFK* exemplifies this linkage in its presentation of a speculative and, in some respects, clearly fictional account of a real, historical event. Similarly, the network television drama series *The X-Files,* which features an ongoing narrative concerning the efforts of a multinational alliance of governments to keep secret the history of human contact with extraterrestrial creatures, often includes episodic story lines that are patterned after actual events. In this sense, the conspiracy narrative is a melding of fact and fiction, and is at its core an attempt to tell a particular kind of story about present conditions through reference to the past. Thus, most conspiracy narratives by definition assert some particular historical truth about the distribution of power.[7]

Although I use a single term, "narrative," to analyze both fictional and putatively historical texts, it is not my purpose to assert either that history is the formal and epistemological equivalent to fiction, that history is simply text or discourse, or that conspiracy theory is merely one narrative interpretation of history among a multitude of other, equally valid ones. Nor, on the other hand, am I arguing that there is an absolute, objective, historical truth whose clear light only illuminates the work of careful, "rational" scholars who resist narrativizing history, and that this truth necessarily eludes those who employ the illegitimate explanations and methodologies of conspiracy theory. Instead, following Fredric Jameson, I begin with the assertion that history "is *not* a text, for it is fundamentally non-narrative and nonrepresentational; what can be added, however, is the proviso that history is inaccessible to us except in textual form, or in other words, that it can be approached only by way of prior (re)textualization."[8] This retextualization, Jameson argues, is *necessarily narrative,* articulating in a contradictory, allegorical fashion "our collective thinking and fantasies about history and reality."[9] Furthermore, the historical narratives that make history are themselves only made intelligible in the narratives' relationships to their historical context, and specifically to what Foucault calls the struggles, strategies, and tactics of power.[10]

This chapter concerns the significance of the cultural practices and forms of this process of narrativizing history and fiction as conspiracy. Its purpose is to describe and analyze this narrative framework, to discuss its seeming "efficiencies" and "coherence" — and, as I will argue, the conspiracy narrative's tendency to excess and incoherence precisely *because* of the incessant integrative operations of its efficient coherence.[11] I will do so with regard to the general structure of three of the most important aspects of the "classical" conspiracy narrative: the role of individual agency within a particular historical situation, embodied in the protagonist who finds, resists, and destroys (or leads the way to destroying) a conspiracy; the dynamic, or what I will term the *speed* and *velocity,* of the conspiracy narrative — its tendency toward a spiraling and dazzling flow of information about a global array of people, institutions, and events; and the attempt to contain the narrative's troubling historical situation and incessant movement within a difficult and often disturbing resolution. To illustrate these characteristics, I use numerous examples but provide more extensive analyses of three conspiracy narratives, each produced in a different medium: the film *JFK,* to which I refer throughout the first part of the chapter; the television series *The X-Files*; and the well-circulated "nonfiction" conspiracy tract *The Gemstone Files.* In conclusion, I discuss those texts that seek self-consciously to subvert the structures and tensions of the conspiracy narrative, using as an example Craig Baldwin's experimental film *Tribulation 99* (1991). My assertion is that conspiracy must be recognized as a cultural practice that attempts to map, in narrative form, the trajectories and effects of power; yet, it not only does so in a simplistic, limited way, but also continually threatens to unravel and leave unsettled the resolution to the question of power that it attempts to address. In attempting to uncover the plot, the conspiracy narrative reveals a longing for closure and resolution that its formal resources cannot satisfy.

The Classical Conspiracy Narrative

General Characteristics of the Conspiracy Narrative

In this chapter, I describe and analyze what I call the "classical" conspiracy narrative, in which the particular conventions of the conspiracy narrative are articulated within the norms and standards of popular storytelling.[12] I am using "classical" in this context to refer to the formal structures and system of production and distribution that constitute the framework within which conventional conspiracy narratives are produced. The "classical" conspiracy narrative attempts to unify seemingly disparate, globally significant elements and events within a singular plot, doing so through the traditional logic of conventional popular narratives, including "causality, consequence, psychological motivations, the drive toward overcoming obstacles and achieving goals. Character-centered — i.e., personal or psychological — causality is the armature of the classical story."[13] Its central point of identification is a character who is able to effect change in himself/herself and in the world, and who, in so doing, brings about what seems a reasonably affirming narrative resolution. The resolution returns that which had been either threatened or captured by the conspiracy (often the nation or all of humanity) to a relatively secure, stable position free from the centralized power of the conspiracy, and it enables the protagonist to resolve whatever personal crises established his or her original motivations that led to or were caused by his or her finding the conspiracy. Although I am delaying discussion of those narratives that actively seek to subvert these conventions until the end of this chapter, as the examples in this section will illustrate, even seemingly conventional "classical" narratives problematize the structures of the conspiracy narrative in their tendency to career toward incoherence and in the difficulty they face in resolving the excesses of their narrative elements.

I will use the term "classical" interchangeably for both fictional and putatively historical accounts, but for the sake of clarity I will separate the initial discussion of what I mean by the term. With respect to fictional narratives, conspiracy does not, at present, constitute a distinct genre or style. It is neither a developed marketing category nor a cultural construct that circulates among producers and audiences of either film or popular novels in the same way that the thriller, mystery, and spy novel (themselves having fairly fluid boundaries) constitute organizing labels under which written and visual texts are produced, advertised, bought, and sold. Fictional narratives that feature conspiracies and paranoid narratives more generally tend to be more prevalent in certain existing genres (especially thrillers), but they are not essential to them.[14] Instead, conspiracy emerges across a limited number of related fiction genres as a recurring explanatory and organizational logic, playing an integral role in the cause and effect that propel a narrative forward, and enabling a text to develop a particular set of oppositions to and challenges for the central protagonist.[15] Like the genres of which it is a nonnecessary element, "conspiracy" works within what Stephen Neale has called a system of "regulated difference" in which individual texts, and the conspiracies represented in those texts, share basic narrative structures and stylistic elements but differ to a limited degree.[16]

With respect to explicitly nonfictional, "historical" narratives of conspiracy, I will also use the term "classical" to refer to those histories that similarly employ a conventional narrative and causal structure for their description of the "real" of history. More specifically, the classical *historical* conspiracy narrative employs what Roland Barthes has called the "reality effect," "an unformulated signified, sheltered behind the apparent omnipotence of the referent," and sheltered as well behind the social prestige of the historical speech act that declares, "*this happened*"; that is, the notion that history refers to the "real" is the product of a historical discourse whose "process of signification always aims at 'filling' the meaning of History: the historian is the one who collects not so much facts as signifiers and relates them, i.e., organizes them in order to establish a positive meaning and to fill the void of pure series."[17] Thus, in historical discourse the real is implied in socially produced "models (destined to make objects 'thinkable') proportioned to practices through their confrontation with what resists them, limits them, and makes appeal to other models."[18] In explicitly historical arguments, the conspiracy narrative presents itself as "objective history" and brings a "realistic" coherence to disparate events through an integrative logic of conspiracy in the same way that popular fictional conspiracy narratives attempt to signify a literary real in a recognizable fictional world. I will discuss both the differences between fictional and putatively historical conspiracy narratives and the tendency for individual texts to operate as a hybrid of fiction and history; however, I want to begin with the observation that there are important and prevalent similarities between the two.

If "classical" describes the general contours of the typical conspiracy narrative, Hayden White's schematic discussion of modes of historical interpretation provides a more specific, "tropological" description of the type of narrative historical interpretation that conspiracy theory employs. Conspiracy theory, both fictional and that which purports to explain actual events, is an explicitly historical argument asserting that some individual or group in the recent or remote past has secretly seized power by illicit means. One of the four different tropes of historical interpretation that White delineates is the "mechanistic" explanation, which reduces historical data "to the status of general functions of general laws of cause and effect that are universally operative throughout all of history." The key illustrative example White uses is Karl Marx's interpretation of history, which attempts to delineate an ultimate cause for the effects of human history and to explain individual events with respect to their ultimate cause.[19] The significance of this explanation for Marxism is not only explicitly political — having derived the cause of human misery, Marx's historical interpretation is intended to lead to a radical transformation of present conditions — but also in its articulation of a historical narrative. The mechanistic trope implies a tragic emplotment in which humanity's attempts "to construct a viable human community are continually frustrated by the laws that govern history." At the same time — and this is clearly its radical political component — it implies the hope for a comic resolution in which the current exploitative structure of social relations "will be dissolved and a genuine community ... will be constituted as [humanity's] true historic destiny."[20]

The tragic present/implied comic future of conspiracy narrative is central to conspiracy theory's mode of interpretation and politics, especially in its delineation of humanity's continual frustration within history by one or a series of ongoing, all-powerful conspiracies.[21] The "classical" conspiracy narrative, fictional and historical, ultimately attempts to resolve this frustration in a different way from Marxism's call for a mass revolutionary movement to overthrow the ruling political and economic order. In the accounts of "real" conspiracies, resolution occurs through the prospect and process of illumination (i.e., finding evidence and containing the conspiracy within an explanation), whereas in conspiracy fiction, the hero or heroes arise triumphant through the ultimate defeat of the conspiracy. The resolution that individual narratives represent or imply enables the imaginary resolution of the conspiratorial crisis through a comic restoration of political order.

The classical conspiracy narrative, then, is composed of certain structural and formal characteristics that individual conspiracy theories, contained in texts that are both fiction and putatively nonfiction, articulate in similar ways. Not quite a specific genre in the formal and social definition of the term, the conspiracy narrative is instead best recognized as putting forth a particular narrative logic that organizes disparate events within a mechanistic, tragic framework. The remainder of this section concerns the more prevalent characteristics of the conspiracy narrative that constitute its specificity as a cultural form and practice.

Agency and Conspiracy

Individual/History/Totality

Virtually every conspiracy narrative turns on a particular moment in which the central character, through investigative skill or by sheer luck, uncovers convincing evidence of a conspiracy. This discovery, and the realization that comes with it, deeply affect how the character perceives the world, and tend equally to affect the pace and the tone of the narrative. I will describe the effect of this "narrative pivot" on the plot's trajectory and velocity more fully in the section titled "Narrative Pivot," but it is sufficient to note here that this is a complete transition for the character: he becomes alienated from an increasingly defamiliarized political and social order, and his everyday life is suddenly vulnerable to extreme danger and violence. The uncovering of this evidence is nothing less than a totalizing conversion, affecting the character's engagement in the social world and his private life. Information has forced on the character a cognitive crisis, and every current and past event becomes subject to reinterpretation in light of a changed world.

This moment also marks the insertion of the individual into history, enabling the hero to know and to act on that knowledge. By "history" I mean the larger political, social, economic, and historical forces that are vulnerable to capture by conspiracy. The narrative pivot has forced the character to recognize what had been secret to him/her and what remains secret to most of the world: the "truth" of history. Having glimpsed this essential truth, the protagonist begins the long and arduous task of successfully effecting change on the increasingly vulnerable larger historical structures that finally are visible to him. This is equally true for fictional narratives and the narratives embedded in "factual" accounts of conspiracy; in the latter, the metanarrative pivot, the point in the writer's life in which the conspiracy reveals itself to him/her (typically described in prefatory comments, or in what Barthes has called the "preformatory opening"),[22] serves a similar purpose in enabling the narrating act contained in the text.

While demanding effective physical action of the individual (gathering evidence, engaging the conspiratorial enemy in mortal struggle, etc.), this relationship of character to history is largely cognitive and based on the collection, sorting, and interpreting of information. The individual can only begin to act by identifying and correctly unraveling the pieces of information that are immersed in history. It is thus through a cognitive act that the hero, in conceiving a "proper" history that constitutes an acceptable final outcome (i.e., the way things were and ought to be), inserts himself into the larger history presented in the conspiracy narrative. Many central characters in fictional conspiracy narratives are professionals in some kind of knowledge industry: in the conspiracy films of the 1970s, the innocent Joe Turner in *Three Days of the Condor* played by Robert Redford is a low-level member of the intelligence services, whereas Bob Woodward and Carl Bernstein in *All the President's Men* and Warren Beatty's character in *The Parallax View* are reporters; *JFK*'s Jim Garrison is a district attorney who plays the role of detective throughout the film; and many of Robert Ludlum's heroes are current or retired spies or, in *The Chancellor Manuscript,* a frustrated historian turned novelist. The same is true of famous "real" conspiracy investigators, such as journalist Danny Casolaro (see chapter 6), who claimed to have stumbled onto a secret, "octopus"-like cabal that allegedly murdered him, and Bruce Roberts, author of the *Gemstone Files* (discussed shortly), who became a spy patterned after Ian Fielding's James Bond in order to research Aristotle Onassis's supposed takeover of organized crime and the U.S. government. Faced with an imposing, omnipotent mystery, these characters turn their professional or well-developed amateur cognitive expertise toward finding, exposing, and, finally, physically challenging conspiracy. Often, their physical capabilities are inadequate or at least incommensurate with their cognitive abilities and with the forces that their opponents can marshal. Narratives at their core are an organization of data, and reading, listening to, or watching them is a perceptual activity — a "way of organizing spatial and temporal data into a cause–effect chain of events with a beginning, middle, and end that embodies a judgment about the nature of the events as well as demonstrates how it is possible to know, and hence to narrate, the events."[23] Accordingly, the cognitive act of interpretation as performed by both protagonist and audience is squarely in the foreground of the conspiracy narrative.

The conspiracy narrative thus relies on this relation of the individual to history, each term necessary to the other for their mutual survival. History, so the conspiracy narrative asserts, needs the individual in order to be saved, while the individual needs history for meaning, for a purpose — whether the purpose is acting in order to thwart the conspiracy (fiction) or revealing the conspiracy to others and urging public action of some sort ("factual" accounts).[24]

"History," then, represents totality in the conspiracy narrative, while individual characters and especially the protagonist are similarly unlimited in their representativeness. Intelligence, curiosity, and an ability to defend oneself from physical attack are recurring but by no means required attributes of the protagonists in most popular conspiracy fiction and in self-descriptions in the work of actual conspiracy theorists. In this respect, their typicality distinguishes them from both the spectacular spy (e.g., James Bond) and the fetishistically military heroics of "New War" movies and novels of the post-Vietnam era (ranging from Tom Clancy's best-sellers to the *Rambo* films and militaristic pulp fiction series).[25] Unlike more literary fictional narratives that utilize elements of conspiracy and feature complicated characters with opaque motives (such as Oedipa Maas in Thomas Pynchon's *The Crying of Lot 49* and virtually all of the characters in Don Delillo's Kennedy assassination novel *Libra*), the protagonists' motivation in popular conspiracy narratives tends to be a straight-forward, unconflicted combination of revenge (often to right a private wrong), nationalism (restoring public order and a nation's "honor"), and an abstract desire for "truth." The conspiracy narrative hero, then, is generically virtuous, and the conspiracy is undefined and seemingly limitless, a banal, almost generic evil. Fredric Jameson argues that this representativeness of character demonstrates a breakdown and subsequent "absolute collectivization" of the traditional functions of characters and roles in contemporary cultural forms in general and conspiracy narrative in particular, such that there is "no longer an individual victim, but everybody; no longer an individual villain, but an omnipresent network; no longer an individual detective with a specific brief, but rather someone who blunders into all of this just as anyone might have done."[26]

JFK's Jim Garrison, patriarchal protector of political and domestic order against an undefined, expansive conspiracy, is exemplary in this regard. He benevolently rules a home filled with wife, devoted children, and domestic servant, keeping them safe from the homosexual contagion of Clay Shaw (Tommy Lee Jones), David Ferrie (Joe Pesci), and the other leading figures of the New Orleans component of the Kennedy assassination.[27] His legal jurisdiction and professional duties as city district attorney are similarly heroic, having virtually no limits. He merely seems to take the case on by accident, as part of his generalized civic duty to impose justice, to protect "the people" from the patricidal conspirators responsible for the president's murder. As the film progresses, the conspiracy grows and demonstrates an increasing power and ability to kill (adding the assassinations of Robert Kennedy and Martin Luther King Jr.) or attempt to bribe its challengers (Garrison is offered a position as a federal judge if he ends his investigation); meanwhile, as husband, father, and district attorney, Garrison is similarly expansive and fertile, with an office swelling with recruits and a renewed, passionate relationship with his wife. At once blandly typical and wildly exceptional in these roles, Garrison comes to represent not simply one of the "children of a slain father-leader whose killers still possess the throne," as he says at the film's climax in his closing statement during the Clay Shaw trial, but the singular Son of JFK, a representative of both the crisis and potential of post–Vietnam America. The conspiracy, on the other hand, is an invisible network, a great collective — the "military-industrial complex," as a retiring President Eisenhower says in the film's opening credits — that constitutes a parallel order to the one Garrison wishes to uphold.

Once inserted into history, able to perceive the totality of social relations, the protagonist's role is precisely to restore bourgeois order. "The conspiracy" has allowed Garrison to glimpse its omniscience and omnipotence. It has also demonstrated the transparency and constructedness of the bourgeois separations between public (the law, assassination, political order, his "family" collective at work) and private (biological family, sexuality, home), as well as between economic and political order. Garrison's goal, however, is to restore order in his own home (reconcile with his wife, resume his role as patriarch) and to so smash the dreaded, looming, but invisible "military-industrial complex" — without, of course, challenging the basic structures of capitalism — that the individual components of bourgeois order will all resume their proper autonomy. In *JFK,* the restoration of order, achieved in Garrison's final courtroom explanation of the assassination (but not in the successful conviction of conspirator Clay Shaw), concerns reestablishing Garrison's control of the public realm of law and the public space of the courtroom by proving the validity of his theory, and in the domestic sphere by reestablishing his position as patriarch. Significantly, this relationship is based on individual revelation, a decidedly liberal notion of political knowledge and resistance in which redemption comes not through collective or movement-based action, but by individual effort. The only true collective or movement in conspiracy theory is that of the conspiracy itself. This secret collective has appropriated power and history, and both power and history must be reclaimed and renewed through the efforts of a singular hero who can restore global order, regardless of whether the rest of the world knows about the threat.[28]

In its totalizing impulse, the conspiracy narrative challenges classical liberal conceptions of the individual political subject. Because all of "history" in these narratives is caused by the hidden truth of conspiracy, the narratives themselves represent and enable a recognition of the totality of history, and specifically of the linkages between public and private, and between the relations of production and political and social order denied in classical liberal thought. Jameson identifies the "utopian" impulse behind the conspiracy narrative's totalizing tendencies by relating conspiracy theory to his notion of "cognitive mapping," an ideological practice in which the individual subject attempts to "span or coordinate, to map, by means of conscious and unconscious representation," the "gap" between the individual's local subject position and the totality of class structures.[29] The relationship between the individual and history within the conspiracy narrative is allegorical, and may "be taken to constitute an unconscious, collective effort at trying to figure out where we are and what landscapes and forces confront us in a late twentieth century whose abominations are heightened by their concealment and their bureaucratic impersonality."[30] The conspiracy narrative, in other words, is one of the few socially symbolic attempts in contemporary culture to confront and represent totality, to reject the ideological divisions between social, economic, and political realms on which a liberal democracy within monopoly capitalism exists. It may be simplistic and wrong — Jameson calls it "the poor person's mapping in the postmodern age," while Michael Denning, in an analysis of the British spy novel that utilizes Jameson's notion of the "political unconscious," notes that "If [spy novels'] plots often provide mystified and mendacious maps to the international order, it is perhaps less the fault of the genre than of the culture and society which can only imagine the relations between nations and peoples through the conspiracies of secret agents and spies."[31] In its attempt to insert the individual into history writ large, however — a historical realm that challenges the alienated social conceptualized within classical liberal thought — the conspiracy narrative needs to be recognized for what it is: a utopian desire to understand and confront the contradictions and conflicts of contemporary capitalism.

Despite its utopian impulse, the conspiracy narrative generally resolves the problematic relation of individual to history with recourse to precisely the social relations that conspiracy's totalizing impulse would seem to challenge. This is not to deny the importance of this challenge, however; the conspiracy narrative, as Jameson notes, is a profound, if simplified and conflicted, reflection on individual agency within the present historical moment.

History through a Gemstone: Bruce Roberts and the Gemstone Files

In its wide, international circulation over the past two decades, *A Skeleton Key to the Gemstone Files* has proved the resilience and continual appeal of its narrative of individual agency and the totality of an international conspiracy. Initially dispersed in 1975 by mail and hand as a photocopy, it has appeared in slightly revised form as an article in the pornographic magazine *Hustler,* as well as in its original form in books, on the Internet, and as the "Kiwi Gemstone," a version augmented with specifics relating the American-focused conspiracy described in the *Skeleton Key* to the political and economic elites of New Zealand. Authorship of the original *Key* is unclear. The document is a purported synopsis of more than a thousand pages of handwritten notes attributed to a shadowy figure named Bruce Roberts; however, a woman named Stephanie Caruana is generally recognized as its "author," having written and initially distributed the much shorter *Key* as a means of circulating the *Gemstone Files*'s basic thesis as widely as possible after Roberts's death.[32] Further complicating matters is the fact that no one other than Caruana and the renowned, deceased conspiracy theorist Mae Brussell claims to have known Roberts and to have seen the actual thousand pages of the Gemstone File itself.[33] Roberts purportedly began gathering the "information" contained in the file when Howard Hughes's Hughes Corporation stole his invention of a process for creating synthetic rubies — hence the title "gemstone." According to Roberts/ Caruana, Hughes Corporation used the process extensively in the development of its laser-beam research. A victim of the global conspiracy he would "uncover," Roberts's motive in developing the files was revenge, and he used the gemstones that he could create as a combination totem/payment in trade for information.

The basic conspiracy that Roberts describes in the *Gemstone Files* is of a postwar world controlled by Greek shipping magnate Aristotle Onassis and an international alliance of organized crime factions. In the complicated, forty-three-year (1932–75) scenario that it covers, the *Skeleton Key* provides the "real story" behind favorite topics of conspiracy and "legitimate" historians alike, including the disappearance of Howard Hughes (Onassis had taken over Hughes's growing U.S. power and influence by kidnapping him, shooting him full of heroin, and covertly running his businesses); the John F. Kennedy assassination (after father Joseph Kennedy arranges for the Mafia to play a vital role in his election, Kennedy had begun to adopt policies that went against Onassis's wishes); Watergate (internecine warfare between Richard Nixon, who was seeking to protect his secret alliance with the mob, and *Washington Post* publisher Katharine Graham, a longtime Kennedy friend who wanted information to protect herself against Onassis); the CIA, Fidel Castro, and the Bay of Pigs (Onassis's attempt to retake control of the Mafia-run island and casinos); Chappaquiddick (Ted Kennedy, blackmailed into working with Onassis, murdered Mary Jo Kopechne because she knew too much); and Daniel Ellsberg and the Pentagon Papers (a faked diversion from both the real purpose of the Vietnam War, which was the control of Southeast Asian heroin production, and the public's questions surrounding the Kennedy and King assassinations). The conspiracy that the *Key* presents is thus extraordinarily comprehensive, presenting an enormously integrative bricolage of mid-1970s conspiracy theories about postwar geopolitics and a horrifyingly complete domination of the world's political and economic system. A brief but detailed document, the *Key* requires careful reading and background knowledge to understand and follow the trail of often obscure references to names, places, and events.

Its narration emanates from a double source, and works to construct Roberts both as an archetypal conspiracy theorist and a conspiracy narrative protagonist — at once creator, central narrative agent, researcher, and historical interpreter. As Caruana has described him, Roberts was not a passive collector of data from newspapers and other secondhand accounts (in a reference critical of Mae Brussell and other conspiracy researchers who conduct their research primarily through the collection of documents), but obtained his information "direct from the source, and from his own experience."[34] Roberts also emerges as a participant-observer, part of the milieu of shadowy figures and secret power in which he purportedly circulated and traded information. For instance, the *Key* describes the bar where Roberts apparently spent many evenings, the Drift Inn in San Francisco, as "a CIA–FBI safe-house hangout bar, where Roberts conducted a nightly Gemstone rap, for the benefit of any CIA or FBI [agent] or anyone who wandered in for a beer."[35] Roberts's work and great heroic acts entirely concern information; he participates by trading in intelligence, and besides his performances in the Drift Inn, his only production is his legendary collection of letters. Although he seems constantly in danger — his car is the victim of a Mafia hit-and-run attack, and at the end of the *Key* he is dying from the "Brezhnev flu" (a "secret" biological weapon originally introduced by American agents into Soviet leader Leonid Brezhnev's lymph system) — his only actions are cognitive and communicative: learn more, interpret, circulate the information through letters.

That the *Key* is written in the form of a chronicle, an unfinished arrangement of events by year rather than in more conventional narrative form, adds to the seeming immediacy and authenticity of the information that Roberts has collected. The *Key*'s chronicle is made up of informative entries placed next to a year or specific date, with entries varying in length from one sentence to a multipage, thorough description of the JFK assassination. The selection, arrangement, and descriptive prose, however, project a clear narrative arc and voice. The narrative begins in media res, as Onassis, already a "drug pusher" who "made his first million selling Turkish Tobacco (opium) in Argentina," strikes a deal with Joe Kennedy to ship booze during Prohibition.[36] Rife with misspellings, some wrong dates, and breathless, sweeping prose (e.g., "1936–1940: Eugene Meyer buys the *Washington Post,* to get control of news media. Other Mafia buy other papers, broadcasting, T.V., etc. News censorship of all major news goes into effect"),[37] the *Skeleton Key* feels as though its author is pausing to write while on the lam from the mob. But its quasi-tabloid, hard-boiled style (reminiscent of Mickey Spillane and foreshadowing the more recent work of James Ellroy) draws the reader in to its comprehensive narrative through its matter-of-fact revelation of gruesome hidden "truths" and the occasional flash of sarcasm, and secret, indecipherable code (e.g., the inexplicable January 1973 entry "The Yellow Race is not in China — the Yellow Race Dead-Fucks Mary Jo Kopechne").[38] Caruana's description of the style of the files, and its influence on the *Key,* are significant in this regard:

> Roberts was not only a mental giant and powerful writer, but
> also a sort of poet. Reading his letters was like reading a

history written by James Joyce in his *Finnegans Wake* period. All of historic time (that is, the threads that Roberts was interested in) tended to be jumbled together in paragraph-long sentences. Some of my "chronologizing" consisted of bits and phrases out of these sentences, and putting them under appropriate dates — sometimes years apart. I stuck to Roberts's own words and phrases as much as I could, since I felt that any interpretation I might make of what might be a "poetic" expression on his part, might well be wrong.[39]

Unfortunately for Roberts, his great unseen modernist historical account has been stripped to its barest narrative essentials, with mere hints at the style, scope, and detail of the promised mother lode of the mythical thousand-page file.

Ultimately, what emerges from the *Key* is the forced insertion of Roberts, as representative of the betrayed America citizenry, into the historical totality of Aristotle Onassis, Howard Hughes, and all of the other "thieves at the top"[40] that the *Key* breathlessly describes. Gathering and interpreting information, Roberts is able to glimpse the totality of his historical moment. Although the narrative that survives in the *Key* already seems comprehensive, it is infinitely expandable: there is no event in the postwar world that is not already, or cannot be, included in this story. But Roberts and Caruana can do little more than describe and circulate this description as best they can. The only measure of revenge that Roberts has gained, and the only resolution his chronicle's narrative seems to reach, is in naming and encompassing the conspiracy. The very glimpse that Roberts gets, and the description that he makes of it, constitute him as a tragic but heroic figure spreading his revelatory gemstones to an ignorant world.

Conspiracy and Narrative Movement

The Skeleton Key, as a condensed chronicle of twentieth-century geopolitics, moves at a bewildering pace across historical events and an international theater of action. As with most conspiracy theories, reading the *Key* requires a map and a cast of characters in order to follow the frequent leaps in the locations and elite figures it claims to encompass. Fictional and nonfictional expositions of conspiracy present the insertion of the individual into a totalizing notion of history at a disconcerting, often incoherent pace, disrupting conventional notions of both time and space. The conspiracy narrative *moves.*

Its dynamic progress emanates from a central paradox at the core of the narrative. The conspiracy theory is at once explicable as a conflict between a central but secret power and an unsuspecting public, and an incredibly complex phenomenon that requires great skill and expertise to find and explain. Indeed, this paradox is at work in the name itself: as a conspiracy *theory,* it is a simplification of a presumptively "complex" reality; but as a *conspiracy* theory, it is a labyrinthine explanation of that which could be, and often is, more easily explained another way. Hence, *JFK* is dismissed both for its simplistic depiction of an all-powerful "military-industrial complex" and for its convoluted attempt to disprove the "simpler" and more "logical" explanation of the lone killer Lee Harvey Oswald. The "history" into which the protagonist is inserted initially appears to be the result of random causes, but it is in fact the result of a quite simple explanation that begins to surface as the narrative progresses from bewildering, frightening incoherence to unity.

This movement is itself bound to the interpretive desire discussed in the previous chapter. Like the conspiracy theorist, the conspiracy narrative protagonist and reader/viewer are propelled forward by the desire to make sense of the historical agent behind the events. Peter Brooks has described the process of "reading for the plot" as a form of desire "that carries us forward, onward, through the text. Narratives both tell of desire — typically present some story of desire — and arouse and make use of desire as dynamic of signification."[41] The narrative movement that I describe here, both structurally and with particular reference to *JFK,* shares with conspiracy theory's interpretive desire a dynamic of signification that progresses by integrating within a singular plot disparate events that occur across vast temporal and geographic horizons.

Speed and Velocity in Conspiracy Narratives

One aspect of the conspiracy narrative's representation of this movement is what Gérard Gennette has termed the "speed" of narrative, "the relationship between a duration (that of a story, measured in seconds, minutes, hours, days, months, and years) and a length (that of the text, measured in lines and in pages).''[42] A narrative that is moving at a fast speed will use quick depictions of a multiplicity of events in brief scenes encompassing a few pages or terse scenes; long descriptions of places and characters, dense dialogue, and extended cinematic tracking shots that set a mood or depict a location in great detail exemplify a slower narrative pace. In fictional and putatively real conspiracy narratives, presented in both written and visual form, the variance in this relationship establishes a certain rhythm, typically gaining in speed as the protagonist approaches, exposes, and foils the conspiracy.

The relationship between the story's duration and the text's length does not exhaust the sense of movement in conspiracy narrative, however. Thus, in addition to "speed," I will use the term "narrative velocity" to refer to the geographic, geopolitical, and cognitive aspects of the conspiracy narrative's movement. The narrative's dazzling representation of and in time is matched by its representation of the conspiracy's and the protagonist's physical and cognitive movement through historical space. An all-encompassing conspiracy is always already (almost) everywhere, always already knows (almost) everything, and has effects everywhere while appearing nowhere. The protagonist, on the other hand, must continually move or rely on numerous, scattered sources in order to collect necessary information, to track the conspiracy and its effects. The fictional conspiracy narrative maps the protagonist's trajectory across the political, spatial, and social order of conspiracy, while the historical conspiracy narrative plots the points of conspiracy's power and appearances.[43] The physical and cognitive movement of the protagonist's progress and the conspiracy theorist's work, necessarily both global and increasingly rapid as the narrative progresses and increases in speed, is what I mean by "velocity."

The conspiracy narrative's velocity is further complicated by the degree to which the conspiracy has achieved what Paul Virilio has called a "state of emergency" through its negation of space and reduction of distance. In a state run by conspiracy, the conspiracy is defined not by its singular position but by its ability to move across space, immediately and virtually unnoticed; in Virilio's words, "the strategic value of the non-place of speed has definitively supplanted that of place."[44] To the extent that the conspiracy has penetrated political, social, and moral order, constitutes an omnipresent threat of total apocalyptic destruction, and is able to communicate and move quickly with-

Before a hearing of the Senate Judiciary Committee on Terrorism, Technology, and Government Information, Senator Arlen Specter (R–PA) stands with "Commander" Norman Olson of the Michigan Militia. Photo by Ray Lustig. Copyright 1995, *The Washington Post*. Reprinted with permission.

NUMBER 14   ISSN 10602-3795 $4.50 ($5.50 foreign)

Cover from *Steamshovel Press*. Reprinted with permission of Steamshovel Press.

Kevin Costner stars as New Orleans District Attorney Jim Garrison in Oliver Stone's suspense drama *JFK*, a Warner Bros. release. Photo courtesy of Photofest.

(Left) Tommy Lee Jones as Clay Shaw, the menacing threat to patriarchal order; Michael Rooker as District Attorney Bill Broussard; and Kevin Costner as New Orleans District Attorney Jim Garrison in *JFK*. Photo courtesy of Photofest.

The Lone Gunmen: conspiracy theorists as a paranoid boys' club.

Cigarette-Smoking Man: conspiratorial agent.

Conspiracy and satire: Anthony Perkins in *Winter Kills.* Photo courtesy of Photofest.

Tribulation 99. Courtesy of Craig Baldwin.

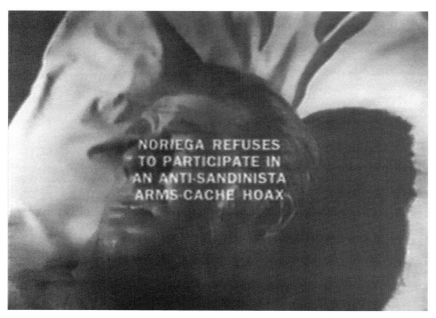

Tribulation 99. Noriega replaced by voodoo-spouting freak! Courtesy of Craig Baldwin.

www.conspire.com.

out being noticed, the narrative that represents it must be global and systematic, capturing the conspiracy's immediacy, omnipresence, and near omnipotence. In its pages, images, and/or sound, it must represent the complexity of near-total, secret control.

In representing conspiracy, in other words, the conspiracy narrative must be able to encompass the world, to posit a new world order. Consider, for example, the dynamic and amorphous properties of the Onassis/mob-related *Gemstone Files* theory that has been malleable enough to explain more recent events as well as events on a different continent (e.g., the "Kiwi Gemstone" document described earlier) without losing its general shape and thrust. Its chronicle form especially facilitates this by allowing dates to be added in the beginning, middle, and end and filled in to the preexisting structure without requiring any substantial changes. As Michel de Certeau describes the operations of historical narrative in general, "[N]arrativization creates a 'depth' which allows the contrary or the remainder of the system to be placed *near* it. Historical perspective therefore authorizes the operation which, from the same place and within the same text, substitutes conjunction for disjunction, holds contrary statements together, and, more broadly, overcomes the difference between an order and what it leads aside."[45] The *Gemstone Files,* like the conspiracy it describes, is narrative as machinic assemblage, devouring all that comes in its path, articulating all new, seemingly random, and often contradictory elements within the expansive framework of the conspiracy, doing so at remarkable speed and velocity across time as well as geographic and cognitive maps of meaning and power. In the *Gemstone Files,* the very act of identifying and chronicling this conspiracy provides a map of power; in fictional narratives or docudramas, such as *JFK,* the protagonist must follow this map with his own cognitive and physical trajectory, tracking, resisting, and defeating conspiracy as the narrative moves headlong toward its resolution.

Narrative Pivot

Conspiracy narratives especially foreground their speed and velocity at significant cognitive turning points for their main characters. Consider, for example, that moment in virtually every mainstream conspiracy-based film and novel when the protagonist gleans a single piece of information enabling him to realize the real nature of the forces that oppose him. This is also the case of many written accounts of real and alleged conspiracies, in which prefatory comments provide the "personal" story of the author who describes that turning point at which the conspiracy became clear to him. This point, a device suggestively termed by narratologists A. J. Greimas and Joseph Courtès the "narrative pivot," condenses the structures and dynamic of the conspiracy narrative within one moment, when opposing forces come into clear focus and the narrative speed and velocity begin to change pace and direction.[46] Greimas and Courtès illustrate this notion by referring to the shift in narrative sequences that occurs in the story of Oedipus, when the moment of discovering knowledge about himself and his previous acts transforms both the actions that follow and the meaning of the acts that have already taken place.[47] They term the protagonist's passing from erroneous to "true" knowledge a process of cognitive doing, an action upon knowledge consisting of an operation that would establish the true or reveal the secret (e.g., pivotal moments in a conspiracy narrative when a source provides the protagonist with crucial information) or an interpretive act that establishes a state of knowledge (e.g., the protagonist's discovery of conspiracy). These cognitive acts then affect what Greimas and Courtès call the "pragmatic": "[T]he acquisition of true knowledge, as a narrative pivot, often provokes a new series of events, capable of unrolling on the cognitive plane, but also on the pragmatic level."[48]

At the narrative pivot, a convergence of information emerges as the protagonist (and, in many narratives, the audience as well) is finally able to make the correct interpretive conclusions necessary to integrate the overwhelming amount of relatively incomprehensible data concerning seemingly disparate events that has confronted him. At this moment, the momentum shifts (though it does not abate), and the hero can finally move toward resolving the violence and deception that caused the narrative's central conflicts. Although the fast pace of cognitive and physical activity (again, coupled and dependent on each other) and the narrative's dizzying, global scope remain, the narrative's quality changes from incoherence to integration. Such blockages are conventional in the mystery and suspense genres, which rely on delay and cycles of frustration and satisfaction of curiosity, but the speed and velocity of the conspiracy narrative's trajectory toward the uncovering of an all-encompassing plot to seize power makes the narrative pivot a liminal point condensing the dynamic of movement in the conspiracy narrative.

Narrative Movement in JFK

For a film whose director claims narrative coherence and efficiency as guiding principles, *JFK* boasts a remarkably disorienting style and set of formal and narrative strategies. The film attempts to map the complex conspiracy of the "military-industrial complex" through an equally complex aesthetic composed of the intricate editing of archival footage and re-creations, varied film stocks, and a layered sound track of voice-over and sound effects. It restlessly presents its intricate historical argument, often bombarding the viewer with an incomprehensible stream of data. Structured as a classical detective story, *JFK* presents so much historical information and speculation, and moves so quickly and so far across an expanse of American political history, that it threatens to overpower the narrative and the argument that it makes about the conspiracy to assassinate Kennedy.

The two most important narrative pivots in the film that break through blockages in the narrative's focus illustrate *JFK*'s manipulation of narrative movement. At both points in the narrative, Garrison's investigation had been stuck; at each point he suspects that Lee Harvey Oswald was not the sole perpetrator of the Kennedy assassination, but he has neither concrete evidence to prove his suspicions nor a satisfactory counterexplanation to displace the dominant one. These pivots initiate shifts of momentum in which Garrison's investigation and the narrative's speed and velocity move in a new, more efficacious direction toward coherence and resolution.

The first such pivot occurs three years after Kennedy's assassination and Garrison's brief, initial interest in the time that Oswald had spent in New Orleans. Garrison's first interview with the suspicious David Ferrie (Joe Pesci) had raised doubts about the allegation that Oswald had acted alone, but the district attorney had no proof of any larger conspiracy, and the FBI had rejected the notion that Ferrie had any relationship with Oswald. Following a title card reading "Three Years Later," Garrison appears on a plane, seated next to Louisiana senator Russell Long (Walter Matthau), who humorously and cynically questions the Warren Commission's findings on the assassination. Reminded of his earlier suspicions, Garrison returns home and voraciously consumes all twenty-six volumes of the report (against the protests of his concerned wife) and imagines the testimony contained therein — visually represented through disjointed flashbacks and dream sequences that re-create both the witnesses' testimony and the actual events to which they are testifying. Oliver Stone's commentary on this sequence demonstrates his conception of the formal and narrative representation of an investigation into conspiracy:

> I wanted to do the film on two or three levels — sound and picture would take us back, and we'd go from one flashback to another, and then that flashback would go inside another flashback, like the [testimony of witness] Lee Bowers.... We'd go to Lee Bowers at the Warren Commission and then Lee Bowers at the railroad yard [on the day of the assassination], all seen from Jim's point of view in his study. I wanted multiple layers because reading the Warren Commission report is like drowning.[49]

The meeting with Long has redirected Garrison and the narrative from a point of stasis to the thrashing about of an investigator "drowning" in a sea of data and disembodied voices of (often dead, as in the case of Lee Bowers) witnesses reliving and describing their experiences at different moments in different places.

As the investigation develops, the narrative often changes speed, especially as Garrison comes closer to evidence of a conspiracy. In gathering information, Garrison and his staff obtain the testimony of witnesses, each of whom relives his or her experience of the assassination through flashback. The relentlessness of this evidence is at times overwhelming — it is difficult to recall a mainstream Hollywood film that allows so many ancillary characters flashbacks. *JFK* signals these flashbacks with quick edits and different visual styles and film stocks (e.g., from color to black and white, and from high to grainy resolution), fracturing the film's temporal rhythm and disrupting the relationship between the duration of the film's story (Garrison's investigation), its narrative form (the logic and sequence of the film's representation of Garrison's investigation), and the film's act of "narrating" (i.e., the film itself and the time that it takes to present the narrative). Mapping an enormous amount of space across not only a wide range of time, but also within a particular compressed period, the film attempts to show where the main conspirators were and what they were doing before the assassination, as well as the precise location of everyone at every moment along the presidential motorcade and in Dealey Plaza at the time of assassination.

The master narrative of conspiracy that can explain the information that Garrison collects appears at the film's second narrative pivot, during Garrison's meeting with "X" (Donald Sutherland), the fictional "inside" source that Garrison consults when his investigation seems to be reaching an end and is increasingly threatened by shadowy, powerful forces. In previous scenes, Garrison has been offered an appointment in the federal judiciary if he drops the case, and he has witnessed David Ferrie's crazed, incomprehensible monologue hinting at the broader outlines of the conspiracy. The scene with Ferrie is visually disconcerting, shot at a bizarre array of angles and film stocks and edited at a rapid, dizzying pace. Ferrie spits out quick, confusing explanations about Jack Ruby and the CIA's role in the assassination, shouting at Garrison, "Oh man, why don't you stop? This is too fuckin' big for you! Who did Kennedy? It's a mystery, wrapped in a riddle inside an enigma. Even the shooters don't fuckin' know! Don't you get it yet? I can't be talking like this. They're gonna kill me. I'm gonna die!" Ferrie's paranoia is irrational, beyond even the complex explanation Garrison will deliver in the film's final act, yet his prediction of his own demise is soon proven true. Ferrie ultimately proves to be more persuasive than even Garrison, and the character's impenetrable explanations and Pesci's exuberant performance undercut the seemingly neat explanation that the film attempts to provide.[50]

X, by contrast, provides precisely the grand plot that Garrison lacked and Ferrie could not coherently explain, enabling the district attorney to integrate the evidence he had previously collected. X's explanation is interspersed with real archival footage and reenactments of secret meetings and documents implicating Lyndon Johnson in the assassination. This montage stands in contrast to Ferrie's monologue, which received no visual corroboration and is especially difficult to follow because of the pace of Ferrie's delivery and the disorienting, quick edits.[51] X has arrived from outside the narrative, unexplained and virtually without introduction, to redirect the chaos that the film's narrative and formal strategies have developed and that Ferrie's monologue has intensified. After the interview with X, Garrison's cognitive and "pragmatic" acts begin to have greater effect: he arrests Clay Shaw (the menacing gay leader of the New Orleans part of the assassination) and finally begins to uncover and place before the public "the truth" behind the Kennedy assassination in an extended courtroom sequence. The narrative's direction has been altered from Ferrie's (freakish homosexual) chaos toward the authoritative, coherent voice of X.

JFK's valiant but problematic attempt to map conspiracy in narrative form threatens to move so quickly, at such speed and velocity, that it resists integration and coherence. As Art Simon notes, "the montages that structure so much of *JFK* resist linearity, pivoting on so many conflicts of scale and texture, color and temporality as to form any investigator's worst nightmare."[52] David Ferrie's paranoid affect seems a more rational response to the narrative he attempts to tell than does X's detached calm in delivering his masterful narration. *JFK*'s relentless movement through the evidentiary minutiae of the assassination both authenticates and undercuts its attempt to assume an authoritative historical voice — it is exhaustive and exhausting, integrative and incoherent.[53] This dynamic between narrative hypermovement and resolution, so prevalent in *JFK* but always at work in the conspiracy narrative, is the topic of the next section.

Conspiracy and Closure

Resisting an Ending

Closure, although problematic in the conspiracy narrative, does exist.[54] The classical conspiracy narrative generally attempts to resolve the complex and multifarious conflicts and crises it presents. The fictional narrative typically provides an ending that implies that the narrative's movement has, if only temporarily, stopped. Yet, the more that the conspiracy has been able to consolidate power and hide its existence, threaten those who attempt to discern it, and hurl conflicting and often incorrect knowledge at the protagonist (and by implication the audience), the more difficult it is to achieve the convergence of the narrative's conflicts and the containment and resolution of the complex plot by novel or film's end. In some texts, the impossibility of complete convergence and closure is the result of generic and industrial constraints; *The X-Files,* for example (analyzed in the next section), can only resolve individual, episodic stories, but cannot fully disclose and overthrow the larger government conspiracy until the run of the television series itself finally ends. In other narratives, however, an otherwise "successful" resolution of the narrative's central conflicts may remain implicitly disquieting — depending on the enormity of the conspiracy that had been defeated — or explicitly open-ended, if the narrative hints that new conspiracies may arise in the future.

In the putatively historical conspiracy narratives, the very act of narrating, of bringing theoretical coherence to discrete events, is itself an act of closure in its resolution of the question of power; that is, closure is the conspiracy itself, typically described in the work's introduction as history's protagonist. All that follows this act of identification is merely evidence of conspiracy. The resolution that follows, however, like the closure in conspiracy fiction, is often incomplete and disquieting. Certain explanations may be unsatisfactory, contradictory, or incoherent, and the final call to resist the conspiracy can seem hollow and pointless if the conspiracy — the historical closure — is too complete, too powerful.

Consider, for example, this explanation of the book *The Unseen Hand: An Introduction to the Conspiratorial View of History* from its Introduction:

> It will be the position of this book that a conspiracy does indeed exist, and that it is extremely large, deeply entrenched, and therefore extremely powerful. It is working to achieve absolute and brutal rule over the entire human race by using wars, depressions, inflations and revolutions to further its aims. The Conspiracy's one unchanging purpose has been to destroy all religion, all existing governments, and all traditional human institutions, and to build a *new world order* (this phrase will be defined later) upon the wreckage they have created.[55]

Chapters in *The Unseen Hand* discuss individual agents of the conspiracy in roughly chronological order, from secret societies such as the Illuminati (chapter 8) to communism (chapter 9), particular incidents of importance such as the Russian Revolution (chapter 10) and the Korean War (chapter 28), and areas of conspiratorial power such as the Federal Reserve (chapter 16) and "world government" (e.g., the United Nations) (chapter 33). To the extent that the book's final chapters call for active resistance to the conspiracy, *The Unseen Hand* resists a complete resolution to history. By its very existence and its goal of educating true Americans to the evils of communism and the "new world order," the book proposes to challenge the historical narrative that it so fully describes in its first four hundred pages. Yet, as I will argue with respect to fictional conspiracy narratives, its detailed and grandiose description of an all-powerful conspiracy makes effective resistance seem improbable, if not impossible. As a narrative resolution to the formal problem of a seemingly meaningless history, the "unseen hand" of conspiracy is a satisfactory explanation; as a form of historical closure, however, it *must* be revealed, resisted, and unraveled in the future that would follow the reading of the final page. The more complete the formal closure of conspiracy, the more difficult would be a satisfactory conclusion to history.

For formal and ideological reasons, this containment and resolution of the conspiracy narrative are crucial for fiction and nonfiction alike. The thriller genre, of which the fictional conspiracy narrative is a subset, demands some form of resolution that reaffirms the protagonist's agency, whereas the integrative historical narrative to which the nonfiction narrative aspires demands some form of coherence, an emplotment of discrete events such that they make some sense. Moreover, the larger historical structures placed in danger by the conspiracy — including capitalism and the democratic system of the Western nation-state in most contemporary American conspiracy theories — must be made safe and reaffirmed by the narrative's end. Thus, narrational velocity must be directed toward integration and coherence, and must lead to resolution. The coupling of velocity and the demands of narrative resolution, however, often leaves an affective residue of suspicious unease and fear that do not respond fully to the narrative's resolution. The conspiracy, in other words, can and generally does survive the happy ending despite the narrative's, the protagonist's, and ideology's best work.

This kind of contradiction — simultaneously moving toward and away from closure and coherence — is at the heart of narrative progression. The "desire" of the narrative — that is, the cultural assumptions shared by authors and audience, and developed in generic conventions — is contradictory: in Peter Brooks's words, narrative moves "toward ... [its] end which would be both its destruction and its meaning, suspended on the metonymic rails which tend toward that end without ever being able quite to stay the terminus."[56] Conspiracy narrative's excessive momentum—a trajectory intended to plot, reveal, and resist conspiracy in narrative form—makes this dynamic of movement and end especially difficult. For the fictional narrative, the end often cannot resolve, much less destroy, the conspiracy described; for the historical narrative, events resist explanatory closure, which itself comes to resist the promise of redemption toward which the narrative itself is intended to lead. Closure always comes, but resolution rarely arrives.

The conspiracy narrative is also productive in constructing conspiracy out of discrete events. The authoring of conspiracy in narrative form is of course an act of creation (assuming as well an act of interpretation), and the chronological and thematic "finding" of conspiracy in the progression of discrete, historical events is an act of reconstruction performed by protagonist and audience alike. Yet, the process of fictional production faces delays and hazards. Roland Barthes describes the paradoxical dynamics of the text as follows:

> [T]he problem is to *maintain* the engima in the initial void of
> its answer; whereas the sentences quicken the story's "unfold-
> ing" and cannot help but move the story along, the hermeneu-
> tic code performs an opposite action: it must set up delays
> (obstacles, stoppages, deviations) in the flow of the discourse;
> its structure is essentially reactive, since it opposes the in-
> eluctable advance of language with an organized set of stop-
> pages.[57]

It is, in Barthes's terms a "considerable labor" to keep the enigma open, to keep the conspiracy from swallowing author, protagonist, and audience.[58] The greater the narrative production of conspiracy, the more difficult its defeat— its revealing and destruction within the fictional narrative and its revealing and future destruction in nonfiction—in the narrative's closure. Even conventional Hollywood fare such as the Mel Gibson/Julia Roberts vehicle *Conspiracy Theory* (1997) cannot resist hinting at film's end that the conspiracy the protagonists had presumably defeated still pursues them in black helicopters (heard and then seen over the closing credits) and might still have the ability to create earthquakes in Turkey that endanger a visiting U.S. president.[59] Closure that would otherwise seem to lead toward a repudiation of the Gibson character's wild theories and his integration into the properly heterosexual bourgeois order, in other words, cannot be satisfactorily achieved without a winking signal that perhaps Gibson's "paranoia," created through a mind-control experiment performed perhaps by a secret part of the U.S. government, is well founded. It is as difficult to keep the enigma closed as it is to keep it open.

The X-Files *and the Problem of Serial Conspiracy*

The X-Files (1993–present) situates this dynamic within the formalistic and institutional framework of the hour-long television series drama. The series exemplifies the formal characteristics and problems of the classical conspiracy narrative: protagonists inserted into the "truth" of history, continually required to process bewildering information gathered quickly from around the world and outer space, and an episodic dramatic form whose pace quickens as tension mounts in the final act, and whose resolution seeks to reaffirm the motivations and effectiveness of its protagonists while at the same time leaving a disquieting sense of dread at the expansive power of conspiracy. Instead of the relatively contained classical cinematic narrative form, in which the film's end effects some form of resolution, the weekly television series presents a continuing serial narrative developed within smaller episodic narratives that are resolved by the end of the show's final act. Thus, although a specific investigation within a police procedural series may come to an end by the episode's closing credits, certain narrative strains — ranging from small personality quirks to melodramatic personal elements that are central to the show's main characters — are kept alive to be picked up and developed the following week.

The X-Files focuses on FBI agents Fox Mulder and Dana Scully, who are assigned to investigate those cases, known as "X-Files," that cannot be adequately explained through conventional investigative work. Mulder is the character most interested and immersed in the highly specialized epistemology and lore associated with the field of the "X-Files," which includes cases that seem to indicate the existence of extraterrestrials and a governmental conspiracy to cover up their existence, as well as crimes and unexplained occurrences related to occult practices and the paranormal. Scully, on the other hand, is the

skeptical empiricist who rejects Mulder's theories so long as they lack sufficient scientific proof (she is a medical doctor) and logic. Most episodes spend
the first three of their four acts establishing and almost fetishizing some bizarre
phenomenon, and, in their final act, barely resolve — or, quite often, deliberately leave unresolved — the phenomenon's seemingly inexplicable cause with
ambiguous or complicated explanations. Few threats are entirely dispelled by
the closing credits, whether or not the episode's story is continued the following week. Open-ended, darker, and more foreboding even than *JFK* — which
also fails to destroy the conspiracy by its closing credits, but at least confidently proposes and presents some explanation that captures "truth" within a
master narrative — *The X-Files* exemplifies the ambivalent resolution of the
conspiracy narrative.

Episodes often recycle unexplained stories from the mainstream and tabloid
news, as well as from the subcultures surrounding tales of alien abduction and
the like.[60] In this continual reference to well-circulated events both real and
imagined, *The X-Files* owes as much to the long-running anthology series *Unsolved Mysteries,* as well as to the 1970s television series *The Night Stalker,*
as it does to the police procedural/mystery series it might otherwise more formally resemble. Indeed, in transposing the marginal worlds explored in such
shows, *The X-Files* celebrates the unexplained and suspicious within a more
conventional, mainstream format, with bigger budgets and better production
values, playfully legitimating and asserting the need for the seemingly "illogical" fears of nondominant explanations for phenomena such as crop circles
that the show puts forth. This is most apparent in the recurring and popular
characters known as the "Lone Gunmen," three men who publish a magazine
by that name that focuses on government conspiracies. The show pokes gentle
fun at conspiracy- and UFO-related subcultures through these paranoid bit
players, whose roles are both ironically and affectionately performed. It is significant, however, that the Lone Gunmen and their sources of information often supply Mulder with crucial knowledge that enables him to begin or advance his investigation of governmental and extraterrestrial secrets.

One integral aspect of the ongoing series narrative is Mulder and Scully's
gradual recognition of the degree to which mysterious forces at work within
the federal government are involved in various types of suspect activities, such
as secretly capturing alien life-forms, using alien technology for military uses,

and possibly aiding aliens in their program of abducting humans for research. The book *The Truth Is Out There: The Official Guide to the X-Files,* part of the merchandising juggernaut orchestrated by the Fox network and its fellow subsidiaries of Rupert Murdoch's News Corporation, describes this series narrative of conspiracy as the show's "mythology," and asserts that it has come to "define the series as much as [*The X-Files*'s] trademark creepiness."[61] In episodes that include such conspiratorial elements, the narrative progression is formulaic: Mulder and Scully begin to investigate a phenomenon; they stumble upon or learn of some impediment put forth by governmental forces, and in the process often ascertain knowledge through informants who are themselves part of the government; and when the agents finally seem close to both an explanation of the phenomenon and incriminating evidence of the government's duplicity, their quest is thwarted and they must begin again in the next episode with little to show for their investigation and adventures. One important recurring character, a member of the governmental conspiracy known as the "Cigarette-Smoking Man" (or "Cancer Man") for his ever-present cigarette, began to assume a more visible role in the lead-up to the second season's cliffhanger finale in which he left Mulder to die in a burning boxcar filled with dead alien bodies.[62] In the second and third seasons, he became Mulder's most important adversary and was able to stop each of Mulder's investigations into the conspiracy before the agent was able to reach the cognitive epiphany of knowledge and proof of the "truth."

The individual episodic resolution of the particular "X-File," in short, cannot resolve the ongoing series narrative of the larger conspiracy. The truth, as the opening credits in the show's first season assured viewers, may be "out there," but Mulder and Scully can only catch a brief glimpse of it before it once again melts away before them. As series creator and executive producer Chris Carter has remarked concerning the tensions between the series narrative's need for openness and the commercial demands for the classical narrative of the hour-long drama: "We have long, tedious arguments about the network's desire for 'closure.' But it's hard to put handcuffs on aliens every week and throw them in the slammer."[63]

The episode "The Erlenmeyer Flask," the first season's finale, exemplifies this ongoing narrative tension between resolution and mystery that is critical not only to *The X-Files* but also to the larger conspiracy narrative of which the television series often makes use.[64] In this episode, Mulder and Scully come the closest that they had throughout the first season (and, arguably, through the fourth season of the show) to irrefutable evidence of a government coverup when they discover—after a tip from Deep Throat, Mulder's secret government informant—an almost fifty-year-old secret program to experiment with the genetic composition of alien beings. The program alters the genes of human subjects by injecting the tissue and bacteria of extraterrestrials whose space-craft have crashed on Earth. Following Deep Throat's cryptic leads, Mulder and Scully find Dr. Terrance Berube, a genetic specialist who has successfully saved six terminally ill human subjects by injecting them with alien tissue and bacteria. One of these subjects, Berube's friend and former colleague Dr. William Secare, is at large, and the secret "black organizations" within the military that initiated Berube's work attempt to kill Secare before the experiment is made public. Secare's alien genes enable him to elude capture by allowing him to breathe underwater and emit toxic fumes from his blood when shot. By following Mulder, a government team, led by an ominous character named "Crew-Cut Man," finally apprehends and kills Secare. When Mulder himself is captured after becoming sick from his exposure to the toxic fumes produced by Dr. Secare's body, Deep Throat's intervention enables Scully to steal "the wellspring," the original alien body from which the experimental tissue had been taken, as a commodity to exchange for Mulder's life. However, government/conspiracy agents kill Deep Throat during the trade for Mulder. In the episode's epilogue, Mulder calls Scully late at night to tell her that the FBI is shutting down the X-Files team because, Mulder suspects, powerful government figures fear that he and Scully are coming too close to the truth. This uncertain future serves as the cliff-hanger with which the first season ends.

"Erlenmeyer" exemplifies a number of ongoing conflicts between the larger series narrative of conspiracy and the demands of the episodic television drama. For the series narrative to continue, no single episode can resolve it; thus, for the protagonists to remain as such, they can never fully succeed. Mulder and Scully cannot right the course of the larger history in which they have been inserted, and any triumphs they achieve can be at best cognitive. If the truth is out there, they can find some part of it, but they cannot finally learn the totality of "truth," and they certainly cannot expose it. This constitutes a crisis not only for the survival and legitimacy of the protagonists—Mulder and Scully can never crack their biggest case — but also for the legitimacy of the moral order that they are supposed to uphold, which remains unrestored after every episode and every season.

Mulder's relationship with Deep Throat (whose name is an obvious reference to Woodward and Bernstein's still-unknown "source" for their Watergate stories in the *Washington Post*) in this episode and throughout the first season illustrates this quite well. Mulder's source had often given him intentionally deceptive information — the end of the episode "Fallen Angel," for example, shows Deep Throat working for the government's conspiracy in telling another government agent that by allowing Mulder to remain an FBI agent, the government could better monitor and suppress what he learns.[65] In "Erlenmeyer," however, Deep Throat seems to have switched sides. Mulder would have no inkling of this particular government program without his informant's direct intervention. Neither of the agents achieve very much by themselves, and both require Deep Throat's information and direct assistance for virtually every individual clue they find and every conclusion they make in their investigation. Deep Throat's role in the episode demonstrates the very limited agency that Mulder and Scully have in their attempts to fight and expose conspiracy; by the end of the episode, Mulder, the one who perceives conspiracy, has been rendered helpless, his chief informant presumed dead, and, in the epilogue, his position within the FBI, crucial to his access to information and the FBI's incomparable resources, is uncertain. Indeed, even Deep Throat admits to Mulder and Scully that "there are limits to my knowledge," and that some covert operations are even "unknown at the highest levels of power." The agents could not begin gaining knowledge without someone else's initiation; they were unable to retain vital evidence they had gathered, and are left with seemingly little chance of gaining more information in the future. Conspiracy constitutes too powerful a force to be contained and satisfactorily resolved at the end of the season finale, overwhelming the presumed narrative agency of the FBI and its finest young agents.

Yet, the series narrative that *The X-Files* and "The Erlenmeyer Flask" *does* successfully resolve concerns not the exposure of conspiracy, which of course cannot be fully attained without jeopardizing the series's essential conflict, but the gaining of knowledge. For Mulder, the believer, such knowledge is experiential: through his investigations, he follows clues that lead him to the computer-controlled tanks that hold the subjects of Dr. Berube's experiment and to Dr. Secare, even if the agent is unable to save the evidence to prove his suspicions. The scientific Scully obtains her evidence in hard, scientific form, through a scientist at Georgetown University's Microbiology Department who performs computer analyses that find alien DNA in blood from Berube's lab. The ultimate story line to which the larger narrative arc of the show's first season has led reaches its denouement when the skeptical Scully finally concedes to Mulder that "I've always held science as sacred. I've always put my trust in the accepted facts. . . . For the first time in my life, I don't know what to believe." In lieu of the impossible resolution of the conspiracy, Scully's epistemological crisis and break due to "hard" evidence, and her insertion into the interpretive practices of "Spooky" (his nickname within the FBI) Mulder, is the series narrative's resolution of their previous hermeneutical duality. Scully now believes, and when Deep Throat whispers his dying words "Trust no one" to her, she is interpellated as paranoid investigator of conspiracy. The conspiracy cannot be defeated within the narrative; instead, the narrative can be resolved only through the characters' gradual realization of its existence. It is significant, then, that the first season's "cliff-hanger" concerns whether the agents will continue to be able to gain more knowledge though their work investigating the X-Files.

Of course, the serial nature of the network television schedule requires an ongoing narrative, and so the success of *The X-Files* requires the reopening of the "X-Files," while the Mulder-believer/Scully-skeptic dynamic requires the latter to renounce, or at least suspend, her acceptance of Mulder's interpretive practices. In addition, by the next season's second episode, the series introduced a new source (named "X") to replace Deep Throat.[66] Unlike *JFK,* whose narration ends at the film's close and whose narrative ends with the verdict in the Clay Shaw trial, the serial narrative of *The X-Files* is dependent only on the institutional structures of network television (such as audience ratings and the decisions of network programmers and producers). Unbounded by series closure (at least not yet), the show's "mythology" may expand across television seasons, onto new continents and perhaps into outer space — not to mention into a film, books, music, magazines, comic books, and trading cards, and "official" conventions and merchandise — and, ultimately, anywhere the Fox television network (which broadcasts the show), Twentieth-Century Fox Film

Corporation (which produces and distributes it), and their bosses at Rupert Murdoch's News Corporation can sell or license it.[67] *The X-Files* is an ongoing narrative of secret government perfidy that by design cannot reach closure, put forth through the ever-expanding channels of one of the most powerful private figures and media conglomerates of the contemporary era.

Unraveling the Plot
Conspiracy Theory and the Subversion of Narrative Form

In its serial structure, *The X-Files* foregrounds the problematic closure of the classical conspiracy narrative, demonstrating, on a weekly basis, the difficult task of moving forward toward its protagonists' ultimate uncovering of the "truth" of history while delaying this revelation for at least another week (or, while still successful, another television season). *The X-Files* is a dramatic example of the ways in which the formal structures of the classical conspiracy narrative are vulnerable to continual unraveling. Even the most seemingly generic texts such as the *Gemstone Files* and *JFK* challenge the notion that conspiracy theory relies on a static, formulaic conception of history and power. The formal narrative structures of conspiracy might explain power in an ordered, seemingly rational way, but the excesses they produce continually subvert the order that they create. Conspiracy theory represents the desire for, and the possibility of, a knowable political order; yet, in its disturbing revelations and uncertain resolution it also implicitly recognizes the difficulty of achieving transparent, equitable power relations in a capitalist democracy. Despite its professed intentions of uncovering the plot, the classical conspiracy narrative is inherently ambivalent about uncovering the "truth" of power and the possibilities of a different future.

This dynamic is even more prominent in those narratives that seek to subvert the formal structures of the classical narrative, including "postmodern" novels such as Don Delillo's *Libra* (on Oswald) and Pynchon's *The Crying of Lot 49,* experimental films such as *Tribulation 99: Alien Anomalies under America,* and mainstream popular novels and Hollywood films that undermine generic expectations through satire (as in, for example, the work of author Richard Condon, and especially his novel *Winter Kills* [1974] and its film adaptation [1979]) or by adopting some of the mannerisms of European art film (e.g.,

The Parallax View [1974]).[68] Whereas the classical narrative attempts to retain coherence and structure in spite of its crises of agency, incessant movement, and ambivalent closure, these texts seek explicitly to challenge the protagonist's heroic agency posited by the conspiracy narrative, to splinter structure and coherence, and ultimately to refuse the limitations of formal conventions by producing open-ended texts with multiple perspectives and no master narrative with which to explain and restore order. Delillo's dismissal of *JFK* is illustrative of this distinction: "Regardless of [Stone's] imagination I don't think [*JFK*] was anything but an example of a particular type of nostalgia: the nostalgia for a master plan, the conspiracy which explains absolutely everything."[69] *Libra* and other postmodern, experimental, and satirical works provide a "respiritualization" of the conspiracy narrative, constructing "a world in which dark, unnameable psychic forces are in play, forces which, like those of magic and divinity, are not subject to the physical law we think we are bound to obey,"[70] and in doing so refuse the attempt to enclose such forces within the classical, "nostalgic" conventions of individual human agency, comprehensible historic forces, and closure.

Tribulation 99, a faux documentary by Craig Baldwin purporting to reveal the truth about a conspiracy of space aliens who had arrived on earth three millennia ago from the planet Quetzalcoatl, demonstrates this quite well. The film includes ninety-nine brief sequences ("tribulations") with explanatory voice-over narration that purport to "expose" various aspects of this conspiracy. The tribulations, composed of quick cuts of bizarre images and filmed sequences, are pieced together in a rough and jumbled editing style, separated by title cards such as "Earth's Creatures Flee in Terror," "1972: Watergate Martyrs," and "E.S.P.: El Salvador's Poltergeist" written in the tabloid style of *Weekly World News.* The film's visual imagery relies on "found" footage from nature and science films, documentaries of natural disasters, science-fiction and monster movies (especially from the 1950s, but also from later films such as *Westworld*), cheap Mexican pulp movies, James Bond films, and footage of the Kennedy assassination. The musical sources also include "found" material such as the theme from the television series *Mission Impossible,* as well as a spooky, slowed-down rockabilly version of "Ghost Riders in the Sky."

The film's narration, which ties these scattered sources into something that seems to resemble narrative coherence, brings together numerous pieces of conspiracy and ufology lore. At various moments, the description of the Quetzalcoatl plot refers to the Skull and Bones society at Yale, the CIA, the United Fruit Company, Central American politics, the Bermuda Triangle, legends of Atlantis, Easter Island, and the depletion of the ozone layer. After briefly noting the alien origins of the Quetzalcoatls, the narrative focuses on the post–World War II period, where it displays an exuberant anticommunist mania in its descriptions of Quetzalcoatl-led revolutions throughout Central and North America. According to the narration, these uprisings enabled the aliens to appease their alien gods by offering human sacrifice; thus, any counterrevolutionary or colonialist undertakings performed by the American military and intelligence agencies were a righteous attempt to fight these pagans from another planet. Patching together Cold War rhetoric with a psychotic fixation on satanists, werewolves, aliens, and androids, the film claims that Fidel Castro was an alien (look at how many assassination attempts against him failed!); virtually all indigenous peoples' movements against American and corporate exploitation were caused by the Mayan Indians' secret pact with the Quetzalcoatls; the assassination of Salvador Allende was necessary to stop him from rotating Earth's alignment; Grenada was invaded because it had been taken over by vampires (as illustrated in *Tribulation 99* through footage lifted from the *Blacula* films); Eugene Hasenfus, whose plane was shot down over Nicaragua as part of a mission to aid the contra rebels, was delivering Bibles, not guns; and the United States invaded Panama because former CIA asset Manuel Noriega had been abducted by the Quetzalcoatls and replaced with a werewolf.

As a formal exercise, *Tribulation 99* demonstrates not only that the detritus of popular culture and geopolitics can serve equally well as the material of conspiracy, but that such material can relatively easily be assembled into an overarching theory through the narrative machinery of conspiracy. As easy as it is to construct such a narrative, this construction is always already relatively incoherent, moving forward with the continual threat of falling apart. Even with the aid of the book based on the film, *Tribulation 99* makes no sense as a whole, the ninety-nine "tribulations" scattering in hundreds of different directions.[71] Although individual tribulations might make some sense—especially in their parody of the official explanations for CIA activity or American atrocities in Central America—attempting to understand the entirety of the Quetzalcoatl plot is futile. Its formal exercise, in other words, is its point: *Tribulation 99* lays bare the narrative and interpretive machinery of conspiracy theory.

Both classical narrative's fetishization of its vulnerable and problematic structures and nonclassical narrative's formal subversions fixate on and manipulate the conspiracy narrative's shape and characteristics. John Frow, in comparing the popular thrillers of Robert Ludlum with Don Delillo's novel *Running Dogs,* has noted that the formal characteristics of the conspiracy narrative offer "a material that can be worked against the grain of the genre. It is the material itself which in part determines the possibility and the limits of its textual working."[72] This material enables coherence and incoherence, closure and its absence, hero and cabal. In conspiracy's narrative structure and possibilities lies its powerful promise to map and explain the power that lies elsewhere. If, however, the structures of the classical conspiracy narrative offer a utopian promise of knowledge and resistance, a cognitive map of power, then they also contain within them the undoing of that promise, the unraveling of that map.[73] Their narrative desire might be to make some order out of the chaos of history and to provide some answer to the riddle of power, but the conspiracy narrative itself offers no programmatic response or emergent politics to replace the conspiracy it so intricately uncovers and explains. Conspiracy theory's resistance is limited to interpretation and narrative, relegating its opposition to the problems of the dominant political order to the realm of a limited hermeneutical resistance to a prevailing linguistic order.[74] Conspiracy theory may emplot power on a narrative trajectory, but in so doing it fails to contradict its own assumptions about the coherence of conspiracy and the possibilities of resistance.

Part III
Conspiracy in Everyday Life

6. Millennialism and Christian Conspiracy Theory

> Peter knew the prophecies concerning the Rapture, but even this
> great apostle didn't have the insight into prophecy that the diligent
> believer can have today through the Holy Spirit.
>
> In our time we can see that current events unlock areas which
> were hidden from the understanding of earlier believers.
>
> —Hal Lindsey[1]

Christian eschatology and millennialism, the study and belief in the end of
human history and the return of Christ in a coming glorious age lasting one
thousand years, have been central to Christianity since its beginnings, and can
be traced back at least to Jewish apocalyptic belief. In the United States, as
well as throughout any area of the world touched by fundamentalist and conservative evangelical Protestantism, there is widespread belief in the imminent
return of Christ and the establishment of his millennial kingdom as prophesied by certain biblical passages. The exact figure of those who believe in an
imminent millennium is impossible to ascertain, but given the large numbers
of American Christians who consider themselves fundamentalist and "born
again" (according to a Gallup poll, as many as one-third in 1986, and probably more now),[2] and the millennium's central role within the dogma of most
fundamentalist and conservative evangelical denominations, such believers certainly number in the millions. A *U.S. News and World Report* poll found that a
relatively large percentage of respondents believe that current fundamentalist
Christian beliefs in biblical prophecy are literally true, and more than half believed that some world events in the twentieth century fulfill biblical prophecy.[3]
In addition, the proliferation of nonfiction books, videotapes, weekly television shows, and novels relating biblical prophecy to human history and current
events demonstrates the ongoing religious and cultural importance of millennialism. In the months following Iraq's invasion of Kuwait in 1990, for example, evangelical Christian publishers rushed more than a dozen prophecy volumes into print, with *Armageddon, Oil and the Middle East Crisis,* by leading
millennialist seminary professor John F. Walvoord, selling more than a million copies in the first months of 1991.[4] By the mid-1990s, one Internet Web site

was even providing continual updates, with an estimated quantitative measurement, of the proximity of eschatological triumph based on current events.[5]

The general model of a historical and futuristic narrative that describes the apocalyptic coming of a millennium has been remarkably resilient, particularly within Christian cultures. Although the apocalypse can be disconfirmed (i.e., it does not happen at a specific moment seemingly prophesied by the Bible), the narrative model itself is not discredited and can remain current through the appropriation of changing cultural and political interests, rival apocalypses, and different historical knowledges and historiographical epistemologies.[6] Despite historical developments such as the defeat of Saddam Hussein and the breakup of the Soviet Union (which, in many theories of the apocalypse, was supposed to march on the Middle East imminently), as well as many attempts both within and outside the church to debunk the theories and historical elements behind apocalyptic narratives, popular Christian eschatology remains a vibrant religious and cultural practice.[7] With the term "popular eschatology," I am referring to texts that provide an accessible and comprehensible, all-encompassing narrative frame or metanarrative that can explain the past, the present, and the future for a mass audience.

Popular, mass-mediated texts that circulate these kinds of narratives warn and proclaim the degree to which biblical prophecy is coming true, thus heralding the return of Christ. They also attempt both to make prophecy a comprehensible aspect of Christian belief and to make the practice of reading about and deciphering prophecy in light of current and historical events a popular activity. Popular eschatology thus serves as a form of historiography, articulating and circulating a method of historical interpretation, a general theory of historical agency, and an underlying structure that points to the direction in which human history travels. This is not, however, a theory and method of research for professional historians; rather, much of contemporary eschatology serves as a form of *popular* historiography that seeks to provide an overarching theory of history in an accessible format in order to call readers to action to participate in the practice of interpreting history.[8]

Popular eschatology also contradicts dominant historical narratives of human progress in its belief in the supernatural determination of human events and in the ultimate irrelevance of human agency in curbing sin and improving the world. Indeed, it seems explicitly to deny the ability of humans to know and fully understand what human history is at all. Its call to challenge received notions of history and for Christians to investigate and "unlock" secret knowledge through the rewriting and rereading of human current events and history (as the best-known popular eschatological author Hal Lindsey does in this chapter's epigraph) seems to constitute an actively resistant cultural practice that struggles over the signs and meaning of history. This type of popular historiography, in its interpretation of current events and history through biblical prophecy and supernatural signs, demonstrates the degree to which the production and reception of history and historical narratives work as a crucial site of cultural struggle over the understanding and representation of the past and the present, as well as the conditions of possibility for the future. Although distinctly religious, popular eschatology shares with the historical narratives articulated by reactionary and progressive groups the attempt to contest "consensus" explanations of historical actions, agents, and forces.[9]

The parallels with and direct connections of popular eschatology to conspiracy theory are both clear and important. Popular eschatology is based on a specific master narrative, it is followed through the active interpretation of events by both prophecy "experts" and many everyday fundamentalists, it is based on a mechanistic theory of power, and it shapes the political beliefs and activities of those who come to believe in it. Further, popular eschatology often echoes, and at times explicitly borrows, the theories of more secular right-wing conspiracy theorists, blurring the lines between eschatology and reactionary conspiracy theories.

My purpose in this chapter is to note the cultural significance of such a form of historiography in relation to the roles of fundamentalist Christians in contemporary American culture and politics, as well as in relation to the seemingly more secular historiography of conspiracy theory. As Lee Quinby argues, "apocalypticism constitutes a regime of truth that blurs religious and secular lines, informing a range of beliefs and practices that include popular culture, fashion, science, social science, technology, and so on."[10] I do not, however, want to consider popular eschatology as equivalent to or defined by "secular" conspiracy; they each emerge from distinct, if at times overlapping, social and cultural contexts. This was the error in the outcry by liberal columnists in the wake of Michael Lind's and Frank Rich's attempts to "expose" Pat Robertson's 1991 book *The New World Order,* which reiterated and relied heavily on the work of current and early twentieth-century right-wing conspiracy theorists.[11] For Lind and Rich, to the extent that Robertson's book reproduced the implications and intonations of Nesta Webster and other earlier and contemporary anti-Semites, he is as much a conspiracy theorist as Louis Farrakhan and a militia leader such as Mark ("from Michigan") Koernke;[12] but to the extent that Robertson was a conspiracy theorist, his book and his understanding of history "have little to do with ordinary evangelical Protestant theology."[13] On the one hand, Robertson's is a loopy and paranoid secular conspiracy theory with (ir)religious overtones; on the other hand, he does not reflect the proper spiritual cast of (true) Christianity. In fact, although *The New World Order* is merely one of many articulations of the very distinctive popular eschatological narrative, its conspiracy theory–like presentation of the relationship between prophecy and current events, as well as its discussion of the proper response of a committed and righteous church, are quite typical of texts produced and circulated within certain sectors of conservative Protestant fundamentalist culture. Robertson's work and the similar, more explicitly proselytizing texts described in this chapter both relate to and are distinct from seemingly nonreligious conspiracy theory, and a proper analysis needs to look at both the affinities and the divergences.

The first part of this chapter provides a general historical background on conservative Protestantism and millennialism in the United States, specifying the religious and social context within which popular eschatology operates. The remaining sections analyze three different types of popular eschatological texts, including "nonfiction" print accounts of biblical prophecy, as exemplified by the work of the phenomenally successful author Hal Lindsey; "nonfiction" prophecy on videotape and weekly television broadcasts that review current events in light of biblical prophecy; and three commercially successful Christian novels whose near-future narrative is closely based on the eschatological master narrative.[14]

Contemporary American Fundamentalism and Conservative Evangelicalism

Contemporary popular eschatology is part of the general collection of religious and social beliefs of the regionally and culturally diverse movements associated with American conservative Protestantism.[15] The historical development of a fundamentalist movement may have been partially brought about, and was certainly hastened, by the circulation of liberal, modernist Protestantism in the nineteenth and early twentieth centuries, and much of the rhetoric of the current movement seems to be a simple and strong reaction against what it perceives as the twin modern evils of humanism and liberalism. There is, however, a strong and well-documented set of beliefs associated with contemporary conservative Protestantism.[16] These beliefs include the final authority of the Bible, the real historical character of God's saving work, salvation to eternal life through the redemptive work of Christ, emphasis on evangelism and missions, the imminent Second Coming of Christ, and the importance of a spiritually transformed life.[17]

Although "conservative" and "modernist" or "liberal" Protestants share some doctrinal principles, their differences are central to understanding the hermeneutical principles, politics, and historiography that are at the core of popular eschatology. From the late nineteenth century onward, modernists have advocated higher and historical criticism of what is seen as an often "metaphoric" (as opposed to an inerrant) Bible, modern scientific beliefs such as evolution, and certain secular aspects of civil society such as the strict separation of church and state. They have emphasized human progress as the continuing manifestation of the powers of God working in and among men and women, and they interpret the Bible as a literary and historical text. They perceive the historical process to be the result of a close relationship between the divine and the historical, and the Bible, rather than serving as an encyclopedia of dogma or a set of prophecies that will literally come true, represents either a historical account of a divine encounter or an ancient model of religious experience.

Conservatives, on the other hand, base their religious beliefs and practices on what they perceive as literal readings of an inerrant Scripture. Pessimistic about modern culture, they view history exclusively through a particular reading of Scripture and emphasize the supernatural and the direct intervention of the divine in historical change. Just as many biblical prophecies were fulfilled within the Bible, so biblical prophecies made in Revelation and other important books that have not yet come to pass will herald the return of Christ. Despite this belief in the supernatural and prophetic, the hermeneutical principles and the more general epistemological assumptions and methodologies of conservative Christianity are by no means antiscientific or even antimodern. As George Marsden has argued, conservatives' notion of inerrancy and the evaluation of biblical readings rely on exact conclusions and literal, logical, almost scientific readings of the text. Their methodology is largely based on Baconian positivism, favoring simple, positive empirical evidence and confidence that these kinds of commonsensical scientific principles will reveal the truth of the Bible's inerrancy, as well as the truth of biblical prophecy.[18] Indeed, respect for the absolute inerrancy of the Bible, as Ernest Sandeen has pointed out, has been so central to conservative American Protestantism that dispensationalism, the dominant theology for understanding biblical prophecy in the twentieth century, was able to win converts during the latter part of the nineteenth century because its hermeneutic "required, in fact presupposed, a frozen biblical text in which every word was supported by the same weight of divine authority."[19] In this sense, the hermeneutical principles of contemporary fundamentalism and conservative evangelicalism bring together specific aspects of a scientific epistemology and a deep belief in the importance of the supernatural. Thus, interpreters read Scripture as if it were modeled after a Newtonian view of physical universe: created by God, the Bible is a perfect, self-contained unity governed by exact laws that can be discovered by careful, modern analysis and classification.[20]

A similar contradiction in the beliefs and social practices of conservative Protestants is their simultaneous rejection of religious modernity and acceptance of aspects of contemporary society and life, and their adaptation, or more precisely, their articulation, of popular religion to modernity.[21] In this somewhat strange articulation of "conservative" dogma, beliefs, and social practices to modern economic and political structures as well as contemporary everyday life, fundamentalism and conservative evangelicalism work as popular forms of religious practice. Part of the appeal of popular eschatology is its appropriation of the contemporary vernacular of the written word, the electronic media, and popular narrative forms.

Fundamentalism emphasizes everyday, individual experience and practice, as well as a personal relationship with various forms of authority, including Christ, Scripture, and one or more preachers, rejecting the higher criticism of modernists precisely because the latter cannot be experienced and is beyond the realm of the average Christian believer. The fragmented denominations of conservative Protestantism allow for a more dynamic relationship among groups of preachers and believers rather than being constrained within tight, concrete hierarchical structures of established denominations that place theological, political, and social control of religious practice away from individual ministers and parishioners.[22]

Fundamentalist and conservative evangelical Christians' very prevalent and successful use of the most modern forms of mass communication displays this combination of secular modernity and conservative Protestant beliefs within popular forms and practices, extending Christian notions of evangelism and American notions of progress to an identification of technology with the Almighty.[23] Practitioners embrace the popular and commercial success of mass-media religion, while the marketplace serves as a crucial metaphor in which such figures as the number of copies of a book sold and the television or radio broadcast rating serve as indices of souls saved and are used as selling points of evangelical effectiveness in further requests for funds.[24] Ultimately, fundamentalists and evangelicals have appropriated the secular techniques and technologies of mass communication in order to develop and represent what Stewart Hoover has called a long-distance, mass "parachurch" of organizations, ministries, missions, revivals, broadcasts, recording companies, publishers, and clubs, which surround the more formal denominations and congregations of American Protestantism.[25] Within the parachurch, members are constituencies interested in what the ministry/media business (such as the *700 Club* or the Trinity Broadcasting Network) or Christian broadcasting star (such as Pat Robertson) with whom they identify can do to spread the gospel.[26]

Similarly, activist conservative evangelicals and fundamentalists who engage in public politics bring "traditional" moral precepts to the contemporary political arena. The mobilization of the portion of conservative Protestant Americans whose religious, social, and political beliefs led them to view the realm of politics as suitable for Christian activity (which many fundamentalists, whose beliefs lead them to reject the secular realm, do not), led to the development in the late 1970s and early 1980s of what has become known as the "New Christian Right." Such political mobilization was not in itself new in twentieth-century American politics, as a number of religious figures before and after World War II used revivals and radio broadcasts to circulate conservative political messages. The New Christian Right, represented most clearly throughout the late 1970s and early 1980s by the very visible Moral Majority and subsequently in the more "grassroots"-oriented Christian Coalition, have focused on a domestic political battle against secular humanism and the perceived immoralism of modernity (exemplified in issues such as abortion, school prayer, feminism, and homosexual rights), as well as on the deployment of greater military resources against communism and in support of Israel. It has achieved large organizational scale and increasing financial and political success through its use of mass communications and direct mail, and has been more inclusive as a political movement than previous conservative Christian political movements by building alliances with conservative Catholics, Jews, and Mormons, as well as with the more secular conservatives of the New Right.[27] It is crucial to reiterate, however, that the New Christian Right and leading figures such as Jerry Falwell and Pat Robertson do not represent the political views and activities of all conservative Protestants, although their relatively successful attempts to portray themselves as such have increased their public and political visibility and importance.[28]

It is important also to note that the exuberant belief in a coming end is not universally embraced by all conservative evangelicals and fundamentalists. *Christianity Today,* one of the most important periodicals intended for conservative Christians, has published articles critical of extremist eschatology, calling for more "reasonable apocalypticists" or critiquing the often error-prone and excessive viewing of current events through Scripture.[29] Further, as Charles Strozier found in his study of fundamentalists, believers espouse a variety of beliefs and approaches to eschatology, often at least partially determined by gender and class, many containing confusing and self-contradictory elements but each sharing a deep longing for Christ's return. Whereas working-class believers tend to foresee the rapture occurring sooner than those of higher economic status, women stress the transformations of salvation associated with Christ's return, while men concentrate more on the destructive and apocalyptic elements of rapture.[30] Some believers, such as those described touring Israel in search of the landmarks of the end time in Grace Halsell's *Prophecy and Politics* (1986) and those living without fear near a hydrogen bomb assembly plant in A. G. Mojtabai's *Blessed Assurance* (1986), shape their everyday lives and beliefs around the thought and assurance of a coming rapture.[31] Others might include the imminent return of Christ as part of their general structure of beliefs without thinking about it or following the voluminous literature, films, and television or the ministries and preachers that center on the end time.

Social historian Paul Boyer seems to capture this variance best in his image of the "world of prophecy belief" as a series of concentric circles, at the center of which is a core group of devotees who invest a great deal of their time and resources on investigating, reading, attending study groups, and listening to and watching various media about the apocalypse. The next circle would include those believers who might not necessarily know as much about or follow the various interpretations of the prophetic biblical passages nor connect such passages with current events to the degree those in the first circle do. Finally, in the outer circle are more secular individuals and groups whose beliefs about and fears of the future may include a latent notion of a coming apocalypse, but whose religious and social practices may be divergent from the dogma and doctrines of conservative Christians. This latter group includes those who, in addition to having purchased Hal Lindsey's books and the volumes of popular eschatology published during the Persian Gulf War, may also read non-Christian prophecy or predictions, such as the many interpretations of Nostradamus or the astrology of Jeane Dixon.[32] At all of these levels, participants may use or even rely on information and theories from explicitly secular and nonreligious sources.[33] Thus, although eschatology is clearly part of conservative evangelicalism and fundamentalism, its importance varies within the lives and denominations that constitute this complex set of movements; it may actively seek information from outside the circle of committed fundamentalists, and it is also absorbed and accepted, to widely varying degrees, into secular society and culture.

Types of Christian Millennialism

In addition to varying in importance for Christian individuals and denominations, eschatology also varies in type. Nearly all forms of Christian millennialism rest on the belief in an extended (one thousand years or more) period, closely associated with the return of Christ, in which a kingdom of God is established on Earth. From this relatively standard belief, there are a number of divisions based on the timing of the coming millennium, precisely how the kingdom will be established and what role the church will play in its coming, and how the millennium fits into the past and the present of human history. The basic disagreement between "postmillennialists" and "premillennialists" (as opposed to "amillennialists," who reject the notion of a literal millennium) can best be understood this way: "*Postmillennialists* believe that Christ will return *after* the church has established the millennium through its faithful and Spirit-empowered preaching of the gospel; while *premillennialists* expect Christ to return *before* the millennium in order to establish it by his might."[34] These are two very different ways of reading and interpreting the Bible, as well as of understanding the historical past, the present state of the world, and the possibilities of the future.

Postmillennialists believe that the kingdom of God is now being extended through the work of Christians in living righteously and spreading the word of the Gospels, winning the world to Christianity, reducing evil, and enabling the church to assume greater leadership over worldly institutions. This activity leads directly to a millennium in which peace and prosperity reign, and closes with the return of Christ, the resurrection of the dead, and the final judgment.[35] This understanding of the Bible's teaching grants the church, as an agent of Christ, a crucial role in preparing and bringing about the millennium, and posits a historical trajectory in which the future is a progression from the past and the present. For many contemporary postmillennialists, this "progression" toward the millennium is a struggle between good forces who work in Christ, and evil (often satanic) forces that seek to limit Christian influence and the "rights" of Christians to practice their beliefs.

Premillennialists differ over the signs and narrative of the coming millennium. This chapter concentrates on the narrative trajectory espoused by dispensational premillennialists, the most active, vocal, and visible of premillennialists.[36] The basic elements of their approach constitute the metanarrative of popular eschatology. For dispensationalists, certain signs will precede the coming of the final stages leading up to the millennium, including the general worsening of human society, the preaching of the gospel to all nations, and more devastating natural disasters and violent wars. Soon afterward, the church will be "raptured" (i.e., "caught up" into the air to dwell with the Lord) and thus saved from the horrific days to follow. A great "tribulation" period ensues after the rapture and before Christ returns to Earth, during which the Antichrist, as the agent of Satan, will rise to worldwide dominance. The triumphant return of Christ at the battle of Armageddon will end the Antichrist's reign, and Satan's power will be bound as Christ establishes his millennial kingdom. An easily subdued revolt led by Satan will briefly challenge Christ's kingdom a thousand years later, and the resurrection of the dead, the Last Judgment, and the creation of a heaven on Earth will follow. Whereas postmillennialists see the kingdom of God being established over and in human time through the winning of individual souls and by an increasingly powerful church, premillennialists perceive the kingdom as coming through a sudden, powerful, and violent transformation that marks a complete break with the preceding period of human history.[37] Within the present day, known as the "church age," there is little hope for success within human institutions and even within the church itself, which is doomed in its attempt to convert and save the world (but which, despite this fact, should not stop trying to spread the Gospels). A personal belief in and relationship with Christ will save the individual, but the judgment at the end of the seventh and final dispensation will wreak havoc and destruction on worldly nonbelievers, and Christ will establish a literal kingdom in Jerusalem for a full millennium, or a thousand years.

Millennialism in the United States

Dispensationalism has become the most prominent form of millennialism among contemporary fundamentalist and evangelical Christians, but millennialism had been a part of many colonists' religious beliefs prior to the circulation of dispensationalist ideas in the post–Civil War period. Jonathan Edwards's confident postmillennialism during the mid-eighteenth century and the religious "awakenings" of his era eclipsed premillennialism as a dominant belief for a long period and helped give rise to nationalist ideologies of the United States as a "redeemer nation" that could best establish the Lord's dominion on Earth.[38] For a number of reasons, over the past hundred and fifty years postmillennialism has lost much of its popularity among conservative Christians, although it has clearly remained important as the secular and political doctrine of nationalism. In particular, the concept of "Dominion Theology" and the Christian Reconstruction movement, both of which are postmillennial in their faith in the advancement of the kingdom of God through history, have gained followers and visibility for postmillennialism over the last few decades.[39] As Robert Clouse has argued, postmillennialism emerges in the political pronouncements of premillennialists who enter the public arena;[40] when Jerry Falwell and many other politically active Christian fundamentalists argue for a return to "Christian values," their desire for change and progress (and faith in the public arena by engaging in it) contradicts otherwise strict beliefs in premillennialism. Such internal contradictions between premillennial politics and rabidly conservative, nationalistic postmillennialism constitute one conflicted terrain on which the narrative and interpretive practices of popular eschatology meet those of right-wing conspiracy theory.[41]

The Civil War helped to destroy some Christians' belief that Christ's kingdom could be realized within their own age and that humanity could bring about its own spiritual or historical development, and postmillennial optimism concerning both the nation's and the church's potential to change the world receded. In addition, as liberal and modernist theologians were influenced by new trends in naturalism and historicism and began to abandon belief in the work of the supernatural in history, conservatives reconsidered many of their assumptions about human progress and the positive transformation of humanity.[42] Earlier, a premillennial movement led by William Miller, whose "date setting" of Christ's return for October 1844 gained as many as a million followers, had returned the notion of Christ's imminent and millennial return to the forefront of American religious beliefs. After their "great disappointment," however, many of the Millerites formed their own denomination, Seventh-Day Adventists, and had little further influence on premillennialism.[43] Despite the seemingly unattractive example of the Millerites, however, premillennialism has become increasingly influential and popular since the latter part of the nineteenth century.

The American visits, proselytizing, and biblical commentaries of British minister John Nelson Darby during the 1870s began dispensationalism's American circulation and popularity during the post–Civil War period. In the early part of the twentieth century, the overwhelming success of the Scofield Reference Bible (1909), which sold millions of copies, carried dispensationalism to a broader public. By the end of World War I, dispensationalism had become so important and compelling that its teachings were a dominant aspect of revivalism.[44] As Timothy Weber notes, in order for any form of premillennialism to persuade American Christians in the latter half of the nineteenth century, it would have to establish two facts: that it was connected to and worked within the evangelical and orthodox teachings of the American Protestant mainstream, and that it was in no way associated with the teachings of the Millerites. From the earliest American followers of Darby to the leading premillennial ministers at the turn of the century, dispensationalism circulated through the structures of conservative Protestantism as a reading of Scripture wholly consistent with the tenets of the evangelicalism of the time. This specific form of premillennialism ultimately found favor with an increasing number of ministers and believers through years of proselytizing of dispensational doctrine in mission revivals and through the conversion of important pastors.[45]

The central difference in millennial understanding between Millerites and dispensationalists lies in the distinction between "historicist" and "futurist" understandings of prophetic events. Historicists believe that biblical prophecies have been fulfilled within history, whereas futurists expect the fulfillments of prophecy to take place in the future. For these two strains of thought, the clock recording prophetic events reads different times: for historicists such as the Millerites and current Seventh-Day Adventists, the clock has already begun and the purpose of eschatology is to ascertain when the world will end and Christ will return; for a futurist hermeneutic such as dispensationalism, the clock is poised to start as prophetic events begin to take place, and no "last days" prophecy will be fulfilled until just before Christ's return. This difference is crucial in understanding how these different forms of millennialism perceive the future and interpret the present and the past. Historicists more often try to ascertain the date of Christ's return by comparing past events, biblical predictions, and the present. On the other hand, while many futurists pay close attention to world events in order to compare them to prophetic statements, most refuse to set a future date for the second coming as, according to oft-cited biblical passages, no one can know the date or the hour of Christ's return.[46] Premillennial dispensationalists interpret the "church age" (or dispensation) of the years from the crucifixion and resurrection to the present as a relatively insignificant period of frustration and waiting, and neither Christ's return nor any important prophetic event will take place within it.

For the dispensationalist, then, the present has little significance above and beyond the spreading of the gospel (which itself is doomed to limited success, if not abject failure, because this is still before the millennium) and providing "signs" through which Bible-reading and -believing Christians can read and sense a coming end. It is this emphasis on sensing a coming end, of attempting to recognize and understand what Hal Lindsey calls "the key that would unlock the prophetic book: . . . the current events that . . . begin to fit into the predicted pattern,"[47] that popular eschatology microscopically investigates. The remainder of this chapter focuses on the grand narrative and master hermeneutic that three different popular eschatological texts share.

The Late Great Planet Earth
Narrative, Commentary, Imminence

Since the early 1970s, the foremost figure in popular eschatology has been Hal Lindsey, a graduate of Dallas Theological Seminary, one of the leading centers for dispensationalist theology. Lindsey's books are mass-marketed by the secular paperback publisher Bantam, which picked up his first book, *The Late Great Planet Earth* (1970; hereafter, *LGPE*), after its initial success with a Christian publisher. They are available in both religious and nonreligious bookstores, deal either directly or indirectly with prophecy, and trumpet on their covers the millions of copies his books have sold.[48] Two important aspects of Lindsey's work have been his emphasis on reaching young people — in addition to clearly directing his work, and especially *LGPE,* toward youth and college-age students, he has lectured about prophecy on college campuses — and his use of other media, including radio and television programs, to spread dispensationalist readings of prophecy. All of his work warns that the end is soon to arrive; in the three decades that he has been a best-selling author, he has continually pointed to current events in the Middle East, the Soviet Union, and what he sees as the social breakdown of the United States as sure signs that this generation is the "terminal" one and that this decade is the "countdown to Armageddon."

LGPE, his first and most famous book, proceeds from a general introduction setting forth the problems of predicting and understanding the future through a brief presentation of biblical prophets ("daring men, sure of the source of their faith and strong in their belief" [9]) and prophecy. Within the book's initial movement, the problem of an uncertain future is resolved through the Bible, which Lindsey describes as accurate in both short- and long-range prediction, particularly about the First Coming of the Messiah. Lindsey focuses on what he and other dispensationalists perceive to be the most important prophecy of the Bible in signaling the final movement toward the end times: the returning of Jews to a sovereign Jewish nation of Israel. The fulfillment of this prophecy "set[s] the stage for the other predicted signs to develop in history" (47).

The remainder of the book concerns these predicted signs; individual chapters focus on the various "players" of eschatological visions of the future: Russia (equivalent to the "Gog" peoples of Ezekiel), which is developing a vast army and confederacy and will march on Israel; the Arabs, who will join with Africans and be led by Egypt in a march on Israel; China and a vast "Oriental horde" of more than 200 million soldiers; and the European Community, which will form a new Roman Empire and dominate the world under its leader, the Antichrist. In addition, Lindsey identifies the current conditions that will prepare the way for the Antichrist as a world dictator, including the rise in crime, wars, famines, and population, all of which will lead many to call for some supreme global authority to control earthly chaos. He describes a spiritual domain in similar peril, decrying the increasing popularity of non-Christian, pagan, and satanic religious practices and an increasing apostasy in the mainstream Protestant denominations. These religions will provide the groundwork for the rise of the false prophet, a master of satanic magic who leads the world even further from Christ. All of these narrative agents enter into the penultimate battle of Armageddon in Israel, causing worldwide destruction and ultimately foreshadowing the return of Christ, who defeats the Antichrist and establishes the millennium.

This is an elaborate, universal narrative that links history, current events, and a singular vision of a violent and apocalyptic future to a particular set of readings of biblical prophecy. Lindsey's narrative is not new; it relies on the basic narrative structure delineated by Darby and the early dispensationalists and borrows from the work of other eschatologists who have linked dispensationalism's readings of prophecy with the present day. The power and influence of *LGPE* and Lindsey himself can be traced not merely to the book's exposition and retelling of the dispensationalist historical narrative, but also to Lindsey's ability to narrate the story in such a way that it draws readers in through his use of language, his presentation of prophecy and Christian faith as direct experiences in which the reader can participate, and his naturalization of the supernatural to explain and resolve humanity's conflicts and fears. Indeed, *LGPE* (along with many eschatological texts intended for popular audiences) continually and excessively interrupts and steps outside of the story in order to comment on how commonsensical, exciting, and truthful prophecy is for Christians and for those willing to give themselves to Christ. This excessive commentary simultaneously draws the reader into the historical narrative and attempts to articulate eschatology as a practice and set of beliefs that the reader can and must practice.

One of the most obvious narrative strategies in *LGPE* is its emphasis on prophecy as direct and experiential, even as its practice engages in the indirect and intellectual pursuits of theology or history. As the introduction to *LGPE* reads, "This is not a complex theological treatise, but a direct account of the most thrilling, optimistic view of what the future could hold for any individual" (vii). Similarly, although Lindsey describes the study of history as "dry bones to some," he promotes the kind of history that *he* studies as fascinating (35). Lindsey provides an ongoing metacommentary on the narrative he constructs: this is exciting, this is fascinating, this is entertaining, educational, and can bring about your salvation to boot. The language that he uses — particularly in *LGPE*, which is very much a product of the late 1960s — is an attempt to articulate and, to a certain extent, parody the vernacular of youth culture. The chapter on the rapture, for example, is titled "The Ultimate Trip," and the one on the apocalypse is "The Main Event." The writing is simple, clear, and declarative; the commentary continually intercedes, exhorting the reader on and into eschatology, and the direct and plain language of both narration and narrative attempt to communicate a highly charged, metaphysical story of the relationship between the material and the spiritual, the thrilling theological and the fascinating historical.

In associating theological and historical interpretation, *LGPE* assumes a one-to-one relationship between the two in which the supernatural intervenes directly within the human and historical. History's role is to provide the manifest evidence of the workings of the spiritual: "As world events develop, prophecy becomes more and more exciting. Also, the understanding of God's prophecies becomes increasingly clear as we look at the Bible and then at the current scene" (77); "The Bible contains clear and unmistakable prophetic signs. We are able to see right now in this Best Seller predictions made centuries ago being fulfilled before our eyes" (7). One reads prophetic eschatology to become engaged in the practice of studying history and current events, and to link the worldly to the supernatural. The proper and exciting study of the end times enables an understanding of the work of the Lord, the true determinant in human history and individual lives.

LGPE's emphasis on promoting this connection between the supernatural, the theological, and the historical draws readers into the *practice* of popular eschatology. As American fundamentalism and conservative evangelicalism emphasize the experience and practice of individual believers reading the Bible and having a personal relationship with Christ, so Lindsey's work extends this emphasis into the practice of thinking human history, current events, and the future through his and dispensationalism's readings of biblical prophecy. Lindsey writes: "Bible prophecy can become a sure foundation upon which your faith can grow — and there is no need to shelve your intellect while finding this faith. . . . We believe that a person can be given a secure and yet exciting view of his destiny by making an honest investigation of the tested truths of Bible prophecy" (7–8). Lindsey continually exhorts the converted and the unconverted to make "honest investigations" into the world of eschatology as well as further into their faith and into the reading of the Bible.

Notwithstanding the notions of the "honest investigation" and individual experience of prophecy, popular eschatology and dispensationalism in particular strongly structure these "individual" readings and experiences within an already-established framework — there are, after all, proper and improper readings of prophecy and current events for Lindsey and others. The verb form of "a person can be given a secure and yet exciting view" positions this "honest investigation" within a passive or at least preconstituted interpretive practice. In this sense, the interpellation of the reader within eschatological practice is also an interpellation into the ideological structures and practices of conservative Protestantism — the reader is called to practice and experience what others preach.

Further drawing the reader into the texts and practices of popular eschatology is Lindsey's continual referral to what he describes as an almost basic human need to know, as well as what he sees as a pervasive fear of the future: "In talking with thousands of persons, particularly college students, from every background and religious or irreligious upbringing, this writer found that most people want reassurance about the future. For many of them their hopes, ambitions, and plans are permeated with the subconscious fear that perhaps there will be no future at all for mankind" (7). The eschatological subject's need for assurance and fear of the future can be resolved, Lindsey asserts, by faith and understanding in Christ and by knowing the past, present, and future through specific readings of the Bible:

> All we need to do is know the Scriptures in their proper context, and then watch with awe while men and countries, movements and nations, fulfill the roles that God's prophets said they would. (65–66)

> As we see the world becoming more chaotic, we can be "steadfast" and "immovable," because we know where it's going and where we are going. We know that Christ will protect us until His purpose is finished and then He will take us to be with Himself. We can "abound in his work" as we trust Him to work in us and know. (77)

Eschatology is itself a historical agent: The ancient Jewish temple on Mount Moriah will be rebuilt for a third time, despite the presence of the holy Muslim Dome of the Rock mosque on the same spot, because "prophecy demands it" (45); when China marches on the Roman dictator/Antichrist at Armageddon, we will know that "[h]istory seems to be headed for its climactic hour" (76). Because the supernatural controls historical movement ("history" heading toward a supernatural "climactic hour"), knowing and believing in the supernatural enables readers to know and be assured of the future.

If "history" moves without human influence, if the realm of human history is merely the stage or the visible level of the supernatural powers that determine events and change, then Lindsey and popular eschatology in general seem to posit a world without human agency. This suggests that observing as events unfold within the "biblical" patterns outlined by "professional" eschatologists is the correct collective response to the narrative frame that Lindsey constructs. The correct individual response is a new or renewed commitment to Christ. Interspersed throughout *LGPE* and all of Lindsey's books — in the introductions, in the final paragraphs of chapters, in the midst of describing a prophetic passage and its relevance today, and, of course, in the books' final words — are calls to salvation:

> The big question is, will you be here during this seven-year countdown? Will you be here during the time of the Tribulation when the Antichrist and the False Prophet are in charge for a time? Will you be here when the world is plagued by mankind's darkest days?
>
> It may come to surprise you, but the decision concerning your presence during this last seven-year period in history is entirely up to you. (126–27)

> As history races towards [the battle of Armageddon and Christ's return], are you afraid or looking with hope for deliverance? The answer should reveal to you your spiritual condition.
>
> One way or another history continues in a certain acceleration toward the return of Christ. Are you ready? (156–57)

Human agency, removed from the historical narrative through the metaphysical power of the supernatural, returns in a limited way in the individual's decision to become a part of the body of Christ, to ensure that she takes her place in the more desirable part of the narrative, the rapture rather than the tribulation. In deploying its historical narrative to define the good from the bad, Christ from the Antichrist, true Christianity from the false prophets and apostasy of New Age and liberal Christian movements, and the agents of God from the agents of evil, popular eschatology presents a decision between two possible choices that, for the model reader, is not a choice at all. Through its excessive articulation of the inexorable movement of history, the historical narrative of Lindsey's popular eschatology places the reader in the text (and, ultimately, in the Bible) by allowing her to "choose" to follow the narrative to its ecstatic resolution (the rapture, Christ's return, the millennium) or be swept aside in the tribulation and left outside of time.

Watching Prophecy Unfold
Popular Eschatology on Television

Nearly all premillennial broadcast programs on television and radio, whether or not they feature Lindsey, reiterate the general narrative framework and assumptions about the relationship between current events and biblical prophecy that appears in his work. What is particularly interesting about end-time television shows, and what differentiates them from the style and medium of nonfiction, mass-market paperback publishing, is the degree to which they articulate popular eschatology through the structure and conventions of the television news and information program. Focused on the most recent events in the secular world, shows such as *Jack Van Impe Presents* (*JVIP*) and *This Week in Bible Prophecy,* which appear on the Trinity Broadcasting Network (TBN), in syndication, and via satellite, present the latest news and concentrate on specific issues that are crucial to the eschatological narrative. *JVIP* boasts a professional set that resembles that of an authentic television newsroom, and Jack and his wife Rexella Van Impe resemble televised news anchors. As the introductory narration proclaims, the *JVIP* show purports to be "a news program analyzing and evaluating world events. From our international headquarters, Dr. Jack and Rexella Van Impe report and interpret late-breaking headlines for millions in twenty-five thousand cities and towns, coast-to-coast in America, Canada, and Europe, making this one of the most important newscasts today."[49] During the announcer's voice-over, images of what look like important news events (an atomic bomb explosion, soldiers at war, official-looking men shaking hands in front of large buildings, etc.) and of Jack and Rexella poring over news clippings flash quickly on the screen.

Both shows borrow heavily from the conventions and values of secular news in other ways, especially in their attempt to present an authoritative, expert exposition of current events. Televised eschatology, however, is more explicit in its interpretive project than mainstream news shows: it presents events only to interpret their significance specifically for a spiritual purpose. Structurally resembling a comedy team's straight-line/punch-line rhythm, both *JVIP* and

This Week in Bible Prophecy feature hosts (Van Impe and Peter Lalonde) explaining the significance of the current events introduced by their cohosts (wife Rexella Van Impe and brother Paul Lalonde, respectively). As the significance of the discrete event for the larger prophetic narrative develops, the cohosts innocently, but also knowingly, attempt to educate the audience both in the larger framework and the interpretive practice that appropriates the "event itself" (associated with the seemingly unknowing cohost's reading of a news report) into the eschatological (produced in the host's prophetic reading of the event). As in Lindsey's books, both the hosts and the cohosts sprinkle each show with wonderment and metacommentary (e.g., "You can't have such an array of signs and not know the Lord is coming soon!"),[50] and each show ends with a call to conversion and belief ("You can sit and be amazed at these things all day long, but will you bow your head to Christ?").[51]

During June 1992, both shows focused particularly on the creation of the European Community (EC; the EC became the European Union [EU] in 1993), understood within popular dispensationalist eschatology as the likely site of the new Roman Empire.[52] This is particularly significant because the EU's location is the possible base from which the Antichrist shall rise, and the formation and ascendancy of the EU are thus sure prophetic signs of the coming end. Van Impe dealt specifically with Denmark's 1992 vote against acceptance of Maastricht Treaty and the effect that this rejection would have on the number of nations in the EU. The number ten is significant in this context because of dispensationalists' belief in the prophetic significance of the appearance of a ten-horned beast described in Revelation 13 and Daniel 7. For Van Impe, who at the time saw Denmark as a nation that would not be part of what would become a ten-nation EU, this event demonstrated how "everything is coming right according to the predictions of the Scriptures as far as the fulfillment of these things is concerned."[53] (In fact, twelve nations, including Denmark, ultimately signed the Maastricht Treaty in 1993.) On the episode of *This Week in Bible Prophecy* broadcast the same week in 1992, the Lalondes advertised a special videotape, for $19.95, on the EU. The brief advertisement for the tape noted that "Students of Bible prophecy have always known that this day [the formation of the EU] was coming. The Scriptures are very clear in telling us that in the last days a revived Roman Empire would emerge, with its nucleus on the European continent. Today many see this superstate as the hub of the

New World Order."[54] Much of the week's episode concerned the EU, focusing in particular on an illustration in *Time* depicting Europe as a woman riding an animal — and, as the Lalondes saw it, as an image of the harlot riding a beast that the Book of Revelation identifies as a sign of the coming end. Furthermore, the Lalondes consider the development of the EU to be the first human attempt since the Tower of Babel to create a "new world order" — the phrase, both dreaded and fetishized by conspiracy theorists, that refers to the ultimate conspiratorial one-world government. In order to illustrate this and to demonstrate, once again, the pervasiveness of signs of the end-emergent global political authority, they used two advertisements by multinational corporations, Xerox and Lockheed, that employ the image of Babel. These images of prophetic signs are not, the Lalondes assured viewers, mere coincidence:

> Some images that have been hidden below the surface for generations are beginning to come forth and we as Christians should see these as signs that the Lord is coming back soon — that exactly what was prophesized [*sic*] in the Bible is beginning to come to pass and it's not only recognized by us, it can be recognized by everyone out there.[55]

In addition to their similarities in structure and content, *JVIP* and *This Week in Bible Prophecy* are quite repetitive over time. Indeed, given the overwhelming significance of time to the eschatological narrative, these television shows emphasize the fact that the hermeneutic they present must necessarily focus on current events and must regularly measure time. Each week's show brings new revelations about the prophetic "meaning" of the events of the previous week, and more specifically during 1992 about the EU, the return of Russian Jews to Israel, further discussion of plans to rebuild the Temple on the Mount, and the possibilities of war in the Middle East. During what seem to be slower periods for popular eschatology, the shows focus on somewhat less momentous current events.[56] In short, the hosts' readings emphasize currency and demonstrate both the immutability of the broad outlines of the eschatological narrative and its flexibility in fitting recent events within the flow of time toward the coming end. The metanarrative structure remains quite stable, but the precise unfolding of events takes place in changeable form. Similar to television news, these shows' hosts literally "anchor" the contingencies of the weekly events within the larger temporal structure of eschatological Bible prophecy. Unlike Lindsey's books, *JVIP* and *This Week in Bible Prophecy* must regularly and continually update and refine their interpretation of worldly events because, given the demands of both the electronic medium and the un- known and unknowable specifics of the eschatological narrative, weekly tele- vision cannot fix the narrative's development in time. As a result, these shows represent more strongly than do Lindsey's books the sense that eschatology is an ongoing practice of interpretation in which the imminence of Christ's re- turn is measured on a regular basis. Extending the texts and practices of sens- ing the end to a different medium, popular eschatological television utilizes somewhat different conventions and allows for the interpretation of immedi- ate events, but retains the same basic narrative structure and style of narration as print-based popular eschatology.

Narrating the End
Millennialist Popular Fiction

The millennialist novel, a "realistic" fictional representation of a near-future end time barely averted through the power of prayer and the work of good Christians, has become an increasingly popular cultural form among conserv- ative Christian readers.[57] Borrowing from popular eschatology in narrative sweep but influenced also by the secular thriller genre, these novels tell the story of a future in which Satan and God wage war on Earth, and the Antichrist and Satan's other agents gain control of the world through the oppression of Christians, the sinful nature of humanity, and apostasy and false religion. Like other forms of popular eschatology, these novels' focus is universal and global; the battle is real and everywhere for the souls of Christians. Yet, like the thriller, the narratives of these novels focus on one or a few characters who attempt to uncover and fight the satanic conspiracy. As models of proper Christian be- havior, these characters are quite conventional, but the novels themselves face a difficult resolution, one related to but quite distinct from the conspiracy narra- tive's closure: How can realistic naturalism, human agency, and narrative clo- sure — so central to the structure of popular fiction — be achieved within a nar- rative structured around an apocalyptic belief in the supremacy of the spiritual, a belief that denies the possibility of realism, humanism, and human triumph?

Another central problem these novels face is creating a plausible narrative that includes the rapture, an element of eschatology that assumes that the saved will be taken up into heaven before the tribulation period. This, of course, precludes all that would be interesting in an apocalyptic novel, and would be best suited for an evangelical tract intended to convert nonbelievers by showing them the terror that the unsaved face during the period of tribulation. Indeed, the film *A Thief in the Night* (1972) represents that very "horror," beginning the morning after the rapture has already occurred; it has been used, apparently quite successfully, in youth missions for decades.[58] Two of the three novels discussed here approach the edge of the millennium only to pull back, leaving the future, as well as the distinction between pre- and postmillennialism, open; the third, Pat Robertson's *The End of the Age,* is firmly postmillennial, and so faces the continual narrative crisis of having its ending entirely foretold before and during the early parts of the novel.

The Illuminati (1991), a very successful novel by Larry Burkett published by the Christian publishing house Thomas Nelson, exemplifies the problematic articulation of the end-time story within popular fiction. Prior to the novel's publication, Burkett was already well known among many fundamentalists for his "biblically informed" financial advice and doomsday predictions concerning federal spending and monetary policies delivered in books such as *The Coming Economic Earthquake* (1991) and his frequent appearances on Christian television programs such as the *John Ankerburg Show* and the *700 Club.* Burkett has repeatedly warned against the "godless" and socialistic spending and budget deficits undertaken by the federal government, and in his warnings the economy — determined by the spiritual world in an interesting reversal of Marxist notions of the base–superstructure relationship — faces the same imminent apocalypse as every other element within a society that has forgotten Christ.[59]

The Illuminati is set at the turn of the twenty-first century, when an agent of Satan, working through a secret group called the Society (with ties to the Druids, the Freemasons, and the Illuminati, whose members have included Mao, Lenin, and Hitler) attempts to prepare the world for Satan's rule. The story includes many of the elements of popular premillennial eschatology, including the imposition of a one-world government, the mark of the beast (a mark on the skin that the devil will require everyone to wear), rising violence against

Christians, "Asian hordes" marching on Israel, and the threat of nuclear disaster. The world averts the end times, however, through the work of underground Christian groups and an innocent computer genius turned hero. Satan does not, however, suffer his ultimate defeat; as the novel ends, the specter of another potential Antichrist looms on the horizon, "chosen to prepare the world for the final conflict that would eventually pit the people of God against the forces of Satan to arise in fifty years" (306).

The novel serves as a morality tale in which Christians learn the importance of both faith and the need to fight the influence of Satan wherever it appears. The list of such influences reads like an accounting of New Christian Right fears: "militant homosexuals" who chant "God is dead, God is dead," carry placards with inverted crosses, and riot and loot homes; the "National Civil Liberties Union," which leads the violent persecution of Christians; the anti-Christian, liberal media, which circulates false information and serves as a tool of the Antichrist; and federally enforced bans on firearm ownership. The novel's description of a conspiratorial "secret society" covertly controlling the political machinations of evil resembles closely the entire history of right-wing paranoia concerning such entities as the Freemasons, the Jews, the Illuminati, the Council on Foreign Relations, and the Trilateral Commission. Importantly, the connection between such conspiracy theories and Christian fears of satanic influence is well articulated in Pat Robertson's book *The New World Order* (1991). Indeed, *The Illuminati* (which was published in the same year) seems at times to be a fictionalized account of Robertson's "nonfiction" description of the workings of Satan in contemporary America.

Through these references to contemporary social and political issues, the novel's landscape references the historical events of the current day, particularly as perceived by Christians who consider themselves under the siege of a hostile government and culture. Yet, this "realistic" landscape serves merely as an epiphenomenal surface for the seething spiritual and supernatural battle waged beneath the surface. The would-be Antichrist, Amir Hussein (a half-Arab, half-Jew Israeli), working through the secret society he manipulates, attempts to control the United States and ultimately the world by turning people against Christ and Christians and exterminating those believing Christians who resist. Christians who do not recognize their dire situation within a superficially secular but in fact satanically controlled world must either rebel or face forced removal to concentration camps. The novel provides no spiritual options besides fundamentalist Christianity: Jews are either dupes or willing accomplices of the Antichrist, while non-Western religions are directly linked to the satanic plot.[60] Secularism is an impossible position because the "spiritual warfare" between good (Christians or moral people who by the novel's end will recognize the spiritual necessity of conversion) and evil is so encompassing that any claim for the nonspiritual merely masks the work of Satan.

Of course, this direct, deterministic relationship between the superstructure of the human and the base of the supernatural is part of the model reader's set of religious beliefs, and the novel works both to confirm and to narrativize this belief—to set the spiritual and contemporary events within a narrative that can carry both forward into a possible future. Although the end is not apocalyptic, the moral lesson is clear: the characters who either retain their committed, personal relationship with Christ or who come to him as a result of the events of the novel are saved, and all of the saved must work together to fight the power of Satan on the human plane. The end is averted, yet still near, and only true Christians can survive the end of the novel and the end of the world.

Like Lindsey's attempt to encompass all of the world's events and document American military strength and that of its enemies, Burkett's book features global geopolitics and technological fetishization, both of which are foremost elements of the satanic conspiracy's massive computerized tracking system and the military engagements manipulated by the Antichrist. Frank E. Peretti's *This Present Darkness* (1986), a precursor to *The Illuminati* in the Christian thriller genre, narrates a far more local series of events associated with a satanic plot to take over Ashton, a small college town in an unnamed state.[61] Peretti's novel has been enormously successful, spawning an audiocassette adaptation and several sequels.[62] As with *The Illuminati,* which featured the pairing of a committed white Christian preacher with a moral yet religiously uncommitted computer genius, *This Present Darkness* follows the simultaneous realization of a local minister and the owner of the town's small newspaper (both of whom are newcomers to the town) that evil forces are at work in Ashton. The beginning of the novel describes a town in radical decline: "For generations Ashton had taken pride in its grassroots warmth and dignity and had striven to be a good place for its children to grow up. But now there were inner turmoils, anxieties, fears, as if some kind of cancer was eating away at the town and invisibly destroying it" (27).

The conspiracy behind this decline includes a psychology professor at the local college who mesmerizes students and prominent locals with her New Age/satanic powers, a powerful man who is secretly buying the town and college through his company, the Omni Corporation, and a legion of evil spirits working to prepare the world for the rise of satanic rule. Thus, Ashton serves as simply one local site within a global plot; occasionally, the novel offers a glimpse into the same worldwide conspiratorial elements on which *The Illuminati* focuses exclusively, including the "New World Order," the "New Age Christ," and the role of the United Nations, the World Bank, and the European Community. Unlike *The Illuminati, This Present Darkness* has a dual, spiritual narrative that represents the determining basis for human action. While the human characters struggle within "the world," the spirits that correspond to their spiritual beliefs fight an invisible war that, through the help of Christian prayer and Satanic "meditation," replicates the characters' worldly struggles. As in *The Illuminati*, humanity averts the end times through prayer, action, and conversion, yet it continues to face the looming threat of evil, as the good spirits fly off in the final scene to protect a successful revival in Brazil from another satanic insurrection.

The popular fictional narrative from which both of these novels borrow requires the use of certain conventions, including a "realistic" setting, one or a small number of protagonists whose rational actions bring forth some kind of change, and a resolution that brings closure to the narrative. However, although the eschatological metanarrative brings closure to the progression of dispensations under which humanity has been judged and resolves the ongoing spiritual battle between the forces of good and evil, it radically calls into question realism and human agency. The apocalyptic biblical prophecies, particularly as they are interpreted and articulated within popular eschatology, provide a violent, fantastic vision of supernatural warfare that allows for little human agency beyond the individual choice of committing one's life to Christ. *The Illuminati* and *This Present Darkness* attempt to resolve this potential representational crisis by positing the spiritual as real (Peretti's novel describes the battle of good and evil as an actual occurrence on a separate plane of action; Burkett presents the potential Antichrist as a real character) and by allowing for some limited human agency (in *This Present Darkness,* human prayer is essential to the angels' battle; in *The Illuminati,* the human characters are able to repel the Antichrist's rise, at least for the next fifty years). Although the eschatological metanarrative provides closure, its ending seems literally unrepresentable within the thriller genre, which seems at best able to promise a heaven on Earth under Christ's kingdom but cannot narrate the ultimate deficiency of human agency necessary to achieve it. For the apocalypse to come, the effort of humans to save the world morally and spiritually must fail. Significantly, neither novel presents this ending, offering instead a contingent resolution to an individual narrative while leaving in place, as a looming threat, the failure of humanity and the saving grace of apocalypse.

Pat Robertson's *The End of the Age* (1995), in contrast, plods forth into the millennium.[63] Unlike both straight and "fictional" prophecy, *The End of the Age* offers no mysteries or riddles to be deduced from current events, and provides little tension as to whether humanity will be saved. From the very first chapter, when word leaks of the impending collision of Earth with a huge meteor plunging into the Pacific Ocean off the coast of southern California, the novel does not hesitate in signaling that the Antichrist is rising and Jesus is returning imminently. *The End of the Age* begins by focusing on two families who are able to escape from what will soon become the devastated and uninhabitable West Coast, and who end up in the survivalist camp of evangelist John Edwards outside Albuquerque. The meteor, the novel quickly relates, not only eliminates life in the western United States, but because of the giant tidal waves, volcanic eruptions, nuclear accidents, and earthquakes caused by the meteor's impact, as well as the resulting cloud of volcanic ash that blankets the Earth, most of the world suffers terribly. Meanwhile, satanic elements in the American government, acting through the Hindu god Shiva, seize power and promote New Age religion, "deviant" sexual practices, widespread drug use, and the persecution of Christians throughout the world.

The novel is odd for a number of reasons, especially given the position of its author as an important political figure and activist in the religious right. The spiritual warfare it describes between Satan and God so overpowers human agency that, other than by providing moral and material support for Christians who cannot reach Edwards's compound and by saving a few more souls, the most that believing Christians can do is to take refuge in the prophetic scriptures of the Bible. Indeed, whole passages in the middle of the novel describe impromptu Bible-reading seminars that Edwards leads for the lucky California survivors, providing at once the novel's central lesson (Christ will return and save believers from an awful fate) and scriptural justification for the novel's story elements concerning who will be the Antichrist, and when and from where he will arise. By the end of the first of these lessons, before the midpoint of the novel, the entire second half of the novel is foretold in this exchange between Edwards and Dave Busby, a former star athlete and follower of Edwards who is further along in his study than the others:

> "After the attack by the horde of demons, people will no longer be thinking rationally. They'll be willing to give political power to anybody who's able to restore order and get the world moving again. Then, the devil will bring out his satanic savior, the man of sin we call the Antichrist. For a short time, he will rule the world."
>
> "Then comes the fourth quarter," said Dave Busby, jumping to his feet, "and the good guys will win!" (164)

By Part Two, when the book changes its focus from the practice of interpreting prophecy at Edwards's survivalist camp to the rise and fall in global power of the Antichrist, the typical elements of popular eschatology follow in rapid succession, including the victory of a "New World Order" (the title, of course, to Robertson's controversial work of "nonfiction"), the tattooing of the "mark of the beast" on an unsuspecting populace, and the gathering of satanic forces for a final battle in the Middle East. Heavenly angelic forces protect the camp, and then proceed quickly and easily to defeat the Antichrist's forces in a final battle. In an extremely strange passage in the novel's climax, however, Robertson (through Edwards) makes the bold prophetic argument against his premillennial competitors that the final battle does not take place at Armageddon, but at Jerusalem, "[d]espite the popular notion of the last several years" (399). Even in describing the arrival of the kingdom of God, prophetic interpretation remains central to *The End of the Age* and, for Robertson, the fundamentalist eschatological experience of the millennium.

Unlike *The Illuminati* and *This Present Darkness*, *The End of the Age* both confidently presents what the end times *will* be like and asserts the pleasures and necessities of interpreting prophecy. Having luckily survived the natural disasters of the meteor and its aftermath, the two California families can only truly become part of the Christian survivalist camp and thus enjoy the wonders of the millennium by recognizing and understanding the signs of the "end of the age." Although it may be a prophetic narrative with the ultimate in happy endings, *The End of the Age* is less interesting for its attempt to describe the return of Jesus and the millennium in the realist prose of the popular novel than for its consideration of and argument about prophetic interpretation itself.

Popular Eschatology as Historiography and Conspiracy Theory

Popular eschatology works within and helps to define further the religious practices and beliefs of contemporary conservative Protestants. It is articulated within the general structures and belief patterns of most fundamentalists and conservative evangelicals and helps to win converts and to bind believers through reassurance, faith in the imminent return of Christ, and emphasis on the individual experience and practice of faith in understanding and preparing for such future events as the rapture and the millennium. Eschatology also helps to extend religious faith and practices into the everyday lives of believers; if Christ's return is imminent and can happen at any time, then one must be prepared at all times for horrific destruction and ecstatic rapture. Hope and fear can prove motivational for believers attempting to follow a disciplined, holy life. As Timothy Weber writes, "Premillennialists may not have developed a new Christian lifestyle, but they used their beliefs about the second coming to fortify some of the slipping behavioral standards they shared with other evangelicals."[64] In addition, premillennialists have been among the most active in missionary and proselytizing activity, spreading the word of the coming end (like Lindsey himself) through ministries and mass communications.

Popular eschatology also has a number of important effects on the political and social practices and views of many conservative Christians. First, because of Israel's role in the end times, most believers in biblical prophecy throughout the rise of premillennialism from the nineteenth century to the present have been strong Christian Zionists, arguing not only for a sovereign Jewish state but also for a well-armed Israel that can defend itself and strike against what many fundamentalists see as inherently evil Arabs who threaten Judeo-Christian order.[65]

Second, many popular eschatological texts lean toward right-wing conspiracy theory, particularly in their patriotism, fears of a one-world government, virulent anticommunism, and calls for a strong military — all of which would seem to contradict their sublime longing for Christ's return from a spiritual realm over which humans have no power. Eschatology's problematic patriotism exemplifies this tendency. The presence of the United States in biblical prophecy is the subject of much debate between eschatologists; indeed, although Lindsey's *LGPE* works from the assumption that the United States must inevitably lose power and cede authority to the Roman dictator (84, 150, 173), his later work seems to imply that although the ultimate downfall of the world will sweep away all nations, the United States can remain strong until rapture by making its foreign policy more strongly anticommunist, destroying the evils of the "welfare state" and governmental bureaucracy, building up a strong military, praying, and continuing to support Israel.[66] This conflict between the inexorable fate foretold in the apocalyptic narrative and the growing desire among conservative Christians, particularly since the rise of the New Christian Right, to change America for what they see as the better can only be contingently resolved. The eschatological work and political tracts of more politically involved Christians such as Pat Robertson and Tim LaHaye demonstrate this problematic resolution; LaHaye argues that the tribulation is not necessarily going to come about soon and could be forestalled by the public work of Christians, and Robertson's premillennialism does not deter his political activism.[67] Similarly, millennialist fiction attempts to resolve the demands of the thriller narrative with the imminent end posited by eschatology by resolving the single narrative through heroic, Christian agency and prayer, while keeping alive a near-future threat that the end will come regardless.

Finally, one of the most important aspects of popular eschatology that works within many of the teachings and political views of conservative Christianity is the tendency to view historical and current events in terms of vast conspiracies led by knowing and unwitting agents of Satan. The tendency to divide reality into antitheses of good and evil, and to place such antitheses within a historical narrative that seeks to understand the natural through the supernatural, leads to a specific type of cognitive understanding and mapping that structures the interpretation and understanding of events.[68] In this respect, the degree to which popular eschatologists such as Hal Lindsey, Jack Van Impe, and Pat Robertson share many of the fears and conspiracy theories of the John Birch Society and other far-right-wing groups is not particularly surprising. This way of narrativizing the past, present, and future leads one to view the world as the domain of secret and dangerous groups that seek to undermine and destroy Christian beliefs and values.

Ultimately, as Lee Quinby has argued about apocalypticism in general, popular eschatology constitutes a Foucauldian "regime of truth that operates within a field of power relations and prescribes a particular moral behavior." At once it narrows conventions for understanding, iterating, and acting on the meaning of history, and it constructs a vast network for the proliferation of discursive and nondiscursive practices of eschatology.[69]

I want to conclude by returning to my original discussion about the implications of popular eschatology in the conflicts over the social and political meaning of history. Popular eschatology relies on the construction of a historical narrative, structuring discrete historical and current events into a dynamic and all-important narrative frame that can adequately explain for believers a world seemingly beyond the realm of human understanding and agency. It presents the "reality" of historical events (and the importance accorded to currency and factual information, as we have seen, is great) in a way that has meaning, in an explanatory plot that can adequately and meaningfully account for this reality. A historical narrative, as Hayden White argues, "reveals to us a world that is putatively 'finished,' done with, over, and yet not dissolved, not falling apart. In this world, reality wears the mask of a meaning, the completeness and fullness of which we can only imagine, never experience."[70] The individual eschatological narrative — whether in the form of a "nonfiction" book on prophecy and current events, a televised prophecy/news program, or a novel that fictionally represents the movement toward the last days — works between the individual events reported in it (whether they are biblical, "real," or "fictional") and the larger structure of the Christian eschatological narrative as it currently survives, and attempts to provide a form of resolution and closure between the natural and the supernatural.

The reader/viewer who can successfully move between these realms and who recognizes, comprehends, and accepts this narrative frame can thus further understand both the information represented by these accounts of discrete events and the larger narrative at work in them. The ongoing framing and re-framing of present and historical events within the larger narrative demonstrate the intense will to know in eschatology, a continuing quest for transparency and sharply defined images and information. The biblical provides a combined timetable, map, and script; the annals of human history and current events are a shifting and mobile text; and the practice of popular eschatology is an ongoing attempt to match the latter with the former in order to know the coming future.[71] Ironically, this process works as a form of secular forecasting (such as, for example, weather forecasts, the work of political pundits, or even the interpretation of non-Christian "prophets" such as Nostradamus) that attempts to "see" and "know" the future through models of the past.[72]

This narrativization of the past serves a crucial role in the understanding and experience of time. As John Gager argues, the Book of Revelation serves a similar purpose as psychoanalytic therapy, attempting to transcend the line between a real and dangerous present and a mythical future. Indeed, this line is not merely transcended, it is suppressed; the future is at work in the past and the present, which serve as both preludes to and signs of the great days to come. The triumphant visions with which all popular eschatological texts end thus do not merely describe future events, they "transcend the time separating present from future, to make possible an experience of millennial bliss as living reality. Just as the therapeutic situation is the machine through which the patient comes to experience the *past* as present, so the myth is the machine through which the believing community comes to experience the *future* as present."[73] Ultimately, as Frank Kermode notes, in eschatology the end is not merely imminent, it is immanent — present in the whole of history and the individual life is the promise of the End.[74] Popular eschatology serves as both narrative and interpretive practice, fulfilling the desire to provide a complete explanation of historical and present events as well as suppressing the dangers and threats that these events represent.

Clearly, such fulfillment is "ideological" in the sense that it displaces the possibility for recognizing and enacting real structural social change for current and past problems in favor of an abiding belief in a metaphysical solution. Popular eschatology, in its racist and patriarchal articulation of conservative Christianity, is also dangerously reactionary. Yet, the social narrative of the end times is not simply the production of a passive, impotent public; although it works within and is clearly articulated to the more general lack of a plausible social and historical imagining of a better past, present, and future, its utopian impulse and its creative agency allow the practices of popular eschatology to work not unlike what Fredric Jameson calls "fabulations," postmodern novels (such as, for example, E. L. Doctorow's *Ragtime*) that retell and recast history as parody and fantasy:

> Fabulation . . . is no doubt the symptom of social and historical impotence, of the blocking of possibilities that leaves little option but the imaginary. Yet [the] very invention and inventiveness [of the "fabulation"] endorses [*sic*] a creative freedom with respect to events it cannot control, by the sheer act of multiplying them; agency here steps out of the historical record itself into the process of devising it; and new multiple or alternate strings of events rattle the bars of the national tradition and the history manuals whose very constraints and necessities their parodic force indicts.[75]

Agency, in other words, is no longer perceived as functional in the historical process — the individual can do little but be saved through a personal and meaningful relationship with Christ — but is very much in play in the practice of historicizing, in participating in the ongoing rethinking and reconstruction of the popular eschatological narrative. The notion that "anyone" can understand prophecy and relate it to current events, by comparing the nightly news to Revelation, points to a form of popular historiography that interpellates the subject as historian rather than as historical actor. Further, the ecstatic promise embedded in this interpretive practice — ultimate redemption, becoming one with the body of Christ — casts eschatology as more than mere historiography and as transcendent experience of and obsession with the sublime. The eschatological subject is not passive: she "chooses" to be born again, to practice her faith and adherence to religious and social principles, to evangelize, to pore over the Bible, to watch current events, read historical accounts, and consume prophetic interpretations — and, ultimately, to sense the end. The everyday eschatological life promises the transcendence of the everyday.

This is very much a political process, in which a competing construction of the past, present, and future makes sense of and activates religious and political beliefs and practices.[76] As the work of self-constructed outsiders attempting to question and struggle against what participants perceive to be dominant, humanist ideologies, popular eschatology participates in the conflict over the politics of history and the history of politics. Such struggle demonstrates the importance associated with the power to represent the past (and the future) and the degree to which religious, racial, ethnic, gender, and sexual minorities and dominated groups must continually attempt to articulate their histories and visions of the historical process against the dominant, "consensus" history.

This returns us to the discussion in Part I. Just as it would be easy to label conspiracy theory as paranoid, so it would be to simply dismiss popular eschatology as the bizarre metaphysical fantasies of fundamentalists. To do so, however, would be to make two errors: first, as Paul Boyer argues, it would simplify the dynamic processes of religious belief and the everyday lives and actions of millions of people within a rather flat, static notion of sickness;[77] and second, it would fail to take into account the ongoing political struggle to represent and understand the past. Eschatology and conservative Christianity in general are clearly ideological in the sense that, as Ernesto Laclau argues, any attempt to describe a singular, unified, and ahistorical social — whether by Marxists, Christians, or consensus historians — is ideological in its misrecognition of the play of and struggle over meaning and the process of society.[78] Yet, in demonstrating the conflict over history in the realm of the popular, texts and practices that attempt to sense the end also represent the struggle over the interpretation and narratives, as well as the meanings and possibilities, of the past, present, and future.

7. The Conspiracy "Community"

The technological and cultural expansion of "alternative" media—including newspapers, fanzines, noncommercial radio and television, and computer bulletin boards and networks—has enabled wide distribution of and access to theories and information among a wide variety of individuals and groups interested in conspiracy theory. The uninitiated in conspiracy can learn of theories through independent bookstores, nonmainstream political magazines (particularly on the right), shortwave radio, and computer on-line networks and bulletin boards. Neither logging on to the Internet nor learning of relatively obscure publications with a circulation of a few thousand copies is easy and equally open to all, and the computer Web sites and bulletin boards, fanzines, and other cultural forms that make up the "conspiracy media" seem for the most part to be heavily dominated by white males.[1] Yet, the on-line and fanzine conspiracy theory networks are open to anyone with a computer and modem or a couple of dollars and a few stamps. Conspiracy media often indiscriminately present a relatively diverse range of conspiratorial views, and they invite participation (bulletin boards and computer news groups are intended for the "posting" of messages) and encourage others to start an outlet to distribute their own theories (as in contemporary fanzine culture and the much older heritage of the political broadside, each of which champions a "do-it-yourself" and speak-your-mind ethic). Although alternative networks of political information are not new, the current era is marked both by the sheer number and range of media that are used and the large amount of content that is available.

In some ways, conspiracy media outlets and computer networks constitute a kind of wider conspiracy "community" consisting of smaller, more tightly knit factions focused on a singular theory or individual theorist. I employ the term "community" with some irony, in that the conspiracy "community" of researchers, information, and analysis that on-line and print communication has helped to expand represents a central paradox of conspiracy theory politics. The conspiracy researcher is by definition a loner, existing in continual fear of contamination by the conspiratorial Other. The popular conception of the conspiracy investigator is of a solitary figure with a well-earned sense of distrust: Robert Ludlum's characters work alone, as did Ronald Malcolm, Robert Redford's character in *Three Days of the Condor*; JFK assassination conspiracy researchers are known for their vituperative condemnation of one another's work; and investigative journalist Danny Casolaro (discussed later in this chapter), a tragic hero for many in the conspiracy community, died the archetypal conspiracy researcher's death — alone in a West Virginia hotel room, under suspicious circumstances, while tracking down sources. Researchers and dabblers are notoriously cranky, wary of outside interest and help, and difficult to get along with. The old joke about leftists — get four of them in a room and they will start four different journals — is just as true of conspiracy theorists, who would probably come up with four (or more) different theories to explain any contested political event or figure. In some ways, what I will describe is less a community than a dysfunctional family in which researchers inevitably return to each other, even if they do not agree. Conspiracy theorists need like-minded souls — they are their own best audience, even if they do not all get along. I use the term "community," then, for its implications of a group of individuals with a shared set of assumptions who engage in ongoing communication, rather than for its notion of an idealized collectivity.

The "community" that I describe in this chapter is a difficult construction composed not only of individual researchers and enthusiasts spread across the United States and around the world, but also of the media that circulates their ideas and responses and the conferences that occasionally draw them together in one space. If anything, this research community is a shadow copy of the ideal academic community of scholars, with journals, annual meetings, and collaboration that works toward a common intellectual goal. At the same time, this community includes the well-known academic tendency to intense competition involving expansive egos, ill will, and petty bickering. The ability to form a collective enterprise — which would include such basic elements as winning converts, forming alliances among differing groups, creating common goals and statements of goals, and the like — is essential to any political movement. The conspiracy community, however, can hardly imagine a collective, or even much more than a small, self-contained cell; full of suspicion and competitiveness, its most important unit is the contentious individual researcher collecting and placing seemingly distinct pieces of information within a singular explanatory frame.

Assassination conferences are wonderful examples of this conflicted notion of community. At the Second Annual Midwest Symposium on Assassination Politics, held in Chicago in April 1992, professional, published researchers and amateur assassination "buffs" in attendance shared a common bond in strongly suspecting (perhaps even knowing) the worst about what happened to the Kennedys and Martin Luther King Jr. In coming together, attendees were able to exchange information, compare competing theories, view evidence, purchase books, share a meal, and discuss such common foes as uninformed Warren Commission apologists and the mainstream media that fails to take such conferences seriously. These meetings (there is also a larger annual JFK conference in Dallas, as well as, in recent years, separate conferences in Providence, Rhode Island, and Washington, D.C.) provide a public space for interaction and support, and foster a more collaborative spirit among a group of individual researchers. This neither guarantees agreement nor ensures the absence of vocal and bitter disputes during question-and-answer periods following panel presentations.[2] Although such arguments and competition do not threaten the broad alliance that assassination researchers have made to petition the federal government and other bodies to open sealed records, the difficulty of reaching a broad consensus about the perpetrators of the Kennedy assassinations makes the researchers' ultimate goal — coming to agreement with one another and persuading the American public — that much more difficult to attain.

It is this tension between individual research and theory and the collective enterprise of conspiracy theory and conspiracy community that this chapter discusses. I begin with a description of the alternative media through which this "community" is constructed, and conclude with an analysis of the narrative of the death and life of Danny Casolaro, and the way in which this narrative circulates throughout the community.

Alternative Media and the Conspiracy "Community"

Although conferences are successful in creating a physical space and opportunities for the coming together of like-minded, though often combative, individuals, various types of alternative media attempt to reconstruct conspiracy theorists' problematic and paradoxical sense of community through print, electronic media, and computer modem. The former two types of conspiracy media are by no means new; the history of the distribution of conspiracy theory in America through broadsides, pamphlets, periodicals, books, and, more recently, broadcast and shortwave radio, stretches back to the earliest years of the United States.[3] During the postwar period, anticommunist, McCarthyite groups on the right such as the John Birch Society produced books and magazines, and regularly met in local chapter meetings, while on the libertarian left *The Realist,* an important countercultural publication run by Paul Krassner, which, during the 1960s and early 1970s, helped to publicize the work of writer and radio show host Mae Brussell through publication of some of her articles. More recently, the explosion in visibility of and networking among militia groups, described in chapter 2, has led to greater distribution of militia-oriented and sympathetic far-right publications. Although mainstream media coverage often portrays the "movement" as national in scope, most groups are local or at best regional in membership, and no large, visible alliance among groups emerged in the years following the siege at Waco.

Some of the most widely circulated print media are the racist, right-wing Liberty Lobby's weekly newspaper, *The Spotlight,* the Lyndon LaRouche organization's biweekly *Executive Intelligence Review,* and independent fanzines such as the quarterlies *Paranoia* and *Steamshovel Press,* which combine more "serious" material with an ironic approach more allied with the perspective on conspiracy theories discussed in chapter 8. Conspiracy books are available at some smaller, independently owned local bookstores, and, increasingly, through mail-order services such as Flatland and Tom Davis Books in California, A-albionic in Michigan, and Newspeak (which has both a store and a catalog) in

Rhode Island; in addition, larger national militias such as the Militia of Montana offer books and magazines through catalogs. Chuck Harder's nationally syndicated shortwave and AM radio show *For the People* often focuses on conspiracy-related issues, while community radio and cable access television shows such as Dave Emory's *One Step Beyond,* a long-running radio show on KFJC in northern California, and *Broadsides,* a Chicago public access cable television show that regularly features researcher Sherman Skolnick, exemplify the more limited, but still vibrant, broadcast- and cable-based conspiracy media. Militias employ broadcast media as well, and especially shortwave radio, which "Mark from Michigan," whose alleged affiliations with convicted Oklahoma City bomber Timothy McVeigh focused mainstream media attention on him, utilized to become a nationally recognized militia leader.[4]

Computer telecommunication, the newest and most interactive medium used by conspiracy theorists, has emerged as one of the most popular and important resources for the circulation of information and theories. The World Wide Web has become the most rapidly developing public part of the Internet, and the Web pages of individuals, groups, and commercial enterprises that circulate conspiracy theories and information about them have proliferated accordingly. Militias, fanzine editors, *X-Files* fans, and a wide assortment of other interested parties have "constructed" sites, many of them quite complex and ingenious, that mix text and graphics to explain and represent their interests in conspiracy.[5] Significantly, the ability of Web pages to "link" to one another has enabled the emergence of a never-ending hypertext network where the interested can endlessly track theories about historical or recent events from site to site, finding duplicative and often conflicting information from one place to the next. Conspiracy on the Web serves as a virtual representation and experience of the endless interpretive process of conspiracy theory, forever suggesting new links to follow and information to appropriate.

Another important way to circulate information on the Internet is via electronic mail, and particularly E-mail lists that distribute copies of all posted messages to anyone who subscribes. Since the early 1990s, the most prominent electronic mail list has been Conspiracy Nation (originally called Conspiracy of the Day), run by Brian Redman. Unlike USENET news groups and many other electronic mail lists, Conspiracy Nation is not interactive, but instead circulates approximately one message per day, sent by Redman to subscribers.

The message might feature an interview with a conspiracy theorist or information source, an excerpt from an article with "significant" information, or an article by Redman himself. Consistently providing responses to late-breaking news stories, Conspiracy Nation has provided an important and immediate interpretive gloss on conspiratorial elements around the world.

One of the most well read computer forums for discussion of conspiracy theories is the "alt.conspiracy" news group on USENET, a set of news groups supported primarily by the UNIX mainframes of commercial service providers and at institutions of higher education, research institutions, and private employers, and accessed via individual Internet accounts. News groups are composed of messages (known as "posts") sent by individual users through the site from which they connect to USENET. Significantly for alt.conspiracy, the prefix "alt." refers to a specific "hierarchy" for groups that discuss "alternative ways of looking at things"; other such hierarchies include "comp." for computer-related news groups and "rec." for news groups that concern hobbies, recreational activities, and the arts.[6] Alt.conspiracy is by no means the largest or most popular USENET news group, but it is a relatively busy one: it was the 130th most popular out of 3,121 in the monthly USENET survey of July 1994, which estimated that ninety-eight thousand people had at least browsed through the alt.conspiracy message index once during the month.[7] A number of contributors post more than once a week, often more than once daily, and hundreds of "articles" are posted per day. Posts to alt.conspiracy are often "cross-posted" (i.e., posted on more than one news group) to other groups, including the news groups for UFO believers (alt.alien.visitors) and for Rush Limbaugh fans (alt.fan.rush.limbaugh).[8] As militias became more prominent, their presence on USENET became such that the news group misc.activism.militia was established, and it has since become a very active list. Messages posted by militia members, supporters, and opponents are often cross-posted to alt.conspiracy, and include numerous theories and information purporting to prove the existence and imminence of the "New World Order."[9] In addition, the news group alt.conspiracy.jfk was established in the months following the release of the film *JFK* and the ensuing controversy; as interest in the assassination declined, it became a less busy site largely dominated by the more empirically oriented researchers and enthusiasts of the Kennedy assassination.[10] Individual USENET news groups devoted to gun control or President Clinton discuss alleged conspiracies that focus on a single issue, such as the fear that the government is scheming to take every citizen's gun or allegations about the policies and perfidies of the Clinton presidency.

A number of commercial on-line services, such as America Online and CompuServe, also have discussion forums for political issues that attract those interested in conspiracy, and as these services have increasingly been connected to the Internet, subscribers to these services have become better able to take their discussions into the alt.conspiracy groups. Along with the publicly accessible computer realms of the Internet and commercial on-line services, a number of private computer bulletin board systems include conspiracy as a specific focus. These private services are usually run by one person with a computer server, one or a very limited number of dial-ups (i.e., phone lines for users dialing in with their computer modems), and a local (as opposed to toll-free) dial-up number. Because they have heard of a private bulletin board system (BBS) from word of mouth, local contact, or through the occasional promotional post on the Internet, those who dial in to private BBSs tend to be more knowledgeable and active as researchers or readers of conspiracy theories.

Although some "posts" to conspiracy-related computer services include extensive transcripts of relevant radio shows and articles from mainstream and obscure periodicals that are often reprinted without permission, the majority are brief statements, questions, or responses to previous posts. Frequent contributors to alt.conspiracy vary in political background, and include followers of Lyndon LaRouche, members of the John Birch Society, true believers in UFOs (who have their own news group, alt.alien.visitors), left- and right-wing critics of government actions, and left- and right-wing skeptics of conspiracy theories in general. The level of discourse on alt.conspiracy is generally quite contentious along two axes: between believers and skeptics, and between believers in competing conspiracy theorists.[11]

The most vitriolic disputes emanate from the former type of conflict, as skeptics face continual public abuse and accusations of either being dupes of the ruling elite's ideology or purposefully funneling disinformation into a forum of political truth. Skeptics themselves are not innocent of contributing to these conflicts (known as "flame wars" across USENET), and many of their critiques or dismissals of conspiracy theories are as abusive as those to which they are subjected. Yet, skeptics also play an important role in extending debates and solidifying diverse theories and theorists against a common, present enemy. Between 1992 and 1994, for example, during periods when Chip Berlet of Political Research Associates (see chapter 3) and Ted Frank, then a law student at the University of Chicago, actively critiqued posts on topics such as who runs the Federal Reserve, Lyndon LaRouche's theories, or the credibility of well-known conspiracy theorists such as Bo Gritz and Fletcher Prouty, the alt.conspiracy news group was particularly active. Since then, a larger number of skeptics, especially militia opponents who critique and satirize the large militia presence on the Internet, have joined the fray. In such cases, the series of responses to an original post (which are grouped together within the message index and referred to as a "thread") can grow quite long as participants present, refute, or ignore theories and rebuttals to them, make charges and countercharges, and initiate attacks that can quickly become increasingly vitriolic. At the same time, competing theories can cause intense disputes. This is the case in a forum such as alt.conspiracy.jfk, where flames can erupt over the most minute forensic evidence, as well as in disputes between and among theorists and skeptics espousing different political and religious beliefs.

This vehement, often mean-spirited argumentation demonstrates the problem of communicating across conspiracy theories, and of articulating conspiracy theory as a collective enterprise. If the regular contributors of alt.conspiracy constitute a public community, it is a community based as much on suspicion, excessive competition, and dispute as it is on the distribution of evidence and opinion, conversation, and mutual support. Perhaps more appropriately, computer communication of conspiracy theory often takes place in the meeting of like-minded souls in the more interpersonal realm of electronic mail (as well as on private computer BBSs), where conversation and the circulation of information remain more private and secure, especially through the use of secure encryption. Fearful of contamination (by the annoying skeptic, the ignorant novice, and the treacherous disinformant) and surveillance (by government agencies such as the CIA and the FBI, which are constantly rumored to be "watching" the Internet), conspiracy theorists find the creation of an electronic "town square" virtually impossible; the "community" can only really take place in a private realm away from the public or, for a limited period of time, at events such as assassination conferences. It is significant and more than a little ironic that those who accept the conspiracy narrative, which so often posits a loss of an authentic relationship to nation, community, and government, find it so difficult to construct an alternative, collective, working model of scholarship and resistance.[12]

Danny Casolaro
The Body Expired, the Figure Transformed

The lone, heroic investigator serves as the reference point through which interpretation, narrative, politics, and, ultimately, community flow. Resistance begins (and often ends) with the work of one extraordinary person who is able to interpret disparate events and forces correctly in order to bring about the salvation of some vulnerable entity. This figure is as integral to the "real" world of conspiracy theorists as he or she is for conspiracy fiction; the individual researcher — such as Bruce Roberts of the *Gemstone Files,* Lyndon LaRouche, and Mae Brussell — functions for his or her followers in the same way that the tireless hero represents and effects the restoration of proper political order in fictional representations.

One of the most resonant such figures within the conspiracy "community" is Danny Casolaro, a virtually unknown investigative journalist who was found dead in a motel room in Martinsburg, West Virginia, in August 1991. While conducting research on a relatively obscure, alleged scandal in the U.S. Justice Department under Ronald Reagan's attorney general, Edwin Meese, Casolaro apparently became convinced that he had uncovered evidence pointing to a series of interlocking scandals, including the funding of the Nicaraguan contra rebels through arms sales to Iraq that constituted the major parts of the Iran–contra scandal, as well as the "October Surprise," illegal deals made with Iranian hostage holders by members of Reagan's 1980 presidential campaign to delay the release of American hostages until after Reagan's defeat of Jimmy Carter.[13] Prior to his death, Casolaro had told friends and colleagues that these seemingly isolated "scandals" were the product of a much larger cabal of secret groups, which he provocatively termed the "octopus" — the conspiracy whose tentacles seemed to reach everywhere. Purportedly close to finding evidence that would conclusively prove the existence of the octopus, Casolaro was, according to suspicious friends, family, and conspiracy theorists, "suicided" — murdered in a way that looked like self-inflicted asphyxiation.

The reporting and discussion of Casolaro, his research, and his death by the conspiracy "community" demonstrate the power of this lone figure, whose murder signified a premature and unsatisfactory ending to the narrative of his life and work. Casolaro has become a point of identification for conspiracy theorists, a figure who signifies exit from the realm of theoretical speculation and into the (murdered?) body of the innocent (i.e., free of fear and free of guilt) investigator. His research, presumed to have reached a point close to realization, and his life, presumed to have ended just before he could attain his goal of uncovering the vast conspiracy he called the "octopus," represent the peculiar completion of the conspiracy narrative, of conspiracy's Desire: the knowledge that never fully arrives, the resolution that never fully closes. The trail of connections that Casolaro left, traced throughout the conspiracy media and "community," are endless. Danny Casolaro has come to represent the promise and danger of the individual for the conspiracy collective, of the perils of the mortal body as it is inserted into the politics, narrative, and interpretation of conspiracy.

The scandal that Casolaro initially pursued concerned Inslaw, a company that designed computer software for law enforcement. Inslaw had developed a powerful program named Promis, designed to enable prosecutors to track thousands of defendants and cases in the criminal justice system across the United States. Originally a nonprofit company supported by grants from a federal law-enforcement agency, the company later became a private corporation and worked as an outside contractor for the Justice Department on a specially enhanced version of the software. The version developed under this contract was eventually installed in twenty U.S. attorneys' offices across the country. The Department of Justice refused to pay the company for its work, however, leading Inslaw to file for bankruptcy. Inslaw sued the Justice Department, initially winning a $6.8 million-dollar decision in bankruptcy court that was upheld in 1989 by a federal district court. A federal court of appeals dismissed the case on technical grounds, however, and the U.S. Supreme Court has refused to hear any of Inslaw's further appeals of the appellate court's rulings.

Bill and Nancy Hamilton, founders and owners of Inslaw, have alleged that Promis had been pirated by Earl Brian, a friend of Attorney General Edwin Meese, and sold abroad, becoming an integral part of legal and illegal surveillance programs run by American intelligence services. The Hamiltons assert that Brian had attempted to purchase or destroy Inslaw and, failing that, stole the company's main asset. Brian's theft was then protected by Meese and his Department of Justice for personal and professional reasons, leading Justice to refuse to pay Inslaw for the software that the company had developed.[14] The Judiciary Committee of the House of Representatives heard the Hamiltons' allegations and called for an investigation by an independent prosecutor. The committee, chaired by Representative Jack Brooks (Democrat of Texas), came to this conclusion despite the unwillingness of the Bush Department of Justice to allow congressional oversight into the case.[15] However, Department of Justice Special Counsel Nicholas J. Bua, appointed by Bush Attorney General William Barr, found "no credible evidence" that Brian and Justice officials conspired to steal the software. The Hamiltons subsequently complained about the "secret" preparation of Bua's report and the fact that they had no opportunity to examine or question the evidence.[16] Federal investigations into the more sensational allegations have effectively ended, although Inslaw's suit against the federal government is still under consideration by a federal contracts appeal board. In May 1995, the U.S. Senate passed Senate Resolution 114, which would have finally put the Inslaw case before the U.S. Court of Federal Claims, and also contained provisions to compensate the Hamiltons should the court rule in their favor. Further, the resolution granted Inslaw full subpoena power to investigate its claims.[17]

The procedural history of the Inslaw litigation seems fairly arcane, but many of the allegations concerning why Justice refused to pay, what happened to the software, and the results of various investigations into the fate of the company and its computer program have been incorporated into spectacular charges of corruption and conspiracy. The "Inslaw case" had been a public concern of some in the conspiracy community since before Casolaro's death (Dave Emory, for example, had associated Inslaw with Iran–contra and other scandals on his radio show *One Step Beyond* just a week prior to the discovery of Casolaro's body), but over time the dead journalist's body has become just as important in many conspiracy theorists' discussions of Inslaw as the scandal itself. The mystery lingers: What did he know, what was he working on, and who was he meeting in Martinsburg, West Virginia — home of the national computer center of the Internal Revenue Service and less than two hours west of Washington, D.C. — on the night that he died?[18]

Danny Casolaro had been chief reporter and, briefly, owner of the Washington-based trade publication *Computer Age*. With some previous experience in conspiracy-related investigations (in the late 1970s he had investigated some of the alternative explanations of Watergate), his transition from computer reporter to investigative journalist/conspiracy researcher and the expansion of his investigation from computer software threat and governmental abuse to the shadowy and conspiratorial power of the "octopus" were relatively quick and complete. As a 1993 profile in *Spy* magazine described, Casolaro had become obsessed in ways that committed conspiracy researchers know only too well: "He worked on [his investigation] 16 hours a day, staying on the phone past midnight, sleeping only 2 or 3 hours a night, talking with quasi-spooks and bona fide spies, chasing leads, always enlarging his vision of the Octopus."[19] One of Casolaro's most important sources was Michael Riconosciuto, a computer programmer with some experience in clandestine work (allegedly for the CIA) and with a reputation among skeptics and critics of conspiracy theory for embellishing his stories with fanciful fabrications. Riconosciuto has claimed that Earl Brian's alleged theft of Promis was a payoff from Edwin Meese for Brian's assistance in the "October Surprise" negotiations. As articles in both mainstream and conspiracy-related periodicals have revealed, Casolaro followed the trail from Inslaw through the "October Surprise" and into covert arms dealing during the Reagan administration (particularly to the contras), the collapse of the savings and loan industry, and a multiplicity of illegal practices allegedly perpetrated by the CIA.

The debate over Casolaro's sources is an important one in evaluating his research. Although Casolaro had developed contacts besides Michael Riconosciuto — including, according to some reports, federal and intelligence sources, as well as at least one source with connections to organized crime — Riconosciuto's name and questionable credibility often arise in connection to Casolaro. In addition to accusations of lying or stretching the truth toward the fantastic, Riconosciuto was arrested on drug charges, which, he and his defenders claim, were filed in retaliation for his testifying before the Brooks Committee's investigation of Inslaw. Chip Berlet (see chapter 3), for example, has argued that Casolaro's notion of the "octopus" was a fantasy built on information from faulty sources, particularly from the Christic Institute and the LaRouche organization.[20] The disappearance of Casolaro's notes and files from his hotel room leaves supporters and critics with little evidence to evaluate his research beyond family and friends' recollections of discussions with him about his work and a brief, rejected book proposal that contains neither evidence nor sources.[21]

The very lack of "hard" evidence in Casolaro's life and death produces an excess of signification for conspiracy theorists. This is particularly the case in the attempts by conspiracy theorists and Casolaro's friends to unravel the mysteries of his murder. The two clues that seem to implicate foul play most clearly are Casolaro's missing files, filled with notes and references, that his friends and family say he never left unattended, and the embalming of his corpse without the authority of his family and before they had even been notified of his death (illegal in the state of West Virginia), which virtually destroyed the chances for an accurate autopsy. In addition, paramedics and police on the scene, assuming the cause of death to be suicide (his wrists were cut and there was a plastic bag secured around his head with rubber bands), bungled evidence necessary for a murder investigation. Family and friends question whether Casolaro, apparently in good spirits prior to leaving for West Virginia, would have killed himself; they also have doubts about a terse suicide note that seemed out of character for a verbose writer.[22] Short of a confession, the mystery of Casolaro's death will remain a narrative that will not reach full closure, his prematurely embalmed corpse a body that refuses to disappear. Coupled with his investigation, Casolaro's dead body makes him a particularly compelling figure among conspiracy researchers precisely for what it is not able to speak.

The signs of Casolaro's murder and the conspiracy he attempted to uncover resound throughout the conspiracy community, where accounts of both appeared in virtually every conspiracy-related forum in the months following his death. The fanzine *Paranoia* reprinted an article on Casolaro from the Liberty Lobby's publication, *The Spotlight,* on the third page of its premiere issue, and *Steamshovel Press* editor/publisher Kenn Thomas has written several articles and a book that make bold and fanciful connections beyond the already extraordinary ones covered in the more mainstream press. These connections to conspiracies hither and yon include: elements of the JFK assassination, because through Casolaro's sources in the Gambino crime family he apparently was able to meet with E. Howard Hunt, who some in the research community implicate in the Kennedy assassination (Hunt, of course, also connects Casolaro's investigation to Watergate); Lee Harvey Oswald himself, who links to Casolaro in a number of nebulous ways, the most prominent being that, "in lieu of all the facts, the best speculation makes both look like hapless patsies in a game of control played by larger, more invisible forces";[23] the foreign banks Banco Nazionale del Lavoro and Bank of Commerce and Credit International (BCCI), and thus the illegal arming of Iraq and Saddam Hussein before the Persian Gulf War; then-governor Bill Clinton's alleged assistance in covering up the use of a small airport in Mena, Arkansas, for drug and gun smuggling as part of the Reagan White House's efforts to aid the contras in Nicaragua; and, finally, the coverup of information concerning UFOs, connecting Casolaro through his investigation of an alleged factional split in the intelligence community, one side of which appeared in memoranda "ostensibly documenting the retrieval of aliens" from a legendary UFO crash in Roswell, New Mexico, in 1947.[24]

An article on the *Gemstone Files* (see chapter 5) nicely places Casolaro at the end of an extended and extensive conspiracy narrative:

> Industry discovered in its infancy that a domestic population can be colonized as lucratively as a foreign one. Urbanization served the crude necessities of industry, while destroying long-established social structures as basic as the family. Transforming the nation into a protector of corporate rights over and above citizen's [*sic*] rights has made-over the national character as an extension of industrial domestic colonization. The promise of a "new world order" arising from the dust in the dried-up sea of promises has been signed with the inky deception of a fleeing, multi-legged cephalopod. Freedom lovers intrepid enough to challenge the veil of secrecy for a glimpse of the truth as it writes in the clutches of an American shadow government in the employ of organized corporate criminals often as not die premature and mysterious deaths. Enter and as quickly exit Joseph Daniel Casolaro.[25]

On his community radio show a week after Casolaro's death, Dave Emory connected Casolaro's "political assassination" to an entire postwar history of such events:

Whenever a major investigation breaks with regard to the intelligence community, it is always followed and accompanied by a wave of very mysterious deaths. This has been the case in so many different investigations that we've looked at in the past: the Iran–Contra investigation, Edwin Wilson's trials, the assassinations of John and Robert Kennedy and other people, . . . a massive series of deaths in connection to the investigation of the Vatican banking scandals and the other machinations relevant to the Propaganda Due Lodge, a bogus Masonic lodge in Italy that became a crypto-fascist government for Italy and was inextricably linked with NATO. Unfortunately, as I've said, this country has given itself for so long to the obviously incorrect view that we do not have political assassinations that it makes it very difficult for anyone to approach a tragic death like Joseph Daniel Casolaro's [with] any kind of objective framework.[26]

The grand narrative of instrumental power, brutal exploitation, sensational murder, political scandal — all linked to Danny Casolaro's death. Originally one of those engaged in uncovering these linkages, Casolaro himself became immortalized as one of conspiracy's most recent victims and mysterious pieces of evidence.

Kenn Thomas's description of the circumstances surrounding the murder scene and investigation in fact assumes that Casolaro was a victim of conspiracy's insatiable and inevitable appropriation of everything. "The all-to-familiar [sic] pattern, of course, brings to mind the dictum that if They control the coroner, They control the city. . . . Most of Casolaro's notes and his manuscript disappeared, to [sic], naturally."[27] The "familiar," the "natural" — where else would such events become not merely possible, not merely probable, but certain, except in the narrative structures of conspiracy? Indeed, it is Casolaro's body that itself produces the "octopus," as a radio host on WBAI, the Pacifica radio station in New York City, stated one month after the reporter's death:

[This story] is just so amazing, because it really started with a blurb in the *New York Times* that said a reporter looking into a case was found dead. And now we're talking about people who were involved in the so-called "Secret Team" [a term used most often by the Christic Institute in its failed lawsuit against a number of figures in the U.S. government], the "Octopus," almost like a secret government in the United States.[28]

Constructing a narrative that would include such descriptions was, apparently, not foreign to Casolaro himself. A book titled *Secret and Suppressed: Banned Ideas and Hidden History,* published by Adam Parfrey's Feral House (which also produced *Apocalypse Culture*), includes the first publication since Casolaro's death of the journalist's book proposal (which at that time had the biblical title *Behold, a Pale Horse,* after two verses in Revelation). In it Casolaro wrote:

> An international cabal whose freelance services cover parochial political intrigue, espionage, sophisticated weapon technologies that include biotoxins, drug trafficking, money laundering and murder-for-hire has emerged from an isolated desert Indian reservation just north of Mexicali. . . .
>
> I propose a series of articles and a book, a true crime narrative, that unravels this web of thugs and thieves who roam the earth with their weapons and their murders, trading dope and dirty money for the secrets of the temple.
>
> *Behold, A Pale Horse* will be a haunting odyssey that depicts a manifesto of deceit, decisions of conscience, good and evil, intrigue and betrayal. . . .
>
> Possession of a secret is no guarantee of its truth, and while [the] allegations [of the conspiracies and incidents that he describes in the proposal] by a handful of people are indeed remarkable, they are also wrought with undocumentable details — at least thus far[—]and veils of deniability masking the necessary spine for a traditional journalistic effort. It is for this reason that *Behold, A Pale Horse* is subtitled *A True Crime Narrative.*[29]

How else could such a narrative be read by current readers except with a slightly different ending that includes its author's death? Casolaro's demise thus has meaning, signifying the possibility of a tragic ending to the conspiracy narrative. Perhaps the best statement of the inspiring meaning of Casolaro's death comes from a freelance reporter and friend of Casolaro, who stated in an interview on New York's Pacifica Radio affiliate:

> Well, I think what has to happen is exactly what Danny Casolaro intended to happen. And that is to understandably tie all of these events together because they are, in fact, all linked. And only under those conditions — and if our Congress and our Senators regain their intestinal fortitude to do their job (and I don't mean just [give] themselves pay raises, but actually monitor what's going on within the judiciary and within the executive branches of government, as they are supposed to do to maintain our balance of power), maybe then the citizens can rely upon obtaining some answers.[30]

All of these extensive narratives and explications of Casolaro, as well as Kenn Thomas's description of Inslaw's Promis as "the software that figured prominently in events leading to the suspicious death of writer Danny Casolaro in a West Virginia hotel room in 1991,"[31] come to signify Casolaro's role in Inslaw (or vice versa) and, more important, as his story is circulated, Casolaro's role in the conspiracy community itself. Significance (meaning and identification) only results from the stitching of the individual into the conspiracy. The author of a rejected book proposal becomes significant when he dies a suspicious death, creating a context in which the proposal's meaning and accuracy begin to take on an aura of the real.

Discussions on alt.conspiracy of Casolaro and his work were particularly vibrant in 1991 and 1992, and information on the entire Inslaw case continues to be circulated widely in books, articles, and the World Wide Web. This circulation exemplifies the degree to which the deceased reporter has become a collective figure of identification within the divergent individuals and groups that constitute the conspiracy "community." Articles on Inslaw and Casolaro that had appeared in such periodicals as the *Village Voice, Barron's,* and the *Napa Sentinel* (a northern California community newspaper that ran an extensive investigative series on Inslaw) were transcribed and posted along with transcriptions of radio interviews with such prominent figures as Bill Hamilton of Inslaw, Michael Riconosciuto, and the *Napa Sentinel's* Harry Martin. Web sites still contain numerous articles (some of them culled from alt.conspiracy or obtained otherwise through the Internet) on Inslaw and Casolaro both because of the proliferating connections between his research and late twentieth-century conspiracy theories and because the alleged theft of Inslaw's Promis allegedly can be used to augment the government's already powerful surveillance capabilities.[32] The discussion and investigation have continued, with the suggestion made through E-mail groups, on USENET news groups, and on the World Wide Web by a figure named J. Orlin Grabbe that Casolaro's murder was connected to Bill Clinton and the death of Vincent Foster.[33]

Invoking Casolaro, some regular contributors to alt.conspiracy in early 1992 began to discuss potential alliances within the conspiracy "community" that could be built through the the Internet and USENET. Suggestions that people holding differing theories could at least come together in opposition to a common enemy are not infrequent on alt.conspiracy, but during February 1992 the notion that "the net" itself could provide the structure for conspiracy investigation as a political practice of resistance took on new meaning. Had Danny Casolaro been on "the net," one contributor reasoned, and had he been aware of the ability to circulate information through it and use it to make contacts with other researchers and interested parties, he might have been able to further his investigation and better protect himself and his work before his death. Perhaps, the writer suggested, creating a "Casolaronet" and a "Danny Casolaro Foundation for Online Journalism," while perhaps a "pipe dream," could enable the spirit, if not the body, of the dead journalist to live on.[34]

The death and life of Danny Casolaro thus demonstrate that conspiracy theorists use the Internet not merely to distribute information and ideas, but also as a forum for the formulation of political and cultural practice. "The net" circulates Danny Casolaro and becomes a public space for others prepared to enter the conspiracy metanarrative of which he had become a part. Participants in these discussions of Casolaro's work and death are *not* (as the diverse and competing theories circulated in print, on television and radio, and through computer modems demonstrate) political activists able to form alliances and a cohesive group in order to advance a specific agenda. Rather, Casolaro can draw together divergent theories and cantankerous theorists by the lack of specific knowledge of what exactly he was working on: his voice silenced, his notes missing, all that is left to speak is his corpse; and his corpse, in the circumstances in which it was found, fits quite well into the popular conspiracy narrative and thus into one of the few aspects of the conspiracy "community" that *is* collective: its mythology of a simple antagonism between "the people" and the ever-elusive, ever-conspiratorial power bloc. Casolaro's significance, ultimately, is his position as an individual, almost mythical, figure, stepping out of the realm of fictional narratives, on whose body these divergent theories and theorists and this "community" can build the desire for the impossible identification and closure of conspiracy.

8. Conspiracy Theory as Play

This award-winning game reveals what you've always suspected.
Secret conspiracies are everywhere! THEY really are out to get
you . . . so you'd better get them first.
 —From the box of *Illuminati: The Game of Conspiracy*[1]

A somewhat oddball collection of predominantly young (fifteen to thirty years old), predominantly white, and predominantly male convention-goers, most of them affiliated with a number of different but overlapping "underground" interests, wandered the halls and gathered in the ballrooms of a relatively small, mid-priced Atlanta hotel in September 1992. They were attending Phenomicon, "America's Most Dangerous Convention," a weekend gathering of cyberpunks, hackers, conspiracy theorists, members of the "Church of the Sub-Genius," book and fanzine publishers, role-playing game players, and fans of underground comic books. This was one of the world's largest gatherings of hip nerd sub-cultures in one building — a mix of alienated youth, mildly subversive adults, and the cottage industry that they have developed to serve themselves. Among the honored guests invited to speak and participate in the convention's panels were widely known individuals in one or more of those "subcultures," including Bruce Sterling, noted cyberpunk novelist and spokesperson for the science-fiction subgenre's movement; Jonathan Vankin, whose profile of conspiracy theorists, *Conspiracies, Cover-ups and Crimes,* had recently been published in a paperback edition;[2] Adam Parfrey, owner of Feral House Press and editor of *Apocalypse Culture,* an influential collection of essays and rants on "the fear-inspired upsurge of irrationalism and faith, the clash of irreconcilable forces, and the ever-looming specter of *fin de race*" in contemporary culture;[3] and the Reverend Ivan Stang and Kerry Thornley, founders of, respectively, the Church of the Sub-Genius and Discordianism, two farcical antireligions.

As with similar gatherings (such as comic book, record, and sports card conventions), enthusiasts with different interests represented in a single event (e.g., *Star Trek* and *Star Wars* fans at a sci-fi convention, or collectors of cards for different sports or from different eras) were at once separate and mixed; although, for example, the role-playing game enthusiasts tended not to hang out with the hackers, and the Sub-Genius "followers" at times disrupted the proceedings of conspiracy theory panels, there was a remarkable fluidity to the interests and an eclectic variety of offerings to sample and with which to become involved. Televisions and VCRs in two meeting rooms played nearly around the clock during the weekend, showing tapes such as a documentary on Wilhelm Reich, the legendary camp films *Robot Monster* (1953) and *Unidentified Flying Objects: The True Story of Flying Objects* (1956), and an anthology of television and film clips on the Kennedy assassination. Well-known and unknown experts filled meetings with theories and practical advice on everything from publishing fanzines to fighting censorship, and in panels on the topics "Vampires: Myth or Reality," "Introduction to S&M," "Atlanta's Position in the New World Order," and "Conspiracy-a-Go-Go."

One commonality among the groups and meetings at Phenomicon was a sense of knowing, bemused detachment from the "apocalypse culture" to which the convention participants belong. Conspiracy, weird science, weird sex, hacking through the privatized data world of cyberspace — each assumes a profoundly dystopian time in which the hip seek fun and pleasure in the center of the apocalypse. Parfrey's description of the second edition of the collection he edited best summarizes the approach much of the conference seemed to take: "It was my recurring childhood game to believe that I could avert disaster (car crashes, atomic bombs, etc.) by imagining the calamity while holding my breath. It is entirely possible that *Apocalypse Culture* is the outgrowth of this kind of puerile superstition."[4]

Of the conspiracy theorists in attendance at Phenomicon, many (but certainly not all) were as much fascinated and removed from the "paranoia" that they practiced as they were a part of it. By imagining conspiracy and holding their breath, they were feeling the excitement of playing paranoia while keeping the disaster it assumes in abeyance outside the convention hotel. Conference participant Jonathan Vankin has described this game as the "conspiracy rush": "a zap of adrenaline that hits when you apprehend a higher truth; the revelation sensation, I call it. Your mind expands, or so you believe. Everyone else now appears slower, plodding through life a little stupider than you thought they were before."[5] The "rush" may be a form of revelation, but it is *not,* Vankin wants to maintain, a revelation that discloses a necessary truth. Like Parfrey, Vankin attempts to retain some critical distance from "puerile superstition" and an illusory experience of knowledge, and both writers observe rather than identify with the lives of those who interpret and enter into the narratives of apocalypse and conspiracy. This distance is important; neither Vankin, Parfrey, nor Robert Anton Wilson (whose influential writings are discussed in the next section) would claim a committed politics of conspiracy. Instead, they seek to describe and engage with the American fascination with the aesthetics and pleasures of conspiracy theory, in an approach laced with playful irony. Recognizing and conceptualizing this "rush" — the excitement and laughter of "finding" and "following" conspiracy — is a crucial step in understanding the contemporary cultural fascination with conspiracy theory and the affective engagement that some of conspiracy theory's practitioners experience in it.

Illuminatus! and the History of the World

Through his writings and public appearances, Robert Anton Wilson has become one of the figures most closely identified with conspiracy theory as a form of ironic play. He is best known for a trilogy of novels, *Illuminatus!,* written with Robert Shea and originally published in 1975.[6] The epigram of book 1 of the trilogy's first novel, taken from Ishmael Reed's novel *Mumbo-Jumbo,* boldly proclaims: "The history of the world is the history of the warfare between secret societies." Shea and Wilson's work attempts to present such a history, albeit a particularly knowing, parodic, fictional vision of conspiracy as a central theme in human development. Together, the three novels (*The Eye in the Pyramid, The Golden Apple,* and *Leviathan,* currently packaged in one large volume) include their own myth of human creation, an explanation of everything from the lost island of Atlantis to cryptography, goddess worship, and the I Ching, a review of the trilogy itself ("The authors are utterly incompetent — no sense of style or structure at all" [238]), as well as sex, drugs, and an apocalyptic form of rock and roll, the latter of which is itself an integral part of the conspiracy. Although it holds some high literary pretensions in its disruption of conventional notions of narrative, perspective, time, and space, the trilogy works within the conventions of science fiction and fantasy, the genres with which it is generally stocked in bookstores.

In the years since the trilogy was published, both *Illuminatus!* and Wilson, who has become far more associated with the trilogy than the late Robert Shea, have reached cult status among many readers. Moreover, the trilogy's story, characters, and spirit have moved far beyond the printed text: *Illuminatus!* has been adapted into a five-part dramatic cycle produced in Liverpool in 1976; it heavily influenced the successful Illuminati role playing and board games (discussed later in this chapter); it has helped to draw new "members" into the Discordian and Sub-Genius "religions"; and it has found a large audience among computer enthusiasts.[7] In addition, Wilson's writings in the intervening years include fictional "prequels" to *Illuminatus!* (the "Historical Illuminatus Chronicles," which includes, as of 1998, three novels, *The Earth Will Shake* [1981], *The Widow's Son* [1985], and *Nature's God* [1991], with plans for at least one more) as well as collections of nonfiction essays and aphorisms that return to many of the themes of the trilogy.[8]

Illuminatus! concerns a coordinated effort by a number of central characters to thwart an apocalyptic conspiracy by a group calling itself the Illuminati. The Illuminati's plan is to rule the Earth by slaughtering a huge audience at a rock festival held in Ingolstadt, Bavaria, and, in so doing, achieve immortality. Since long before the trilogy was published, actual countersubversives have warned the world about a secret society called the Illuminati that had worked throughout history to seize power and/or foment revolutionary discontent among intellectuals and the masses, purportedly through conspiratorial, occult means. Founded in 1776 by Adam Weishaupt, a professor of religious law at the University of Ingolstadt in Germany, the Illuminati actually *did* exist in late eighteenth-century Europe as a secret group within the already secretive society of Masons. Promoting revolutionary ideas, specifically against both church and state, the Illuminati were outlawed ten years later, and, as a "secret society" of subversives, were finished.[9] The Illuminati's reputation continued to grow throughout Europe, particularly among monarchists and other conservatives in the aftermath of the French Revolution who perceived the Illuminati to be the secret element behind all revolutionary movements in Europe. The lengthy list of such countersubversives includes John Robison and the Abbé Augustin Barruel in nineteenth-century Europe, Nesta Webster in early twentieth-century Britain, and even contemporary American evangelist Pat Robertson, all of whom have warned of the manipulation of politics by a small, secret group of powerful members of the occult. More than just a secret society, however, the conspiracy in *Illuminatus!* involves supernaturally evil elements, such as the Illuminati's attempt to raise a battalion of Nazi soldiers held in suspended animation beneath a lake outside Ingolstadt, and, on the side of "good," the benign power of Eris, the goddess of discord, who helps to save the world from the evil group's plans.

Shea and Wilson are by no means conventional conspiracy theorists. In fact, their trilogy is an extensive parody of the fear of conspiracy, and through continual reference to alleged secret societies and various well-known and obscure theories about them, *Illuminatus!* becomes a subversion of conspiracy theory through parodic humor and excess. As conspiracy folds into conspiracy and it becomes increasingly difficult to identify the political orientations and goals of groups and individual characters (not to mention the convoluted relationships between them), the trilogy emerges as an anarchic treatise about a world in which conspiracies have run amok. Indeed, the trilogy explicitly advocates anarchism, criticizing and parodying both right- and, to a lesser extent, left-wing conspiracy theories and politics in favor of a composite of left anarchism and economic libertarianism. In the trilogy, two main characters embody this alliance: Simon Moon, a young hippie anarchist associated with the student movements of the 1960s and practitioner of tantric sex and hallucinogenic experimentation; and Hagbard Celine, an older libertarian capitalist entrepreneur who travels the world in first-class accommodations, including a large nuclear-powered submarine. These two seemingly disparate positions are relatively complementary in their shared opposition to mainstream dualities of "left" and "right," and in their disdain for monopoly state and/or private control over power, property, and human behavior. While working relatively independently throughout the trilogy, Simon and Hagbard ultimately act together in the climactic scene to foil the Illuminati's attempts to cause mass destruction and seize material and metaphysical power. *Illuminatus!* associates "conspiracy" with the manipulation of mainstream politics and supernatural powers by unseen forces, and ultimately with any form of power and control by the left or right; resistance, on the other hand, is the struggle against any such "politics" and form of power, and for freedom from coercion by the state, religion, and particularly conspiratorial groups.

Most of the three novels focuses on five characters: Celine and Moon, the two "adepts" in the ways of political resistance to conspiratorial groups and of the supernatural; and three "innocents," Saul Goodman, a New York City policeman, Joe Malik, the editor of *Confrontation,* a left-wing magazine based in New York, and George Dorn, a reporter for *Confrontation.* As the novels progress, the three "innocents" learn various versions of the history of the struggle for power, as well as how to recognize, interpret, and resist conspiracies that seek to control humanity. The narrative begins with an investigation of the disappearance of Joe Malik and the bombing of the *Confrontation* offices (located, significantly, near the Council on Foreign Relations, an elite international policy group often feared in right-wing conspiracy theories). Investigating the bombing, Saul finds on the premises of *Confrontation* a series of memos that refer to an "Illuminati Project." The memos document references to the Illuminati in a wide variety of publications — from the *Encyclopaedia Britannica* to *Playboy,* from radical social theorist Jacques Ellul to the John Birch Society. Because these individual pieces of evidence make little sense on their own, they require some sort of deduction; Saul's method of sorting through them is to use his "intuition," a process of "thinking beyond and between the facts, a way of sensing wholes, of seeing that there must be a relationship between fact number one and fact number two even if no such relationship is visible yet" (23). Saul's interpretive process, we learn, developed out of his "dissatisfaction" with a wide range of "official explanations" of American foreign policy and political assassinations (51). For Saul, the progression from an interpretive method that "senses wholes" toward a conspiratorial imagination is logical: if there are reasons to be suspicious of an "accidental" theory of history and "official" historical explanations, and if one senses wholes and relationships among historical facts, then conspiracy becomes a possible explanatory framework.

Saul's "intuition" quickly becomes the shared mode of understanding for a host of other characters, especially the increasingly "illuminated" innocents. George Dorn, one of the other central characters transformed by Hagbard Celine, responds in this way to one of Celine's many — often contradictory — explanations of the narrative's odd, conspiratorial events:

You've just tied two hundred years of world history up in a theory that would make me feel I should have myself committed if I accepted it. But I'm drawn to it, I admit. Partly intuitively — I feel you are a person who is essentially sane and not paranoid. Partly because the orthodox version of history that I was taught in school never made sense to me, and I know how people can twist history to suit their beliefs, and therefore I assume that the history I've learned is twisted. Partly because of the very wildness of the idea. If I learned one thing in the last few years, it's that the crazier an idea is the more likely it is to be true. (200)

Much of *Illuminatus!* concerns this process of initiation into a form of ongoing hyperinterpretation, in which the explanatory framework built at one point in the trilogy must be destroyed and rebuilt in order to explain new evidence and new "crazy ideas" of a different conspiracy.

Characters are not the only ones initiated; as Dorn, Goodman, and Malik are educated in the hermeneutic of conspiracy almost simultaneously across time and space, the intrepid reader must similarly work to bring coherence to the scattered and often contradictory pieces of "true," "false," and "speculative" history the novels present with virtually every sequence. For coauthor Wilson, this narrative strategy serves as a fictional representation of quantum physics, a kind of "serious proposal for a more Einsteinian, relativistic model than the monistic Newtonian theories which conspiracy buffs favor" through a narrative built on "indeterminacy and probability, not . . . religious or ideological dogmas."[10] In one collection of essays, Wilson calls this approach "guerrilla ontology," an attempt

to so mix the elements of each book that the reader must decide on each page "How much of this is real and how much is a put-on?" This literary technique seems justified by the accelerated acceleration of new knowledge, new theories, new inventions, and new possibilities in our time, since any "reality" map we can form is probably obsolete by the time it reaches print.[11]

A particularly good example of this process, and one that has become a running joke among fans of *Illuminatus!,* is the episode in the second novel in which Saul begins to "see the fnords." In an advanced stage of his transformation from innocent to adept, Saul wakes up one morning, begins reading the *New York Times,* and continually sees the "word" *fnord!* in a story about an angry dispute between the United States and the Soviet Union. Other fear-provoking stories concerning topics such as war and pollution contain fnords at regular intervals. After undergoing a type of deprogramming hypnotherapy, Saul can finally see the fnords and realizes that they are a form of mind control intended to create a docile, hypnotized, and anxious population through the fear of impending emergencies. Saul learns that there is only one release for people under the hypnotic spell of the fnords: because advertisements are the only part of the media without fnords, "only in consumption, endless consumption, could [people] escape the amorphous threat of the invisible fnords" (438–39). The Marxist critique of consumer society thus has its perfect conspiratorial explanation, and only by learning to peer through the hypnotic ideology of fear and repression, as Saul has done, can one begin to see the extent of the conspiracy — can one begin, literally, to "see the fnords."

The conspiratorial twist on a classic critique of media propaganda and commodity fetishism is only one in a series of uses that the trilogy makes of the rhetoric of late 1960s and early 1970s dissent and seeming paranoia. Much of the "evidence" to which the novels refer was part of the fodder of conspiracy theorists of the time, and remains so today. Beginning with the subtitle of the first novel's opening chapter ("From Dealey Plaza to Watergate . . ."), *Illuminatus!* reads like a virtual encyclopedia of conspiracy theory, including references to the Lincoln assassination, the U.S. military's development of germs for biological warfare, and the ruling elite's manipulation of public fear through fabricated "threats" of communists in the Cold War and planted rumors of invading aliens in UFOs. The trilogy even extends conspiracy theories' obsessive excesses of confusing connections and conjectures by referencing other fictional works: a British intelligence agent, code-named 00005, patterns himself on Ian Fielding's James Bond character; Richard Condon's novel on mind control, *The Manchurian Candidate,* is described as the result of an Illuminati information leak of the realities of brainwashing as a military weapon; and different subversive groups share the "Tristero" postal system at the heart of Thomas Pynchon's *The Crying of Lot 49*. Ultimately, the trilogy features a dizzying series of references to conspiracy theories real and imagined, rewarding the reader who comes to it with previous knowledge and leading interested "innocent" readers into the realm of deepest suspicion and a vast body of fictional and historical literature.

Its references to the John F. Kennedy assassination are particularly telling of the trilogy's use of "real" conspiratorial events. Early in the first novel, Shea and Wilson describe Lee Harvey Oswald's attempt to shoot Kennedy from the Texas School Book Depository, which is frustrated by shots from the Triple Underpass and the grassy knoll that occur before Oswald has the opportunity to fire (28); the second novel includes a scene that focuses on John Dillinger's (one of the John Dillinger quintuplets, all of whom survived the shooting of a different man in front of the Biograph Theater in Chicago) attempt to shoot Kennedy on the grassy knoll, which, like Oswald's, is also frustrated, this time by an unnamed killer who fires before Dillinger has the opportunity (514–16); and finally, in the "real" solution to the assassination, Hagbard tells Joe Malik that the man who actually committed the assassination of Kennedy was a true "lone-nut" gunman (but not Oswald). Of course, even this final "solution" is met with "proper" skepticism, as Malik replies: "You sound very convincing, and I almost believe you" (586–87). References to "real" conspiracies might be a central feature of *Illuminatus!,* but in its often farcical, fantastic play with such conspiracies, the trilogy neither presents a "true" theory nor even identifies the possibility of a final, "true" explanation for the unsolved riddle of the JFK assassination. The conspiratorial hermeneutic of "sensing wholes" never fully reaches the "whole" it seeks; rather, its ongoing play of interpretation finds its purpose and pleasure in ongoing conjectures about and refusals of a singular truth.

The initiation into this hermeneutic is, for the trilogy's innocents, a process of transformation through which one acquires both knowledge and the ability to correctly perceive and interpret the historical, political, and spiritual "real" (such as it is). Specifically, the "adepts" continually teach the "innocents" to question all forms of accepted "reason" and "truth" through manipulation, lies, drugs, induced hallucination, and religious and political instruction. Their transformation into "adepts" occurs through a painful learning process because, one character is told, "illumination is on the other side absolute terror. And the only terror that is truly absolute is the horror of realizing that you can't believe anything that you've been told" (278). By the end of the trilogy, Joe Malik complains to Hagbard Celine, after hearing Hagbard's countless contradictory explanations of himself and the plot, "You're just an allegory on the universe itself, and every explanation of you and your actions is incomplete. There'll always be a new, more up-to-date explanation coming along a while later" (695). In such a situation — and again, the reader's position is analogous to Joe's, given this dialogue's position immediately prior to another in a long line of "explanations" of the significance of the trilogy's penultimate scene — the role of the innocent (and the reader) is to ponder, both critically and humorously, a further explanation of the "truth."

If the play of the hermeneutic of conspiracy theory and suspicion leads to greater knowledge, the ability to see connections between seemingly disparate events is also necessary to save the world. An ongoing dynamic throughout the trilogy concerns the shape and dimension of the larger conspiracy against which the adepts struggle. The conspiracy's meaning and the alliances among those fighting with and against it change with virtually every contradictory and confusing piece of evidence and explanation. Following the mutating connections between groups and events is so difficult for character and reader alike because the Illuminati have created a conspiracy that looks like randomness, an orchestrated plan whose enactment looks like sheer coincidence. Individual pieces of the conspiracy might be visible because, as Simon explains, "It amuses the devil out of [the Illuminati] to confirm their low opinion of the rest of humanity by putting things up front like that and watching how almost everybody misses it" (133). Only Hagbard, Simon, and others associated with them have the ability to integrate individual pieces into an interpretive framework, and they quite literally save the world by correctly interpreting and acting on that interpretation. As Hagbard says to Joe Malik, "Anybody who tries to describe their operations sounds like a paranoid" (270). "Paranoia" is a necessary condition to perform heroic acts.

As the trilogy twists and reconfigures the mass of fictional evidence and prominent and obscure intertextual references into an ironic catalog of conspiracy theory, this heroically paranoid hermeneutic becomes inexorably linked with humor. Hagbard informs Joe Malik about this central theme of the trilogy in the following exchange:

"Trickery is your *métier,*" Joe [Malik] said bluntly. "You are the Beethoven, the Rockefeller, the Michelangelo of deception. The Shakespeare of the gypsy switch, the two-headed nickel, and the rabbit in the hat. What little liver pills are to Carter, lies are to you. You dwell in a world of trapdoors, sliding panels, and Hindu ropetricks. Do I suspect you? Since I met you, I suspect *everybody.*"

"I'm glad to hear it," Hagbard grinned. "You are well on your way to paranoia. . . . Just remember: *it's not true unless it makes you laugh.* That is the one and sole and infallible test of all ideas that will ever be presented to you." (250; emphasis in original)

The trilogy's relentless use of puns, scatological acronyms (BUGGER, "Blowhard's Unreformed Gangsters, Goons, and Espionage Renegades"; KCUF [note its backward spelling], "Knights of Christianity United in Faith"), and outlandish escapades similarly place paranoia within a context of laughter. Such is the play of conspiracy; as the *Principia Discordia,* the "sacred document" of Discordianism, a "text" and "religion" that heavily influenced *Illuminatus!,* claims,

The human race will begin solving it's [*sic*] problems on the day that it ceases taking itself so seriously. To that end, [Discordianism] proposes the countergame of NONSENSE AS SAL-, VATION. Salvation from an ugly and barbarous existence that is the result of taking order so seriously and so seriously fearing contrary orders and disorder, that GAMES are taken as more important than LIFE; rather than taking LIFE AS THE ART OF PLAYING GAMES.[12]

Like the game of Discordianism, the hermeneutic proposed and enacted by *Illuminatus!* is nonsense, a type of play meant for fun and pleasure. As Wilson told an interviewer from a publication for conspiracy theorists named *Conspiracy Digest,* skepticism might be "liberty's greatest ally," but "chronic suspiciousness, or suspiciousness without a sense of humor, can be just as blinding and limiting as the naïve submissiveness of the masses."[13]

Illuminatus! thus establishes a number of influential ways of understanding conspiracy: as a form of interpretation, as a form of play, and ultimately as a form of cultural practice that seeks to decipher events in a simultaneously paranoid and humorous way. Reading the trilogy, its prequels, and Wilson's often similar nonfiction is itself an enactment of this practice — one that is followed up and extended in other texts and practices that similarly enact the "sensing of wholes" as a source of pleasure and play.

Playing Conspiracy
Conspiracy as Fun and Games

A tongue-in-cheek compendium of conspiracy theories titled *It's a Conspiracy!*, and authored by the "National Insecurity Council," includes in its introduction a description of the situation in which its author first conceived it: "This book began in France in 1990, when three vacationing American couples met at a dinner party. Knowing nothing about each other, they groped for something to talk about. At first the conversation was self-conscious. Then somebody mentioned JFK's assassination. Suddenly they had a lot in common, and plenty to talk about."[14] In short, conspiracy is a parlor game, a kind of trivial pursuit for Americans abroad, a nice way to break the ice at parties.[15] On the Internet, such playfulness can become the idea for a Web page. On one site, you can "Make Your Own Conspiracy Theory" in the manner of the children's travel game Mad Libs, where blindly filling in blanks under subject headings that ask for personal information, important historical dates, and leading conservative and liberal figures can enable the Web surfer to create an individualized, tongue-in-cheek right-wing conspiracy.[16] A very humorous and clever site tracks different conspiracies as though they were competing teams in a sports league, tracking recent news events to see which conspiracy team currently "leads" the "National Conspiracy League."[17]

Yet, discussing, studying, and documenting conspiracy is not a source of fun solely for the upscale demographic of the author of *It's a Conspiracy!* or the lucky Web surfer who happens upon the conspiracy Mad Lib and sports league. Two games designed by Steve Jackson Games of Austin, Texas (publisher also of games on time travel, space aliens, and "swashbuckling," and particularly famous for an FBI raid of its office and computers while it developed a game on cyberpunks), a card game and a role-playing game both named "Illuminati," enable players not merely to track or discuss but also to enact the practice of conspiracy.[18] In these games, conspiracy is at once a frightening aspect of human society about which one should be paranoid and a source of amusement and competition. If conspiracy buffs are, in Robert Anton Wilson's words, "adrenaline freaks,"[19] in search of the rush or "zap" of adrenaline that Jonathan Vankin has described, these games domesticate adrenaline in fictional roles and competitive entertainment in which participants can indulge their desire to "experience" conspiracy and paranoia for a few hours or for however long a role-playing game runs.

The Illuminati card game has relatively clear rules and goals for players: the objective is, simply, "to take control of the world."[20] Four to six contestants begin the game by drawing and placing facedown on the table one of the eight "Illuminati" cards, each representing a different group engaged in secret competition to take over the world and each a reference to a group from conspiracy theories, science fiction, or some equally obscure, ironic, subcultural source. The eight Illuminati groups include "The Bavarian Illuminati," whose goal "is simply raw power" and, with its powers and relative invulnerability, is the strongest such group in the game; "The Gnomes of Zurich," "Swiss bankers who are reputed to be the money-masters of the world," and who win by amassing money; "The Discordian Society," who "seek to bring all the strange and peculiar elements of society under their banner, and especially delight in confusing the 'straights' around them"; and "The Servants of Cthulu," masters of "arcane powers and inhuman forces" whose objective is to destroy other groups. Each Illuminati card rates that group's powers and income; each player then attempts to use her group's money and strengths to take over lesser groups (which are described on a different set of cards). The success of a takeover is determined by a roll of dice, and the game proceeds until one Illuminati group either controls a certain number of groups (determined by the number of players in the game) or meets the specific conditions for victory outlined in the rules.

The Illuminati card game, like a conventional board game, has a relatively standard duration (one and a half to three hours, except if players decide to use different types of "advanced rules"), and is generally played in one room at one sitting.[21] Although the competition can turn nasty (along the lines of a "classic" board game such as Risk or Diplomacy), GURPS (Generic Universal Roleplaying System) Illuminati is a completely different experience. Rather than playing with a set of strict rules and goals, and in a specific space and for an agreed-upon period of time, players "become" (at least during those times when they are "playing") the roles that they choose or are assigned. In addition, there is far less of a prespecified objective for the players; instead of amassing power, GURPS Illuminati players attempt to gain or protect secret knowledge, depending on the roles that they assume.

The role-playing game consists of a game manager, who designs and manages the shape of the conspiracy and information about it and is in charge of defining the players' roles, and any number of players assuming different character roles outside and/or inside the conspiracy's power structure. Players can assume the roles of investigators seeking to study and expose the conspiracy (e.g., conspiracy theorists, historians, journalists), members of groups that play a subordinate role in the conspiracy (e.g., the military, law enforcement), or members of competing conspiratorial groups that control vast resources and subordinate groups, and seek some larger, secret goal. Obviously, the more people who participate as players, the more complex and interesting the game, and the more people the manager can get involved in the "conspiracy"—such as the person who is not formally in the game but is recruited by the manager to divulge to an unsuspecting player a piece of information that becomes crucial to the game—the more engrossing the action.

Although players and the game manager can use the Illuminati card game as a reference, and a game of GURPS Illuminati will most likely take suggestions from a book published by Steve Jackson Games for groups, roles, and tactics with which to play,[22] much of the pleasure of role-playing games, and particularly of playing Illuminati, comes from the amorphous, anarchic play that results from its relative freedom from set rules and from the limitations of space and time associated with board games. The game manager "authors" at least the framework and contours of the game, yet her role is far more interactive and improvisational than the printed rules that govern the card game. Indeed, the very notion of assuming "roles" in tracking, fighting, and possibly becoming part of a "conspiracy" within a role-playing game is a far different practice from that of "winning" the card game. If "playing" conspiracy is about the creation of fear, dread, and a kind of manufactured paranoia, as well as quest, interpretation, and knowledge, then "experiencing" these emotions and practices in a "role" that threatens and often succeeds in infusing the player's everyday life becomes a more affectively engaging and resonant form of play.

The role-playing game, in other words, enables players to "become" a character in a conspiracy novel (hence the importance of the connections between the Illuminati game and the *Illuminatus!* trilogy)—a "fictional" (i.e., not real) enactment of a fictional representation.

Indeed, the link between the Illuminati game and the conspiracy narrative is an important one for players and manager alike. The GURPS book's description of the game manager's introduction of the basic rule structure to players echoes in many ways the progression of the "classical" conspiracy narrative:

> Most introductions to the Illuminati depend on the "pyramid of evidence." The [game manager] leads them into things slowly, dropping very minor hints that there are mysteries behind the facade of the normal. The [players] can find clues that at first seem to have nothing to do with the current adventure. Only when they follow up on these clues do they start to learn the true nature of the world around them, and the existence of the Conspiracy. One clue leads to another, and each new adventure builds on the previous one. Characters can start off as innocents, totally unaware of the Illuminati's existence, then find that they've become pawns of the Conspiracy. As they peel one level of the "truth" after another, they can penetrate deeper into the structure, until they become conspirators themselves. (46–47)

The manager thus serves as the "author" of an interactive narrative. The GURPS book suggests that the manager either create a "pregenerated" power structure, in which she plans the conspiracy's architecture with care before the game's inception, or employ a more "improvised" method, reacting to the players' moves and strategies as they develop. Groups control vast resources, have a specific purpose (gaining power, destroying certain enemies, etc.), and enjoy control over various subordinate groups. The GURPS book also lays out a series of "requirements" for the successful game manager, emphasizing that the manager should "maintain an ongoing sense of mystery and paranoia" by gradually but continually revealing pieces of knowledge while postponing the ability of players to see the entire conspiracy (10–11). The conventions of the conspiracy narrative are thus in play within an open-ended game format: the characters search for knowledge and need to interpret pieces of evidence within an all-encompassing framework; they suffer an ongoing crisis of agency as they begin to recognize the limitations of their knowledge and action in their insertion into the context of a seemingly all-encompassing conspiracy; their longing to know and to act is frustrated by a world that makes full knowledge and agency impossible; they experience a quickening velocity of intrigue and complex events; and they operate in the midst of a conspiracy that resists and exceeds closure.

As all-knowing author, the manager not only constructs a conspiracy narrative, then, but also reconstructs the precise power relations of which the game is a representation at the level of "designing" a "conspiracy." In a game of Illuminati, one individual, albeit known to and approved by all, creates and controls secret knowledge. In "playing" conspiracy, players submit to a particular relationship to knowledge (controlled by the game manager and kept from the players) and to power (held outside the game by the manager and within the game by any players whose characters are part of the game's ruling group or groups) that corresponds to the arrangement of conspiratorial power. To "play" conspiracy, one must submit to conspiracy. One passage from the GURPS book, describing the ability of the manager to "alter the memories" of one or more players (i.e., the manager can tell a player that something that her "character" remembers from the game was not real but a figment of her character's imagination), illustrates this relationship between manager and players quite well: "This is a particularly twisted ploy to spring on a player. Remember, in a role-playing game the player's memory equates to the [role's] memory; it's the [manager] who decides on what reality is, and that reality might not match either the player's or the character's memory" (118). This mental state seems to approach clinical paranoia, as not only can the subject not protect her memory from the Other, but she cannot fully trust it herself. This is, of course, a highly constructed form of "paranoia" that takes shape within the conventions and structures of the role-playing game narrative. The role of the manager is to *create* this "paranoia"; the pleasure of the role-player is to *experience* "paranoia" as *play,* and the correct strategy of the role-player is to *enact* "paranoia."

The challenge and pleasure of GURPS Illuminati emanate not merely from "playing the game" and researching conspiracy, but also in the more formalistic arrangement of finishing the story as the manager has written it, gaining the knowledge and defusing the power over knowledge that the manager controls. The players' motivation is to solve the conspiracy by uncovering the secrets constructed by its author, and the role of the manager/author is to construct/write a power structure/narrative that continually postpones its solution; which returns us to the central problems of resolving the conspiratorial narrative and ending the interpretive practice of conspiracy theory: If the joy is in the play, how can one continually postpone the game's ending? This is the issue discussed in the section of the GURPS book titled "Victory in an Illuminated Campaign":

> Players used to other role-playing environments and genres will probably have a view of "victory" that is totally impractical in an illuminated campaign. If the Illuminati are really monstrous spiders in a web of intrigue, you can't defeat them. You can only soldier on, struggling to reveal one more layer of the conspiracy, while staying one small step ahead of those who would destroy (or co-opt) you. . . .
>
> Of course — especially if the [manager] sees the Illuminati as a set of squabbling power groups, rather than a monolithic bloc — it could be possible to defeat some of the Secret Masters. And that could make a satisfying ending to the campaign. But if the Illuminati are vanquished, another group is sure to slip into their position. ("The Illuminati are dead; long live the Illuminati.") It's possible that the [players] themselves will become the "new" Illuminati, and may find themselves acting in the same way as the "original" conspirators. (13)

This is the dilemma of the conspiracy theorist in a condensed form. The end of the narrative/game is at once impossible ("you can't defeat them," although you can gain knowledge about and perhaps defeat "some of the Secret Masters," or even "become" one of "them") and, even as an artificial form of narrative closure, marks the end of the pleasure of reading and writing the narrative. Of course, the game's possibilities are endless: at the conclusion of one game, players and manager can immediately begin planning a new one, while any individual game, through a little rearranging of power structure/narrative, can easily become an endless serial. Reaching the end of the game, finally, merely leads the player to resume it, to postpone the "cure" for paranoia because it's so much fun.

Conspiracy, Laughter, and Play

Wilson's work and the play of the Illuminati games present conspiracy theory as a "rush," a form of play, and a source of pleasure; readers and participants assume an ironic and almost mischievous distance from the "paranoid" situation of the characters and roles with which they identify. In this conception and practice of conspiracy theory there is a delight in that which is constituted as the marginal, the sick, the apocalyptic. *Illuminatus!* revels in the carnivalesque of sex and drugs, articulating conspiracy and paranoia to a nostalgic representation of the grand collective party of the 1960s — possibly a historically accurate assertion, but pushed in this case to absurd limits — while the Illuminati role-playing game creates a world in which paranoid fears are not only "rational" but a necessary part of a player's strategy in a world where control over the game's narrative lies elsewhere. This is not conspiracy theory as, say, the John Birch Society or Kennedy assassination researchers conceive it, in which some past historical moment has been tragically lost because of the machinations of a secret, evil group and must be regained; instead, this is conspiracy as a transhistorical structure infusing all of human experience, past, present, and future, and as a positively enervating experience, approaching the manically depressive pessimism of conspiracy theory with an ironic, cynical detachment from its dystopian implications.

This detachment is a rich, contradictory response both to fears of conspiracy and to the present political order. Without necessarily believing any single conspiracy theory — even, arguably, without adopting conspiracy theory as epistemology — Wilson readers and Illuminati players nonetheless celebrate and assume the perspective of the conspiracy theorist. This is a form of what Peter Sloterdijk has termed "cynical reasoning," an enlightened false consciousness that is aware of the ideological practice in which it engages while engaging in it nonetheless:

> It is that modernized, unhappy consciousness, on which enlightenment has labored both successfully and in vain. It has learned its lessons in enlightenment, but it has not, and probably has not been able to, put them into practice. Well-off and miserable at the same time, this consciousness no longer feels affected by any critique of ideology; its falseness is already reflexively buffered.[23]

These forms and practices of conspiracy theory revel in powerlessness, seeking to recapture lost control through revelatory fantasies and role-playing carnivals that infuse a hip, pseudo-"paranoia" with an enervating sense of fun. They are based on the simultaneous acknowledgment and enjoyment of misery and powerlessness. As Slavoj Žižek notes, "Cynical distance is just one way — one of many ways — to blind ourselves to the structuring power of ideological fantasy: even if we do not take things seriously, even if we keep an ironical distance, *we are still doing them.*"[24] Yet, in their utopian moments, they are also a populist rejection of official historical and political understanding through irony and excess, a cheeky, indulgent strategy that delivers anarchic belly laughs to knowing players and exposes official, dominant political ideologies as banal covers for the brutality of power.

I want to expand first on the latter, more favorable way of conceptualizing this specific set of practices and representations. François Roustang argues that laughter provides a significant first step toward a cure for clinical paranoia in that it represents "the smallest conceivable unit of detachment, of difference of removal" from a life lived in fear of the other that the paranoiac has created; that is, in constructing a distance from which to view, with laughter, the all-consuming threat of the dissipation of individuality and limits (for which the paranoiac's theory of an infiltrating enemy serves to define the self), the analysand can begin to construct an identity, a sense of limits, a territory.[25] Such laughter — working in, around, and against the most totalitarian of political possibilities — can allow for what Dick Hebdige proposes when he writes, "We may have to learn to *laugh* our way around whatever sense of dread and crisis may afflict us."[26] Laughter serves as a strategy, in other words, not only of self-realization and healing, but of survival. When conspiracy seems possible, when conspiracy theory's interpretive machinery seems a rational response to a context in which political and economic power are always elsewhere, one must not only resist but learn to laugh and play, to find a point of ironic and critical distance from which a more efficacious resistance can proceed.

Further, the play and laughter of these types of practices constitute some degree of carnivalesque disruption of political order. As Mikhail Bakhtin argued, the Rabelaisian carnival has historically worked as a significant cultural and political transgression of the ordered distinctions between categories such as high and low, and popular and dominant, and serves as a source of social renewal, a practice that could be used to challenge and destroy older orders.[27] As such, the analogy between the transgressions of the carnivalesque and the "play" of conspiracy theory is important. The carnival's material excesses and degradations constructed the body

> not in a private, egotistic form, severed from the other spheres of life, but as something universal, representing all the people. As such it is opposed to the severance from the material and bodily roots of the world; it makes no pretense to renunciation of the earthy, or independence of the earth and body.... The material bodily principle is contained not in the biological individual, not in the bourgeois ego, but in the people, a people who are continually growing and renewed. This is why all that is bodily becomes grandiose, exaggerated, immeasurable.[28]

Conspiracy theory's tendency toward a cognitive totalization of the social in *Illuminatus!* and in playing the "role" of conspiracy thus finds its corporeal relation in the carnivalesque, which similarly disrupts notions of separate spheres of public/private, political/cultural, and so on. In its excesses and role playing, conspiracy theory as play represents an attempt to break free from bourgeois subjectivity and toward an ongoing, all-encompassing game made up of alliances of liberating coconspirators. In transgressing, and thus "resisting," dominant political interpretations, *Illuminatus!* and the Illuminati games subvert the "consensus" interpretation of history and the "rational," sane interpretation of everyday life and politics. Live as though someone were *really* out to get you and the rest of the world becomes an object of desire, a transgression of boundaries between center and margin, sane and irrational, serious and ironic.

Indeed, the "poetics" of such transgression constitutes a far more significant domain than mere subcultural subversion. The carnivalesque transgression of playing conspiracy as a practice of popular cultural politics, as with the carnivalesque in the popular culture of the subjugated classes of the Middle Ages, plays "a symbolic role in bourgeois culture out of all proportion to [its] actual social importance," because "what is excluded at the overt level of identity-formation is productive of new objects of desire";[29] that is, "playing" conspiracy as a game mediates between the dominant mode of political engagement—the acceptance of political "consensus," participation in the pluralist exercises of political elections and interest groups, and so on — and the "extremist" radical populist skepticism of which conspiracy theory is a nonnecessary but significant element. In addition, such radical skepticism of dominant notions of the democratic distribution of power and capital is itself an official Other to the dominant political identity of "citizen," becoming, at the level of the political unconscious, a site of "disgust, fear and desire," of "degraded" popular politics.[30]

But this is not entirely satisfactory. Conspiracy as play may at its best represent a productive and challenging cultural and political practice; it is, however, also quite often a cynical abandonment of profound political realities that merely reaffirms the dominant political order. It may be a source of populist pleasure, but conspiracy theory of this sort also substitutes fears of all-powerful conspiratorial groups for political activism and hope. Even *Illuminatus!*, which posits a utopian collective of right- and left-libertarians, allows for little in the way of democratic, political activism; in order to effect change or fight the forces of evil in Wilson's trilogy, as well as the Illuminati board game, one must join a small group of experts in law, politics, sex, drugs, and the occult. In other words, the conspiracy must be fought by another conspiracy. The Illuminati role-playing game shrinks the basic unit of resistance even further, to an individualist, pessimistic vision of "resistance." "Victory" is virtually impossible, as is a challenge to the larger "conspiracy"; one can merely hope to gain knowledge of the larger narrative that encompasses the player. Nor is political engagement considered to be a possible realm of activity; it has been abandoned as a site of endemic disappointment, an impossible instrument to work individually or collectively on the world.[31]

Although it may be in some way "resistant" to dominant historical and political epistemologies, "populist pleasure" becomes a retreat into debilitating fantasies of all-powerful, secret groups and a powerless, virtually hopeless, citizenry unwilling and unable to sense the truth. In this vanguardist, rather pessimistic vision of the political, the spirited, carnivalesque populism that these texts and practices at times represent is lost.

Afterword: Conspiracy Theory and Cultural Studies

I want to end with a brief consideration of the infamous novel *The Turner Diaries,* whose fetishization of secrecy, obsessive exclusion of the impure, and fixation on the master signifier of whiteness seems like the deranged big brother to the boyhood fantasy of *The Secret Three,* the children's book whose fascination with secrecy, exclusion, and interpretation was mentioned in the Preface.[1] I am interested in exploring the challenge that texts such as *The Turner Diaries* hold for the kind of cultural approach to populism that this book has taken. Regardless of the role that *The Turner Diaries* may have played in inspiring Timothy McVeigh to blow up the federal building in Oklahoma City, its white supremacist fantasy demonstrates the problem facing any attempt to approach conspiracy theory and contemporary populism as a cultural engagement in the political. Here are "the people" resisting "the power bloc" — how can one who is sympathetic to populism respond?

The Turner Diaries describes the origins and success of the "Organization," a secret, exclusive group of racist radicals who lead a civil war against the "System," the Jewish-run cabal that has seized control over the United States with the help of a slovenly and animalistic black population. The System represents for white supremacists the logical outcome of the conspiracies of contemporary politics, emasculated white men and white women living under the constant threat of sexual assault by depraved African-American males; the secretive Organization represents the violent resistance necessary to overcome the Jewish "occupation" and the blacks and "race traitors" who uphold it. The Organization achieves its goal of a purified and sanctified white society through an underground network of terrorists and an almost poetic flood of violence, effected through bombings, mass hangings, and atomic weaponry. Despite its seeming singularity, *The Turner Diaries* is merely the best-known and most fully realized of the numerous tracts that circulate among fascist groups.[2] It is exemplary only in the scope of its vision, the professionalism of its prose, and its relative commercial success among racists and those members of what James William Gibson has called the "New War" culture who are sympathetic to its message.[3] It is matter-of-fact and almost banal in its narrator's descriptions of the events leading up to the civil war, except in its almost poetic representations of brutality and massacre—which may in part explain its success as both recruiting tool and textbook for white supremacist terror.[4]

The Turner Diaries epitomizes an extreme form of conspiracy theory, one that is fully linked to a fascist racism that is not conspiracy theory's necessary result. Accordingly, the novel constitutes an important caution for those wanting to study and rescue populism, and particularly the populist discourse of contemporary culture, for the left. This is at least partially the project of cultural studies and its amorphous, interdisciplinary, politically progressive project. In one of its more extreme instantiations, best exemplified in John Fiske's work, the populism of popular culture—embodied both in its more transgressive cultural texts and in the most active practices of reception of its audiences—is almost necessarily disruptive of dominant power structures, opposed to the "dominant" of "high" or "bourgeois" art, and, when pleasurable, an "empowering" experience.[5] What happens, however, when this disruption, opposition, and empowerment are employed in the service of a genocidal racism, when "the people" is defined as an exclusionary and violent group?

Fiske is no help in beginning to formulate an answer to these questions, if his analysis of the circulation in black communities of theories of African-American genocide perpetrated by whites through HIV/AIDS is any indication.[6] Terming these investigations and theories "blackstream knowledge" and describing them as a resistant practice of creating and disseminating "counterknowledge," Fiske argues that this is a way for blacks to defend themselves from the racist society that surrounds them. The production and circulation of this counterknowledge is active: "Counterknowledge must be socially and politically motivated: recovering repressed information, disarticulating and rearticulating events, and producing a comprehensive and coherent counterknowledge involves hard labor, and hard labor always requires strong motivation."[7] Its work is to identify and circulate widely accepted historical evidence (e.g., the horrific research beginning in the 1930s performed by the federal government in Tuskegee, Alabama, on black men suffering from syphilis that denied them treatment in order to study the effects of the disease) and more controversial conjectures, and to place them all within broad narratives of racial genocide.

The implications of Fiske's argument are that all African-American theories of genocide — including, perhaps, those positing Jewish control of the African slave trade — are presumptively populist and worthy of championing as practices of resistance. Fiske does have his doubts, which he expresses in a moment of self-reflection:

> As I weighed the different bits of evidence in this [study], I found myself pondering which of two possible "wrong" beliefs would have the worse effects — not to believe AIDS-as-genocide if it were true or to believe it if it were not. And I wondered, too, if the answer might not be different for Blacks and whites, for hetero- and homosexuals, for conservatives and progressives. How do I, as a member of the safest group of all (monogamous, white, straight, non-IV-drug-using, and living in a small midwestern town) weigh the Black conservative argument that the belief in AIDS-as-genocide increases African Americans' sense of themselves as victims and thus their helplessness against the Black radical one that the knowledge arms Blacks in their fight against white supremacy and that what makes them helpless is not knowing the weapons deployed against them?[8]

I share Fiske's difficulty in responding to "counterknowledge," as well as his desire to identify with participants' affirmative belief in the evidence they amass and the narratives they construct. I take issue, however, with what could only be described as his unexamined compulsion to champion certain beliefs and practices of "the people" as necessarily right or at least politically defensible (even if politically, historically, or scientifically inaccurate); because, if active, "resistant" readings are to be championed, then one must champion conspiracy theory, which is both active in its interpretation of history and contemporary politics and resistant in its construction of narratives that oppose dominant historical explanations of political and economic power. Furthermore, if one were also to privilege those cultural texts and practices that demonstrate some instrumental political effectuality — by, for example, helping exploited populations to resent or resist certain aspects of the larger structures that exploit them — then the process and results of African-American counterknowledge's search for a white plot to commit genocide could be considered productive, so long as one considers the politics of black separatism to be a productive avenue for the emancipation of the racially oppressed. Yet, the resistance of such counterknowledge is necessarily resistant not only to a quite limited conception of power (based solely on race), but also to historical correction and a politics of solidarity and emancipation by all but the "resistant" group, having defined its interpretation and narrative of the plight of its "people" around certain core links that would preclude linkages to other movements of resistance.[9] Fiske, as a white man, is hesitant to respond — and, in all likelihood, his responses as a white man would not make much difference to those engaged in the production and reception of such "counterknowledge." An African-American historian or intellectual attempting to refute some piece of evidence or larger theory would likely fare no better in affecting its interpretive and narrative machinery; instead, she might be dismissed as incorrect, or even considered to be part of the conspiracy itself.

The inability to respond, argue with, or link this counterknowledge to a broader political movement is troubling enough, but Fiske's approach cannot adequately distinguish between the African-American counterknowledge he would champion and the white counterknowledge of *The Turner Diaries* that he would abhor. Assuming that the readership of *The Turner Diaries* includes — and in all likelihood is largely composed of — working-class white males, it too is a text that has been produced by and circulated within a group demoralized by the effects of capitalism and patriarchy.[10] It too depends on the interpretation and extrapolation of contemporary power within a broad narrative frame that "resists" dominant notions of political and social order.[11] Yet, in order to distinguish between black and white conspiracy theories, Fiske has two choices: distinguish the causes of black and white searches for counterknowledges, or compare their likely effects. To accomplish the first, he could compare oppressions, asserting that one can excuse or believe in African-American conspiracy theories more readily than those of whites because African-Americans have historically been victims of slavery and incidents of terrible brutality and are currently more oppressed than working-class whites. Alternatively, Fiske could compare the political effectualities of the respective theories by arguing that black theories of white genocide are less likely to produce racism and violence than white theories of a Jewish/black conspiracy. Neither of these arguments is empirically or normatively satisfactory. Nor are they adequate enough to develop either a theory of populism that would provide sufficient analytic power or useful strategies for an emancipatory political movement seeking to inform individuals and groups and persuade them to join.

Fiske's notion of "counterknowledge" is thus too abstract to explain the specificities of "resistance," failing both to explain the political and epistemological valences of black conspiracy theory and to provide a theoretical concept that can enable analysis of contemporary populist discourse. Rather, a specific type of a seemingly "resistant" practice such as the "counterknowledge" of conspiracy theory is merely one element of populist discourse awaiting articulation—the link between "the social force which is making itself, and the ideology or conceptions of the world which makes intelligible the process they are going through."[12] The political effectuality of any populist practice, African-American theories of genocide included, occurs within and across social groups at specific historical conjunctures and is not pregiven. Populism as a popular political discourse has its limits, not in itself but in its articulation by and within a particular cultural and political movement.

In its apocalyptic narrative vision and semiotic apparatus, conspiracy theory assumes the coming end of a moment cursed by secret power and a (never-to-arrive) new beginning where secrecy vanishes and power is transparent and utilized by good people for the good of all. It may appear as a righteous apocalyptic that would claim to be acting on behalf of divine or human justice, positing a necessary end to history through dreadful but deserved events that would lead to the victory of the fellow righteous;[13] it may appear as an ironic apocalypse, facing an unavoidable end with distance and cynicism;[14] or it may appear as a sublime vision of an infinite power-inspiring awe, terror, and pleasure, enabling the assertion of regressive authorities that promise protective repression from the great hovering threat.[15] Nascent in all of these appearances is a critique of the contemporary social order and a longing for a better one. Beyond its shortcomings as a universal theory of power and an approach to historical and political research, however, conspiracy theory ultimately fails as a political and cultural practice. It not only fails to inform us how to move from the end of the uncovered plot to the beginning of a political movement; it is also unable to locate a material position at which we can begin to organize people in a world divided by complex divisions based on class, race, gender, sexuality, and other social antagonisms.[16]

Notes

Preface

1. Mildred Myrick, *The Secret Three* (New York: Harper & Row, 1963).

2. Georg Simmel, *The Sociology of Georg Simmel,* ed. and trans. Kurt H. Wolff (New York: Free Press, 1960), 332–33.

Introduction

1. From the album *Retreat from Memphis* (Chicago: Quarterstick Records, 1994). Reprinted with permission.

2. On comic books, see, for example, David Segal, "Pow! Wham! Take That, Uncle Sam: In Today's Comic Book Culture, the Arch-Villain Is the Government," *Washington Post,* 11 December 1995, C3. On movies and television shows, see, for example, Michiko Kakutani, "Bound by Suspicion," *New York Times Magazine,* 19 January 1997, 16; Jeff Gammage, "JFK Killing Takes on Life of Its Own," *Philadelphia Inquirer,* 24 November 1996, E1; John Yemma, "A Penchant for Plots: Conspiracy Theories Are All the Rage in U.S.," *Boston Globe,* 25 September 1996, A1; and Mark Jenkins, "Devil with a Blue Suit On: Government and Authorities as Hollywood Heavies," *Washington Post,* 14 May 1995, G10. On the increasingly susceptible news media, see, for example, Kurt Andersen, "The Age of Unreason," *New Yorker,* 3 February 1997, 40–43. On the Internet, see, for example, Tom Dowe, "News You Can Abuse," *Wired* (January 1997): 53–56, 184–85; Jonathan Vankin and John Whalen, "How a Quack Becomes a Canard," *New York Times Magazine,* 17 November 1996, 56–57; Mark Schone, "The Moron Commission: JFK Is Alive and Well in Cyberspace," *Village Voice,* 30 November 1993, 56.

3. See, for example, Tina Rosenberg, "Crazy for Conspiracies: The 'Elders of Zion' Predates the Internet," *New York Times,* 31 December 1996, A12; Michael Kelly, "The Road to Paranoia," *New Yorker,* 19 June 1995.

4. One series of allegations of secret political manipulation was the "October Surprise" theory, which claimed that during the 1980 presidential campaign, secret arrangements were made with Iranian forces to delay the release of American hostages until after Ronald Reagan's November victory over Jimmy Carter. For an overview of the media coverage of October Surprise, see Steve Weinberg, "October Surprise: Enter the Press," *Columbia Journalism Review* (March–April 1992): 33. The most vociferous theorizing about conspiracy in the mainstream U.S. media, one writer asserted in the *New Yorker,* was the reaction to the bombing of the Alfred P. Murrah Federal Building in Oklahoma City in 1995. Between the immediate response of experts contacted by the television networks who claimed that the bombing was the work of a secret network of Islamic fundamentalist terrorists, to the fear that a secret network of armed militia members posed an imminent threat to the everyday lives of all Americans, the media seemed to assume that a conspiracy did exist — it just wasn't the conspiracy that theorists thought it was. See Jeffrey Toobin, "The Plot Thins," *New Yorker,* 12 January 1998, 8.

5. Gary Webb, "Dark Alliance: The Story behind the Crack Explosion," *San Jose Mercury News,* 18–20 August 1996.

6. For examples of the media and political reaction to Webb's stories, see Tim Golden, "Tale of C.I.A. and Drugs Has Life of Its Own," *New York Times,* 21 October 1996, A1; Carol Morello, "Conspiracy Theories Fuel Crack Outrage," *Philadelphia Inquirer,* 6 October 1996, A1; Michael A. Fletcher, "History Lends Credence to Conspiracy Theories: Among Blacks, Allegations Can Strike a Bitter Nerve," *Washington Post,* 4 October 1996, 1. The ferocious criticism of the CIA by many blacks and the deep suspicion with which they viewed government attempts to respond led CIA Director John Deutch to address a public meeting in Los Angeles. See B. Drummond Ayres Jr., "C.I.A.'s Director Goes to Watts to Deny the Rumors of a Crack Conspiracy," *New York Times,* 16 November 1996, A9. For a thorough critique of the media coverage, see Norman Solomon, "Snow Job: The Establishment's Papers Do Damage Control for the CIA," *EXTRA!* (January–February 1997). For a defense of Webb's reporting and an account of the way the *Mercury News* responded to the criticism by the *New York Times* and the *Washington Post* by not publishing Webb's follow-up series, see "The CIA's Latest Coup," *CounterPunch,* 16 December 1997, 1.

7. Daniel Pipes, *Conspiracy* (New York: Free Press, 1997), 2–5.

8. Ibid., 7.

9. See Fredric Jameson's reading of conspiracy theory as a degraded yet utopian "cognitive mapping" of "where we are and what landscapes and forces confront us in a late twentieth century whose abominations are heightened by their concealment and their bureaucratic impersonality" (*The Geopolitical Aesthetic* [Bloomington: Indiana University Press, 1992], 3).

10. Christopher Hitchens, "On the Imagination of Conspiracy," in *For the Sake of Argument* (London: Verso, 1993), 14.

11. Similarly, the law of criminal conspiracy assumes that secret alliances among individual actors planning a criminal act constitutes a crime in and of itself. The Model Penal Code, an attempt to provide a rational and schematic model on which individual states can base their criminal laws, defines conspiracy as the agreement to engage in or aid a criminal attempt, solicitation, or act (American Law Institute, *Model Penal Code* [Washington, D.C.: American Law Institute Press, 1985], section 5.03 [1], 398–99). On the development of the law of conspiracy in Anglo-American common law, see Robert Spicer, *Conspiracy: Law, Class and Society* (London: Lawrence & Wishart, 1981), 23–30.

12. Paul Sweezy, *The Theory of Capitalist Development* (New York: Monthly Review Press, 1942), 243. For a discussion of the relationship between "plain" or "vulgar" Marxist theories of instrumentalism and conspiracy theory, see Clyde Barrow, *Critical Theories of the State* (Madison: University of Wisconsin Press, 1993), 47–48.

13. On the John Birch Society's relationship to Barry Goldwater and the Republican Party in the early 1960s, see Sara Diamond, *Roads to Dominion: Right-Wing Movements and Political Power in the United States* (New York: Guilford Press, 1995), 62–65; on the relationship between the Christian Coalition and the Republican Party, see Sara Diamond, "The Christian Right Seeks Dominion," in Chip Berlet, ed., *Eyes Right!: Challenging the Right Wing Backlash* (Boston: South End Press, 1995), 44–49.

14. See Gordon S. Wood, "Conspiracy and the Paranoid Style: Causality and Deceit in the Eighteenth Century," *William and Mary Quarterly* 39 (1982): 411; Bernard Bailyn, *The Ideological Origins of the American Revolution* (Cambridge: Harvard University Press, 1967), 95; and Robert S. Levine, *Conspiracy and Romance* (New York: Cambridge University Press, 1989).

15. Slavoj Žižek's reading of Lacan is developed in his *For They Know Not What They Do: Enjoyment as a Political Factor* (London: Verso, 1991), *Looking Awry: Jacques Lacan through Popular Culture* (Cambridge: MIT Press, 1991), and *The Sublime Object of Ideology* (London: Verso, 1989). See also Gilles Deleuze and Félix Guattari, *A Thousand Plateaus: Capitalism and Schizophrenia,* trans. Brian Massumi (Minneapolis: University of Minnesota Press, 1987), and *Anti-Oedipus: Capitalism and Schizophrenia,* trans. Robert Hurley, Mark Seem, and Helen R. Lane (Minneapolis: University of Minnesota Press, 1983).

16. One model the chapter uses to illustrate this is the "plan" constructed by the three central characters in Umberto Eco's *Foucault's Pendulum,* trans. William Weaver (New York: Harcourt Brace Jovanovich, 1989). Eco's theoretical discussions of "interpretation and overinterpretation" also deal with this issue: *The Limits of Interpretation* (Bloomington: Indiana University Press, 1990), and *Interpretation and Overinterpretation* (Cambridge: Cambridge University Press, 1992).

17. This is the title of a very influential collection of essays and rants, put out by a small California publisher, now in its second edition: Adam Parfrey, ed., *Apocalypse Culture* (Los Angeles: Feral House, 1990).

18. Books that the encyclopedic approach include: Jonathan Vankin and John Whalen, *70 Greatest Conspiracies of All Time* (New York: Citadel Press, 1998); National Insecurity Council (Michael Litchfield), *It's a Conspiracy!* (Berkeley: EarthWorks Press, 1992); Jonathan Vankin, *Conspiracies, Cover-ups and Crimes* (New York: Paragon House, 1991); and George Johnson, *Architects of Fear* (Los Angeles: Jeremy P. Tarcher, 1983).

1. Richard Hofstadter and "The Paranoid Style"

1. For a critique of Hofstadter's work on the late nineteenth century Populist movement in his book *The Age of Reform* (New York: Knopf, 1955), a precursor to his similar, later work on "political paranoia," see the critical literature review in Lawrence Goodwyn's excellent *Democratic Promise: The Populist Moment in America* (New York: Oxford University Press, 1976), esp. 600–604.

2. Daniel Patrick Moynihan, "The Paranoid Style in American Politics Revisited," *Public Interest* 81 (1985): 107–27; Daniel Pipes, "The Paranoid Style in Mideast Politics," *Washington Post,* 6 November 1994, C1, C4; " 'JFK': The Movie," *Wall Street Journal,* 27 December 1991, A10; Richard Grenier, "On the Trail of America's Paranoid Class," *The National Interest* (spring 1992): 76–84; Michael Kelly, "The Road to Paranoia," *New Yorker,* 19 June 1995, 60–75. For just a few of the many explicit and implicit uses of Hofstadter in discussions of the militia movement, see chapter 2.

3. William Kornhauser, *The Politics of Mass Society* (New York: Free Press, 1959), 130. Kornhauser cites the influence of Joseph Schumpeter on this aspect of his work (see Schumpeter's *Capitalism, Socialism, and Democracy* [New York: Harper and Brothers, 1947]).

4. John Dunn, *Western Political Theory in the Face of the Future* (Cambridge: Cambridge University Press, 1992), 27 (emphasis in original).

5. Kornhauser, *The Politics of Mass Society,* 16.

6. Edward Shils, *The Torment of Secrecy* (New York: Free Press, 1956), 231.

7. Kornhauser, *The Politics of Mass Society,* 109–12.

8. Gene Wise, *American Historical Explanations: A Strategy for Grounded Inquiry* (Minneapolis: University of Minnesota Press, 1980), 344–45.

9. As John Higham notes, Tocqueville's work was, in fact, out of print throughout the period in which progressive historians were dominant (*History: Professional Scholarship in America* [New York: Harper & Row, 1973], 221).

10. Louis Hartz, *The Liberal Tradition in America* (New York: Harcourt, Brace & World, 1955).

11. Richard Hofstadter, *The Progressive Historians* (New York: Knopf, 1968), 452–53 (my emphasis).

12. C. Wright Mills, *The Power Elite* (New York: Oxford University Press, 1956), 25.

13. Andrew Ross, *No Respect: Intellectuals and Popular Culture* (New York: Routledge, 1989), 55–56.

14. For a discussion of the consensus historians' status as "objective" historians during this period, see Peter Novick, *That Noble Dream: The "Objectivity Question" and the American Historical Profession* (Cambridge: Cambridge University Press, 1988), 321.

15. J. Rogers Hollingsworth, "Consensus and Continuity in Recent American Historical Writing," *South Atlantic Quarterly* 61 (1962): 49.

16. Antonio Gramsci, *Selections from the Prison Notebooks,* trans. Quintin Hoare and Geoffrey Nowell Smith (New York: International Publishers, 1971), 377.

17. Both Michael Rogin and Christopher Lasch have provided effective critiques of consensus historians' and pluralist political scientists' antipopulism, although Lasch does so within an idiosyncratically adamant defense of the entirety of the nineteenth-century populists' program and its current relevance. See Michael Rogin, *The Intellectuals and McCarthy: The Radical Specter* (Cambridge: MIT Press, 1967), and Christopher Lasch, *The True and Only Heaven: Progress and Its Critics* (New York: W. W. Norton, 1991), esp. 217–25 and 445–55.

18. Hofstadter, *The Progressive Historians,* 439.

19. In addition to Hofstadter's oeuvre, see Richard O. Curry and Thomas M. Brown, eds., *Conspiracy: The Fear of Subversion in American History* (New York: Holt, Rinehart and Winston, 1972); David Brion Davis, ed., *The Fear of Conspiracy: Images of Un-American Subversion from the Revolution to the Present* (Ithaca, N.Y.: Cornell University Press, 1971); and John H. Bunzel, *Anti-Politics in America* (New York: Knopf, 1967). The eight-page "Suggestions for Further Reading" section at the end of the Curry and Brown book lists dozens of books and articles on this topic, the majority of which were published between 1950 and 1970.

20. Richard Hofstadter, *The Paranoid Style in American Politics* (New York: Knopf, 1966).

21. Richard Hofstadter, *The American Political Tradition* (New York: Knopf, 1946), viii. See, for example, Novick, *That Noble Dream,* 334, and Higham, *History,* 213. In a later work, ironically, Hofstadter himself cites this sentence to establish and criticize his own earlier political views.

22. Robert Collins has demonstrated Hofstadter's ambivalence to attacks from leftist historians to *The Age of Reform,* his critical history of the populist movement, many of whose arguments would resurface with a vengeance in Hofstadter's discussions of Joseph McCarthy and Barry Goldwater in the following years. Notwithstanding this ambivalence, largely expressed in private correspondence, *The Age of Reform* remains highly influential in elite and mainstream fears of populist movements, and Collins presents no evidence that Hofstadter extended his ambivalence to his more conceptual work on "political paranoia." See Robert Collins, "Hofstadter and the Originality Trap," *Journal of American History* 76(1) (1989): 150–67.

23. Hofstadter, *The Progressive Historians,* 126; and Novick, *That Noble Dream,* 323–24. Hofstadter's description of American politics should not, however, be simpli-

fied into a blithe celebration of American democracy; one of his late works, *The Idea of a Party System* (Berkeley: University of California Press, 1969), demonstrates ambivalence toward the actual history of the formation and practice of the American party system. He does not, however, demonstrate much ambivalence at all to the American ideal — or, more precisely, fetishism — of an organized "legitimate opposition" of one national party.

24. Richard Hofstadter, *Anti-Intellectualism in American Life* (New York: Vintage Books, 1963), 135.

25. Examples of Daniel Boorstin's work along these lines are *The Decline of Radicalism* (New York: Random House, 1969) and *Democracy and Its Discontents* (New York: Random House, 1974). An example of a contemporary conservative embracing the direction toward which Hofstadter's later work was moving is Richard Grenier, "On the Trail of America's Paranoid Class," *The National Interest* (spring 1992): 76–84.

26. Hofstadter, *The Paranoid Style in American Politics,* viii. Parenthetical page references in the text refer to this work.

27. Hofstadter, *The Progressive Historians,* 442.

28. Daniel Bell, *The End of Ideology* (New York: Free Press, 1960), 121.

29. Yet, Daniel Bell, whose confidence in the triumph of consensus and fear of subversion were more pronounced than in the case of Hofstadter, was more willing to acknowledge some degree of justifiable fear in McCarthy's paranoia: "This is not to say that the Communist 'interest' is a legitimate one, akin to the interest of other groups in the society, or that the Communist issue was completely irrelevant [during the heyday of McCarthy]. As a conspiracy, rather than a legitimate dissenting group, the Communist movement remains a threat to democratic society" (ibid., 123). But Bell's essential faith in American consensus and political process distinguishes his fears from those of McCarthy: he argues that such infiltration was an issue of law that should be taken up by courts and not private individuals, lest it becomes an ideological or moral issue and thus "create strains in a liberal society" (ibid.).

30. Perhaps the strongest such equation between left and right among those who followed Hofstadter is James Hitchcock's "The McCarthyism of the Left," in Curry and Brown, *Conspiracy,* 239–51. Hitchcock sees the New Left as a mirror image of McCarthy's anticommunism, including its vision of a conspiratorial "system," its labeling of innocents with terms such as "racist" (there is a strong similarity between Hitchcock's criticism and the anti-"political correctness" diatribes of the 1990s), and its lack of proof and scholarship to support its claims. In light of the disclosures of CIA involvement in subversion of democratic movements abroad and the FBI's involvement in domestic surveillance and treachery, this essay reads today like an odd and dated diatribe against the New Left in an otherwise even-tempered collection of essays. Hitchcock is willing to admit that "there could be" CIA involvement in domestic activities (just as there could have been a "Communist cadre in the State Depart-

ment in 1952"), but for him that does not allow a hysteria that would destroy "the essence of principled liberalism" (251).

31. Seymour Martin Lipset and Earl Raab, *The Politics of Unreason: Right Wing Extremism in America, 1790–1970* (New York: Harper & Row, 1970), 503.

32. Andrew Ross discusses this in great detail in *No Respect*. See esp. 42–43.

33. Joli Jensen's *Redeeming Modernity* (Newbury Park, Calif.: Sage, 1990) provides a good overview of the association often made between "mass society" and the growth of the mass media by both Cold War–era and contemporary intellectuals.

34. Dwight Macdonald, *Against the American Grain* (New York: Random House, 1962), 37. Macdonald had worked through many of these arguments throughout the 1940s and 1950s in different versions.

35. Andreas Huyssen, *After the Great Divide* (Bloomington: Indiana University Press, 1986), 53.

36. Sander L. Gilman, *Difference and Pathology: Stereotypes of Sexuality, Race, and Madness* (Ithaca, N.Y.: Cornell University Press, 1985), 24.

37. Norman Cohn, *Pursuit of the Millennium* (New York: Oxford University Press, 1970).

38. Serge Moscovici, a European social scientist, makes an argument similar to Hofstadter's in describing conspiracy theory as a "mentality" based on individuals' and groups' fears and resentment against minority groups and outsiders. See Serge Moscovici, "The Conspiracy Mentality," in C. F. Graumann and Serge Moscovici, eds., *Changing Conception of Conspiracy Theory* (New York: Springer-Verlag, 1987), 151–69.

39. For a more obvious example of this mutual exclusion, see Seymour Martin Lipset, "The Sources of the 'Radical Right,'" in Daniel Bell, ed., *The Radical Right* (New York: Anchor, 1963), 307–71, and esp. 308–15.

40. Michael Rogin, *The Intellectuals and McCarthy: The Radical Specter* (Cambridge: MIT Press, 1967).

41. Torben Bech Dyberg, *The Circular Structure of Power: Politics, Identity, Community* (London: Verso, 1997), 202–4.

42. An example of a psychologist attempting more explicitly to associate conspiracy theory with pathological paranoia is Erich Wulff's essay "Paranoiac Conspiratory Delusion," in Graumann and Moscovici, *Changing Conception of Conspiracy Theory* (172–89). Wulff defines conspiracy theory specifically as that which covers or fills a lack in the subject. In doing so, he extends Sigmund Freud's notion of the structural relationship between ego and object cathexis beyond the realm of the erotic and into the "external world," which includes both the broader "social heritage" the subject enters into at birth and the more localized types of social association with which the subject engages (175–76). For Wulff, lack is caused by the inability of the individual conspiracy theorist "to cathect the external world with subjective commitment," which in the "healthy" subject results in an ability to "ascribe a dimension of trust" to his or her

perception of the world and to human interaction. In withdrawing cathexis, the afflicted individual assumes "intrapsychic welcome conditions" (172) for a delusional theory of conspiracy, which becomes a defensive structure that "fills" the hole that reality "lacks" (183). The conspiracy theorist thus shares with the paranoid delusional characteristics resulting in a very specific and intense inability to enter into and participate in political and social institutions. Hofstadter's more historical approach to the analysis of the conspiracy theorist describes the "paranoid style" as diverse instances that share stylistic components and general generative mechanisms but retain their historical specificity; Wulff, on the other hand, attempts to make a broader claim about conspiracy theory both as a pathology and as symptomatic of an individual's inability to properly function within acceptable social and political discourses.

43. John Higham, "The Cult of the 'American Consensus,'" *Commentary* 17 (February 1959): 93–100.

2. John Doe #2 Goes to Washington

1. Some news reports explicitly referred to Richard Hofstadter's work. See, in particular, Malcolm Gladwell's "news analysis" on the front page of the *Washington Post*, "At Root of Modern Militias: An American Legacy of Rebellion," *Washington Post*, 9 May 1995, A1, A6, as well as the headline in William Safire's column, "The Political Style," *New York Times*, 27 April 1995, A25.

2. The subcommittee hearing was carried live on C-Span and rebroadcast numerous times in the days following. The hearing was transcribed in U.S. Senate Subcommittee on Terrorism, Technology, and Government Information of the Committee on the Judiciary, *The Militia Movement in the United States*, 104th Congress, 1st session, 15 June 1995, 2. Parenthetical page references in the text refer to this transcript.

3. The literature on the militias has grown exponentially since the Oklahoma City bombing, and the sources I cite in this brief section constitute a small sample of the print media reporting. A word search of *militia* on a news database such as Nexis would likely find thousands of entries, most pitched at the level of a moral panic. Some of the best and most fascinating accounts are by local and regional reporters describing one or two militia groups or individuals in them (for examples, see note 7), while national newspapers and newsweeklies that try to synthesize local reports or emphasize particular figureheads often tend toward hyperbolic, fearful prognostications of imminent revolution — ironically, the very picture that the militias themselves wish to describe.

The full-length books that have been published either for the first time or in "revised and updated" editions after Oklahoma City provide a better overview. In particular, see David H. Bennett, *The Party of Fear: The American Far Right from Nativism to the Militia Movement*, 2d ed. (New York: Vintage Books, 1995), which includes a new chapter on the militias, culled largely from news reports; Jonathan Karl, *The Right to*

Bear Arms: The Rise of America's New Militias (New York: HarperPaperbacks, 1995), which is a quickie paperback by a *New York Post* reporter who is far more sympathetic to the militias and more willing to minimize the danger they pose than any of the other books listed here; and Kenneth Stern, *A Force upon the Plains* (New York: Simon & Schuster, 1996), which is discussed and critiqued in depth later in this chapter. Good accounts by journalists of the violent hate groups active in the 1970s and 1980s, such as the Klan and the Order, include James Coates, *Armed and Dangerous: The Rise of the Survivalist Right* (New York: Noonday Press, 1987); Kevin Flynn and Gary Gerhardt, *The Silent Brotherhood* (New York: Free Press, 1989); and James Ridgeway, *Blood in the Face,* 2d ed. (New York: Thunder's Mouth Press, 1995).

4. The best single article on this issue is Tod Ensign, "The Militia-Military Connection," *Covert Action Quarterly* 53 (summer 1995): 13–16.

5. Bo Gritz is a former Green Beret who became well known years before the militia movement through his allegations not only that the United States intentionally left prisoners of war behind in Vietnam, but that the military did so in order to cover up massive illegal drug operations with which the CIA and parts of the military were involved. His role as a mediator in the negotiations between Randy Weaver and the FBI at Ruby Ridge further enhanced his position. His projects include SPIKE (Specially Prepared Individuals for Key Events), a ten-part paramilitary training course, for which he travels the country instructing paying groups about lock picking, intelligence-gathering maneuvers, cryptography, weapons, and a general approach to self-sufficiency and self-rule; and Almost Heaven, a separatist "community" located adjacent to land owned by the Nez Percé tribe in Idaho County, Idaho. See Jonathan Mozzochi, "America under the Gun," in Chip Berlet, ed., *Eyes Right!: Challenging the Right Wing Backlash* (Boston: South End Press, 1995), 236–40; Timothy Egan, "Idaho Community Built on Hatred and Fear," *New York Times,* 5 October 1994, A1; Samuel S. Jackson, "On the Moderate Fringe," *Time,* 26 June 1995, 56; and James Ridgeway, "Be All That You Can Be," *Village Voice,* 14 January 1992, 21–22.

Based in Indianapolis, Linda Thompson is best known for her two well-circulated videotapes (*Waco: The Big Lie* and *Waco II: The Big Lie Continues*) purporting to disprove federal law-enforcement agencies' accounts of the siege and destruction of the Branch Davidian compound. She gained even greater notoriety within militia circles with her call for an armed march on Washington by a national alliance of citizens' militias in order to "take back" America from its treasonous federal government. The original "ultimatum" calling for the march has been reprinted in Adam Parfrey, *Cult Rapture* (Los Angeles: Feral House, 1995), 317–22; see also Thompson's written statement "SEPT. 19 MILITIA ASSEMBLY CANCELED," posted 8 August 1994 on her computer bulletin board system in Indianapolis and circulated throughout the Internet. These two documents exemplify both the general framework of her conception of the grand conspiracy afflicting America and the pugnacious, macho posture she assumes against any and all who would challenge her authority as self-proclaimed "Acting Adjutant General of the Disorganized Militia of the U.S.A." Full-length profiles of her in-clude Jason Vest, "The Spooky World of Linda Thompson," *Washington Post,* 11 May 1995, D1, D8, D9; and Adam Parfrey and Jim Redden, "Patriot Games," *Village Voice,* 11 October 1994, 26–31 (revised and reprinted as "Linda Thompson's War" in Parfrey, *Cult Rapture,* 298–316); and Maryanne Vollers, "The White Woman from Hell," *Esquire* (July 1995): 50–52.

6. For an early interview with the Michigan Militia founders, see Robert Downes and George Foster, "On the Front Lines with Northern Michigan's Militia," *Northern Express* (Traverse City, Mich.), 22 August 1994 (reprinted in Don Hazen, Larry Smith, and Christine Triano, eds., *Militias in America 1995* [San Francisco: Institute for Al-ternative Journalism, 1995]). For a history of the Militia of Montana, see Marc Cooper, "Montana's Mother of All Militias," *Nation,* 22 May 1995, 714–21.

7. It is this microlevel of engagement that is most overlooked in media accounts of the movement, although the study of this level could produce the most interesting and helpful research. Examples of good reporting on local militias include: Rebecca Shelton, "The New Minutemen," *Kansas City New Times,* 22 February 1995 (reprinted in Hazen, Smith, and Triano, *Militias in America 1995*), on Missouri's 51st Militia, which began in 1993 as a small group of friends concerned with crime, welfare, and schools in order to represent a "conservative silent majority," and vows to be antiracist by kicking out any neo-Nazis and skinheads who try to join; Dale Russakoff, "Grass Roots Rage," *Washington Post,* 5 May 1995, A1, on Meadsville, Pennsylvania, a town that did not have a militia in May 1995 but contained individuals who seemed ready to begin one; and Phil McCombs, "The Making of a Militiaman," *Washington Post,* 22 May 1995, D1, about one man's effort to form the Perry County (Pennsylvania) unit of the U.S. Militia Association.

8. See David Helvarg, "The Anti-Enviro Connection," *Nation,* 22 May 1995, 722–24. In Washington State, one major conflict between environmentalists and loggers, ranchers, and property rights advocates linked to the Wise Use movement, led to a visit by MOM leader John Trochmann. See Kathie Durban, "Environmental Terrorism in Washington State," *Seattle Weekly,* 11 January 1995 (reprinted in Hazen, Smith, and Triano, *Militias in America 1995*). See also Downes and Foster, "On the Front Lines with Northern Michigan's Militia," 22 August 1994.

9. On "freemen's laws," see James Ridgeway, "Freemen's Law," *Village Voice,* 16 April 1996, 22. For descriptions of common law courts, sovereign citizenship, and other attempts by Patriot individuals and groups to reconstitute law in oddball, obfus-catory, and subversive ways, see Richard Sine, "Right-Wing Dropouts," (San Jose) *Metro,* 14 March 1996, 11–13: Hope Viner Sanborn, "Courting Trouble: Emergence of Common Law Courts Raises Concerns among Critics," *ABA Journal* (November 1995): 33; Thomas Heath and Connie Leslie, "A Law of Their Own," *Newsweek,* 25 September 1995, 75; Michael Janofsky, "Home-Grown Courts Spring Up as Judicial Arm of the Far Right," *New York Times,* 17 April 1996, A1; and Angie Cannon, "Right-

ists Now Using 'Courts' to Intimidate Public Officials," *Philadelphia Inquirer,* 24 May 1996, A23.

10. For a thorough discussion of the relationship between contemporary Protestant apocalyptic and conspiracy theory, see chapter 6.

11. The best single work on the history and complex religious beliefs of Christian Identity is Michael Barkun, *Religion and the Racist Right,* rev. ed. (Chapel Hill: University of North Carolina Press, 1997), which updates a work that was less than five years old in order to cover the Oklahoma City bombing and the increasing visibility of the militia movement. The book's new Epilogue makes more sweeping conclusions about the association and ideological connections between Christian Identity and the militia movement as a whole than I would. Although there clearly are some links between the religious racist right and militias, I do not think it empirically supportable given the decentralized, localized, and heterogeneous character of the recent upswing of far-right "grassroots" activity to equate or even associate all such groups, activities, or actors.

12. James A. Aho, *The Politics of Righteousness: Idaho Christian Patriots* (Seattle: University of Washington Press, 1990), 13–20.

13. See William F. Jasper, "More Pieces to the OKC Puzzle," *New American,* 24 June 1996, 4–8; and William Norman Grigg, "Hard Left's 'Right-Wing' Kin," *New American,* 24 June 1996, 23–26. The latter article asserts that such "right-wing" terrorists have been influenced as much by Latin American "Marxist" guerrillas as by true right-wing ideas.

14. On the people who were joining the Michigan Militia in late 1994, see Beth Hawkins, "Patriot Games," *Detroit Metro Times,* 12 October 1994 (reprinted in Hazen, Smith, and Triano, *Militias in America 1995*); and Keith Schneider, "Fearing a Conspiracy, Some Heed a Call to Arms," *New York Times,* 14 November 1994, A1, A14. On the drop in membership after Oklahoma City, see Beth Hawkins, "Damage Control," *Detroit Metro Times,* 26 April 1995 (reprinted in Hazen, Smith, and Triano, *Militias in America 1995*); and Marc Cooper, "Camouflage Days, E-mail Nights," *Nation,* 23 October 1995, 464. As to links to the bomb suspects, Terry Nichols was from Michigan and had apparently attended some Michigan Militia meetings, and Timothy McVeigh had supposedly traveled with Mark Koernke, nicknamed "Mark from Michigan," who also had some ties to the militia. Koernke, best known for his shortwave radio show and widely circulated videotape *America in Peril,* became a prominent figure in the immediate aftermath of Oklahoma City, as rumors spread in the media and on the Internet that he either was involved with or knew beforehand of the bomb plot. A two-part, front-page *Washington Post* series titled "Roots of Anger" attempted to track the lives of McVeigh and Nichols. On McVeigh, see Dale Russakoff and Serge Kovaleski, "An Ordinary Boy's Extraordinary Rage," *Washington Post,* 2 July 1995, A1, A20; on Nichols, see Serge Kovaleski, "In a Mirror, Nichols Is a Victim," *Washington Post,* 3 July 1995, A1, A14. On Koernke, see Susan Schmidt and Tom Kenworthy, "Mich. Fringe Group's Leader Has National Reputation," *Washington Post,* 25 April 1995, A6.

Allegations have also been made by the watchdog group Klanwatch of links between MM cofounder Ray Southwell and the Aryan Nations. See Hawkins, "Damage Control."

15. James Ridgeway and Ivan Helfman, "A Militia of Another Color," *Village Voice,* 17 October 1995, 22–23.

16. James Ridgeway, "The Posse Goes to Washington," *Village Voice,* 23 May 1995, 17, 19. For a profile on Chenoweth, see Sidney Blumenthal, "Her Own Private Idaho," *New Yorker,* 10 July 1995, 27–33; see also Nin Burleigh, "The Movement's Sympathetic Ears in Washington," *Time,* 8 May 1995, 66.

17. Marc Cooper, "The N.R.A. Takes Cover in the G.O.P.," *Nation,* 19 June 1995, 877–82.

18. During his panel session, Olson called Specter "the single-bullet theorist" (U.S. Senate Subcommittee on Terrorism, Technology, and Government Information, *The Militia Movement in the United States,* 98).

19. Daniel Levitas, "Militia Forum," *Nation,* 10 July 1995, 42. An unofficial hearing, held a month later by Congressman Charles Schumer (Democrat, New York), was an attempt to bring such concerns and expertise to the attention of the public and Congress. For an account, see Serge Kovaleski, "Officials at Forum Describe Alleged Militias' Threats," *Washington Post,* 12 July 1995, A1.

20. From Justice Jackson's dissent in *Terminiello v. Chicago,* 337 U.S. 1, 37 (1949): "[I]f the Court does not temper its doctrinaire logic with a little practical wisdom, it will convert the constitutional Bill of Rights into a suicide pact."

21. Michel Foucault, *Discipline and Punish: The Birth of the Prison,* trans. Alan Sheridan (New York: Vintage Books, 1977), 222.

22. Holmes, dissenting in *Abrams v. United States,* 250 U.S. 616, 630 (1919): "[T]he best test of truth is the power of the thought to get itself accepted in the competition of the market. . . ." The actual phrase "marketplace of ideas" is generally traced to an opinion by the liberal Justice William Brennan, in *Lamont v. Postmaster General,* 381 U.S. 301, 308 (concurring).

23. Wayne LaPierre, National Rifle Association fund-raising letter dated 13 April 1995 (cited in Stern, *A Force upon the Plains,* 110).

24. The law ultimately passed Congress as Public Law: 104–132, 104th Congress, 2d session (24 April 1996), Antiterrorism and Effective Death Penalty Act of 1996.

25. For an account of one example of the way the act has been used to deport immigrants based on secret evidence and to impose criminal and immigration sanctions on anyone who provides even humanitarian aid to a foreign organization labeled "terrorist" by the Department of State, see David Cole, "Blind Decisions Come to Court," *Nation,* 16 June 1997, 21–22.

26. For examples of criticism of the bill throughout the stages leading to its passage, see James Ridgeway, "The Long Arm of the Law," *Village Voice,* 21 May 1996,

32; Diana R. Gordon, "The Politics of Anti-Terrorism," *Nation,* 22 May 1995, 726–28; Robert Perkinson, "Oklahoma Fallout," *Z Magazine* (August 1995): 8–11.

27. Mark Koernke, whose videotapes, shortwave radio broadcasts, and acquaintance with Timothy McVeigh made him one of the most infamous militia spokesmen, had been invited to speak but arrived in Washington only an hour before the hearing and sat in the front row behind the panelists (Karl, *The Right to Bear Arms,* 146–47).

28. For the debate concerning Trochmann's alleged ties with the Aryan Nations, see Serge Kovaleski, " 'One World' Conspiracies Prompt Montana Militia's Call to Arms" *Washington Post,* 29 April 1994, A1, A13; Floyd Cochran, "OPINION: Racism Takes on a New Face," *Ravalli* (Montana) *Republic,* 25 August 1994 (cited in Stern, *A Force upon the Plains,* 70); Daniel Voll, "At Home with M.O.M.," *Esquire* (July 1995): 46–50.

29. Tony Ortega, "Affirmative Reactionaries," *Phoenix New Times,* 29 March 1996.

30. Indeed, the "Viper Militia" in Arizona, whose members were arrested in June 1996, reportedly named itself after the snake in this flag. New reports have indicated, however, that this group was shunned by the local militias operating in the same area. See Carol Morello and Gwen Florio, "Viper Militia Vilified by Other Units," *Philadelphia Inquirer,* 4 July 1996, A1. Furthermore, many of the Vipers participated in little more than paramilitary games, and conspiracy charges against half of the members were dismissed by the judge in their criminal trial. See J. William Gibson, "Paramilitary Culture after the Cold War," in Charles B. Strozier and Michael Flynn, eds., *The Year 2000: Essays on the End* (New York: New York University Press, 1997), 180–89.

31. For an excerpt of Bush's speech, see Karl, *The Right to Bear Arms,* 77–78.

32. Indeed, the fanciful notion of "Don't tread on me" being stamped on militia members' foreheads does not seem especially "normal," but instead conjures up images of two groups with which Johnson might not wish to be associated: hippies painting peace symbols and slogans on their faces and neo-Nazi skinheads etching swastikas into the skin between their eyebrows.

33. Morris Dees, *The Gathering Storm* (New York: HarperCollins, 1996).

34. Dees and the SPLC's fund-raising tactics and effectiveness in helping poor Southern minorities have been questioned over the past few years. For a summary of such allegations, see "The Myth of Morris Dees," *CounterPunch,* 15 May 1996, 1–6, and "The Myth of Morris Dees: The Fall-out Continues," *CounterPunch,* 16 June 1996, 3. These articles include allegations that Dees has personally enriched himself through the auspices of the Center (the subhead of the first article calls him "The Civil Rights Movement's TV Evangelist"), that the SPLC offices are a hostile workplace for minorities and women, that Dees and the Center have tried to suppress potential criticism through pressure and smear campaigns, and that the Center merely attempts to take on a few famous cases that in reality help only a handful of people.

35. Dees, *The Gathering Storm,* 6, 104–6, 109, 201, 228.

36. Stern, *A Force upon the Plains,* 13–15.

37. HarperCollins, part of Rupert Murdoch's News Corporation, Inc. empire, published *The Gathering Storm*; *A Force upon the Plains* was published by Simon & Schuster, a subsidiary of Time Warner.

38. Dees, *The Gathering Storm*, 2.

39. Ibid., 67.

40. Ibid., 90.

41. Ibid., 200–201.

42. Stern, *A Force upon the Plains*, 15.

43. Ibid., 79, 197.

44. Ibid., 107.

45. Ibid., 142.

46. Dees, *The Gathering Storm*, 23, 233.

47. Ibid., 238.

48. Ibid., 219–20.

49. Dees, *The Gathering Storm*, 112, 5.

50. Stern, *A Force upon the Plains*, 210–11.

51. Ibid., 210–20.

52. Ibid., 230–38; Dees, *The Gathering Storm*, 182–94.

53. Another book that makes the same argument in a more explicit and extended way is Thomas Halpern and Brian Levin, *The Limits of Dissent: The Constitutional Status of Armed Civilian Militias* (Amherst, Mass.: Aletheia, 1996).

54. Dees, *The Gathering Storm*, 183–84.

55. Stern, *A Force upon the Plains*, 237.

56. Dees, *The Gathering Storm*, 183.

57. Stern, *A Force upon the Plains*, 249–50.

58. Robin Wagner-Pacifici, *Discourse and Destruction: The City of Philadelphia versus MOVE* (Chicago: University of Chicago Press, 1994), 143. On the assault on the Branch Davidians, see Stuart Wright, ed., *Armageddon in Waco: Critical Perspectives on the Branch Davidian Conflict* (Chicago: University of Chicago Press, 1995). See also Christopher Keep's suggestive Deleuzian take on Waco, which asserts that the conflict in Waco was between the apocalyptic Davidian sect and militaristic federal law-enforcement agencies working under the doomsday regimes of Reagan/Bush (not to mention the early Clinton regime, which implemented the actual tragedy) (Christopher Keep, "An Absolute Acceleration: Apocalypticism and the War Machines of Waco," in Richard Dellamora, ed., *Postmodern Apocalypse: Theory and Cultural Practice at the End* [Philadelphia: University of Pennsylvania Press, 1995], 262–73).

3. Conspiracy Theory and Populism

1. Michael Rogin, *Ronald Reagan: The Movie* (Berkeley: University of California Press, 1987), esp. chap. 9, "American Political Demonology: A Retrospective."

2. Rogin also groups conspiracy theorists who perceive the threat of subversion to be real under this term. This makes a certain amount of sense—there are some parallels between the way leftist critics of political elites and conspiracy theorists view the political process—but it simplifies the critical distinctions between conspiracy theory and a radical, popular-democratic theory of power. These distinctions will be discussed in this chapter.

3. Among the most significant accounts of COINTELPRO is Ward Churchill and Jim Vander Wall, *The COINTELPRO Papers: Documents from the FBI's Secret Wars against Dissent in the United States* (Boston: South End Press, 1990). On the FBI surveillance of Martin Luther King, see David J. Garrow, *The FBI and Martin Luther King, Jr.* (New York: W. W. Norton, 1981).

4. See, for example the unsigned editorial " 'JFK': The Movie," *Wall Street Journal,* 27 December 1991, A10; and R. Emmett Tyrrell, "Stone's 'JFK' Fuels Fantasies of Those without Minds," *Bloomington* [Indiana] *Herald-Times,* 4 January 1992, A6.

5. Except for direct quotations, this section is a condensation of arguments that appear in the following: Chip Berlet, *Right Woos Left: Populist Party, LaRouchian, and Other Neo-Fascist Overtures to Progressives, and Why They Must Be Rejected* (Cambridge, Mass.: Political Research Associates, 22 February 1994 [revised; original draft 20 December 1990]); Chip Berlet, "Friendly Fascists," *Progressive* (June 1992): 16–20; Chip Berlet, "Big Stories, Spooky Sources," *Columbia Journalism Review* 32(1) (June 1993): 67–71; David Barsamian, "The Right Woos the Left: David Barsamian Interviews Chip Berlet," *Z Magazine* (January 1992): 38–43; Michael Albert, "Conspiracy?... Not!" *Z Magazine* (January 1992): 17–19; Michael Albert, "Conspiracy?... Not Again," *Z Magazine* (May 1992): 86–88; Erwin Knoll, "Anticonspiracism," *Progressive* (August 1992): 4; Christopher Phelps, "Forget Conspiracy Theories; Reality's Bad Enough," *Guardian* (U.S.), 12 February 1992, 18; James Ridgeway, "It's All One Big Conspiracy," *Village Voice,* 5 November 1991, 19–20. Although I do not wish to equate all of the work of these activists/writers, their critique of conspiracy theory is generally quite similar and their shared assumptions are my focus here.

6. Berlet, "Friendly Fascists," 26–27; Berlet, *Right Woos Left,* passim.

7. Berlet, "Friendly Fascists," 20.

8. Ironically, both Berlet and *Z Magazine,* the periodical that publishes regular columns by Albert and Chomsky, have been accused by at least one conspiracy theorist, Sherman Skolnick, of having ties to the CIA. To criticize conspiracy theory is to be a part of the conspiracy itself, whether as complicit lapdog or full-fledged member.

9. Albert, "Conspiracy?... Not!" 17.

10. Berlet, quoted in Barsamian, "The Right Woos the Left," 43.

11. Noam Chomsky, *Rethinking Camelot: JFK, the Vietnam War, and U.S. Political Culture* (Boston: South End Press, 1993), 38.

12. Berlet, "Big Stories, Spooky Sources," 67.

13. Berlet, *Right Woos Left,* 61.

14. Daniel Brandt, "An Incorrect Political Memoir," *Flatland* 10 (1994): 58. On LaRouche and the Liberty Lobby, see Dennis King, *Lyndon LaRouche and the New American Fascism* (New York: Doubleday, 1989); and Frank Mintz, *The Liberty Lobby and the American Right: Race, Conspiracy, and Culture* (Westport, Conn.: Greenwood Press, 1985).

15. Daniel Brandt, "Cyberspace Wars: Microprocessing vs. Big Brother," *Name-Base NewsLine* 2 (July–August 1993).

16. Alexander Cockburn, "Cockburn Replies," *Nation,* 23 August 1993, 223–24.

17. Berlet, "Friendly Fascists," 17.

18. Barsamian, "The Right Woos the Left," 39.

19. Ibid., 43.

20. The extent of Berlet's analysis in this direction is his admission that conspiracy theories are "often attractive as explanations for the otherwise inexplicable, and are undeniably entertaining"; similarly, Albert compares their appeal, drama, and vividness to mystery novels, and warns that they "can become addictive." This is a welcome admission of conspiracy theory's cultural significance, but is little more than a quick and simple explanation of their "seductive" powers. See Berlet, "Friendly Fascists," 18, and Albert, "Conspiracy? . . . Not!" 19.

21. For an insightful critique of an overly simplistic approach to the analysis of extreme ideological expressions, see Eric Santer's discussion of Freud's homophobic reading of Daniel Paul Schreber's famous autobiographical account of his own paranoia. Utilizing Eve Kosofsky Sedgwick's notion of the open secrecy constitutive of the "epistemology of the closet," Santer's project is in part to open an analytic space that Freud closed in "too quickly specifying the ideological content of the 'closet' before sufficiently analyzing the closet as *form,* as a place where such ideological meanings can be inscribed" (Eric L. Santer, *My Own Private Germany: Daniel Paul Schreber's Secret History of Modernity* [Princeton, N.J.: Princeton University Press, 1996], 44). The closet, Santer argues, is "a site where the drive dimension of symbolic functioning becomes manifest," and therefore where what he calls "the drive dimension of symbolic functioning" is especially visible (ibid.).

22. For a critical account of the important role of right-wing foundations in shaping contemporary policy, see Jean Stefancic and Richard Delgado, *No Mercy: How Conservative Think Tanks and Foundations Changed America's Social Agenda* (Philadelphia: Temple University Press, 1996); James Ridgeway, "Heritage on the Hill," *Nation,* 22 December 1997, 11–18; Robert Parry, "Who Buys the Right?" *Nation,* 18 November 1996, 5–6. Although many of the largest foundations (like Ford and MacArthur) fund some progressive causes, they have neither the political focus nor the coordinated strategy shared by conservative groups. See Michael H. Shuman, "Why Do Progressive Foundations Give Too Little to Too Many?" *Nation,* 21 January 1998, 11. A number of critical accounts of elite, nongovernmental groups during the postwar era provide important historical perspective. See, for example, Holly Sklar, ed., *Trilateralism:*

The Trilateral Commission and Elite Planning for World Management (Boston: South End Press, 1980), for an overview of the role of private, antidemocratic groups in national and global policymaking. Ironically, this book has proven quite popular among right-wing conspiracy theorists, despite its left antielite critique. See also Jerry W. Sanders, *Peddlers of Crisis: The Committee on the Present Danger and the Politics of Containment* (Boston: South End Press, 1983), for an excellent case study of the role of one nongovernmental organization in the promotion of an American military buildup and aggressive foreign policy before and during the Reagan administration.

23. For some critical accounts of the role of finance capital in national and global economies, see Patrick Bond, "The New U.S. Class Struggle: Financial Industry Power vs. Grassroots Populism," *Capital and Class* 40 (spring 1990): 150–81; Kevin Danaher, ed., *50 Years Is Enough: The Case against the World Bank and the International Monetary Fund* (Boston: South End Press, 1994); Mike Davis, "The Political Economy of Late-Imperial America," *New Left Review* 113 (January–February 1985): 6–37; David Harvey, *The Condition of Postmodernity* (London: Blackwell, 1989); and Doug Henwood, *Wall Street* (New York: Verso, 1997).

24. Stuart Hall, "The Problem of Ideology: Marxism without Guarantees," *Journal of Communication Inquiry* 10(2) (1986): 28–44, 37.

25. Ernesto Laclau, *Politics and Ideology in Marxist Theory* (London: Verso, 1977). All parenthetical page numbers in this section come from this work.

26. Ernesto Laclau, "Populist Rupture and Discourse," *Screen Education* 34 (1980): 90.

27. Ernesto Laclau and Chantal Mouffe, *Hegemony and Socialist Strategy* (London: Verso, 1985), 127–34.

28. I will utilize the term *articulation* throughout this work to signify the contingent, nonnecessary connection between different practices, the tenuous (in the sense of nonpermanent) linkages between social practices that come together at a specific historical moment. The term plays on the double meaning of the word *articulation,* which refers not only to expression, but also, in British usage, to a nonnecessary connection in objects such as the "articulated lorry," a severable connection that is made between a truck cab and a trailer. See Lawrence Grossberg, ed., "On Postmodernism and Articulation: An Interview with Stuart Hall," *Journal of Communication Inquiry* 10(2) (summer 1986): 45–60, 53–55.

29. Bonnie Honig, *Political Theory and the Displacement of Politics* (Ithaca, N.Y.: Cornell University Press, 1993), 3. Page numbers in parentheses in this paragraph refer to this work.

30. Stuart Hall, "Authoritarian Populism: A Reply to Jessop et al.," *New Left Review* 151 (May–June 1985): 118. See also Stuart Hall, "Popular-Democratic vs. Authoritarian Populism: Two Ways of 'Taking Democracy Seriously,'" in Alan Hunt, ed., *Marxism and Democracy* (London: Lawrence & Wishart, 1980), 157–85; and Stuart Hall, *The Hard Road to Renewal* (London: Verso, 1988).

31. Laclau, *Politics and Ideology in Marxist Theory,* 162.

32. Lawrence Grossberg, *We Gotta Get Out of This Place: Popular Conservatism and Postmodern Culture* (London: Routledge, 1992), 249–55.

33. See Alan Brinkley, *Voices of Protest: Huey Long, Father Coughlin, and the Great Depression* (New York: Knopf, 1982); and John Higham, "Ideological Antisemitism in the Gilded Age," in *Send These to Me: Immigrants in Urban America,* rev. ed. (Baltimore: Johns Hopkins University Press, 1984).

34. John Frow criticizes both Laclau and Hall for failing to provide a sufficiently complex analysis of class along these lines; see his *Cultural Studies and Cultural Values* (Oxford: Oxford University Press, 1995).

35. Michael Hardt and Antonio Negri, *Labor of Dionysus: A Critique of the State-Form* (Minneapolis: University of Minnesota Press, 1994), 259–61.

36. Mike Davis, *City of Quartz* (London: Verso, 1990), 224–60.

37. On the relations of local cities and communities to national and global capitalism, see Joe R. Feagin and Michael Peter Smith, "Cities and the New International Division of Labor: An Overview," in Smith and Feagin, eds., *The Capitalist City* (Oxford: Basil Blackwell, 1987), 3–34; and Richard J. Barnet and John Cavanagh, *Global Dreams: Imperial Corporations and the New World Order* (New York: Touchstone, 1994). On the difficult, "nervous," but possible and necessary survival of rural culture and communities, see Kathleen Stewart's wonderful *A Space on the Side of the Road* (Princeton, N.J.: Princeton University Press, 1996).

38. For an account of this development, see Herbert Schiller's *Culture, Inc.: The Corporate Takeover of Public Expression* (New York: Oxford University Press, 1989).

39. See Stuart Ewen, *All Consuming Images* (New York: Basic Books, 1988). Although liberal press critics such as Kathleen Hall Jamieson decry handicapping (see, e.g., Jamieson's *Dirty Politics: Deception, Distraction, and Democracy* [New York: Oxford University Press, 1992], and Larry Sabato's *Feeding Frenzy: How Attack Journalism Has Transformed American Politics* [New York: Free Press, 1993]), in fact, as Doug Henwood has remarked, "since the candidates and their scribes agree on most fundamental issues, with the differences coming down mainly to personality and nuance ... who wins and who loses really *is* the story" (Doug Henwood, "Four More Years," *Left Business Observer* 75 [December 1996]: 1).

40. Zygmunt Bauman, *Freedom* (Minneapolis: University of Minnesota Press, 1988), 81–84. See also John Clarke's discussion of the New Rights in the United States and the United Kingdom in *New Times and Old Enemies* (London: HarperCollins, 1991), 163–76.

41. Grossberg, *We Gotta Get Out of This Place,* 277.

42. Jean Baudrillard, *Simulations,* trans. Paul Foss, Paul Patton, and Philip Beichman (New York: Semiotext[e], 1983), 26–30.

43. Zygmunt Bauman, *Intimations of Postmodernity* (London: Routledge, 1992), 197–200.

44. Brian Massumi, "Everywhere You Want to Be: An Introduction to Fear," in Brian Massumi, ed., *The Politics of Everyday Fear* (Minneapolis: University of Minnesota Press, 1993), 30–31.

45. Regina Austin, "Beyond Black Demons and White Devils: Antiblack Conspiracy Theorizing and the Black Public Sphere," *Florida State University Law Review* 22 (spring 1995): 1021. A rare quantitative social-science study on belief in conspiracy theory, performed in southwestern New Jersey in April 1992, found that blacks (and to a lesser degree Hispanics) believed in conspiracy theory to a greater degree than whites. See Ted Goertzel, "Belief in Conspiracy Theories," *Political Psychology* 15(4) (November 1994): 731–42.

46. See John Fiske, *Media Matters: Race and Gender in U.S. Politics,* rev. ed. (Minneapolis: University of Minnesota Press, 1996), 191–216; Patricia A. Turner, *I Heard It through the Grapevine* (Berkeley: University of California Press, 1993).

47. Michael Eric Dyson, "Haunted by Conspiracy," *New York Times,* 27 January 1995, A15.

48. Interestingly, despite this seeming racial specificity of many conspiracy theories and practices, texts and theories occasionally pass indiscriminately between far-right and black nationalist groups. For example, vendors at meetings of the United African Movement in Harlem sell white far-right-wing author A. Ralph Epperson's *The Unseen Hand* (Tucson, Ariz.: Publius Press, 1985) alongside black nationalist books. See Peter Noel, "No Whites Allowed," *Village Voice,* 18 March 1997, 50, 53.

49. James William Gibson, *Warrior Dreams* (New York: Hill and Wang, 1994).

50. Linda Kintz, *Between Jesus and the Market: The Emotions That Matter in Right-Wing America* (Durham, N.C.: Duke University Press, 1997), 109.

51. Although this argument is typically used by those seeking to delegitimate feminist theory and political interventions (see, for example, Sanford Pinsker, "America's Conspiratorial Imagination," *Virginia Quarterly Review* 68[4]) [autumn 1992]: 605, 625; and Robert S. Robins and Jerrold M. Post, *Political Paranoia: The Psychopolitics of Hatred* [New Haven: Yale University Press, 1997], 181), some radical feminist discourse, such as that of antipornography activists, does assume a complicity between power, patriarchy, and heterosexuality that borders on the conspiratorial. See, for example, Andrea Dworkin's *Intercourse* (New York: Free Press, 1987), and *Pornography: Men Possessing Women* (New York: Perigee Press, 1979).

52. On the historical dichotomy between male "rationality" and female "intuition" and the resulting association of masculinity with scientific method, see Valerie Walkerdine, *The Mastery of Reason: Cognitive Development and the Production of Rationality* (London: Routledge, 1988), on mathematical logic and method; and Sandra Harding, *The Science Question in Feminism* (Ithaca, N.Y.: Cornell University Press, 1986), on science generally. On apocalyptic masculinist fantasy, see Lee Quinby, "Coercive Purity: The Dangerous Promise of Apocalyptic Masculinity," in Charles B. Strozier and Michael Flynn, eds., *The Year 2000: Essays on the End* (New York: New York

University Press, 1997), 157. Probably, right-wing (more than left-wing) conspiracy theory assumes differences between virile knowledge and resistance and feminized thought and equivocation, making this gendered difference both nonessential and historical. Compare, for example, Linda Thompson, who proclaims her authenticity as a militia leader through her macho persona and frequent calls for revolutionary actions, with the more domestic Mae Brussell, a "liberal" conspiracy theorist of the 1960s and 1970s whose work consisted largely of clipping articles from hundreds of periodicals and collecting this information in vast file cabinets in her home. See the discussion of Thompson in chapter 2, and of Brussell in Jonathan Vankin, *Conspiracies, Cover-ups and Crimes* (New York: Paragon House, 1991), 86–101.

53. Henri Lefebvre, *Critique of Everyday Life,* vol. 1, *Introduction,* trans. John Moore (London: Verso, 1991), 89–92.

4. The Clinton Chronicles

1. Michael Isikoff, "Conspiracy Theorists Find Foster Case Hard to Resist," *Washington Post,* 13 March 1994, A10.

2. Richard Hofstadter, *The Paranoid Style in American Politics* (New York: Knopf, 1966), 4.

3. On paranoia's paradoxes, see Yehuda Fried and Joseph Agassi, *Paranoia: A Study in Diagnosis* (Boston: Dordrecht-Holland, 1976), 4–5.

4. Interestingly, this same difficult process is central to the state's attempt to persuade a jury of a defendant's guilt in a criminal conspiracy: "[C]onspiracy is by nature a clandestine offense. It is improbable that the parties will enter into their illegal agreement openly; it is not necessary, in fact, that all the parties ever have direct contact with one another, or know one another's identity, or even communicate verbally with their intention to agree. It is therefore unlikely that the prosecution will be able to prove the formation of the agreement by direct evidence, and the jury must usually infer its existence from the clear co-operation among the parties. But in their zeal to emphasize that the agreement need not be proved directly, the courts sometimes neglect to say that it need be proved at all" ("Developments — Conspiracy," *Harvard Law Review* 72[3] [1959]: 933–34).

5. One potentially fruitful use of the term *paranoia* in this context is the concept in psychology of "healthy cultural paranoia," described as "an adaptive mechanism for coping with a life that is plagued by prejudice and discrimination," and specifically the obsessive fears of individual members of minority groups of persecution. To the extent that this term serves merely as a cover for labeling genuine instances of racism as pathology, however, it merely reproduces the limitations of Hofstadter's more simplistic approach. See Christina E. Newhill, "The Role of Culture in the Development of Paranoid Symptomatology," *American Journal of Orthopsychiatry* 60(2) (April 1990): 177.

6. Greg Ferguson and David Bowermaster, "Whatever It Is, Bill Clinton Likely Did It," *U.S. News and World Report,* 8 August 1994, 29–32.

7. Ibid., 29–30.

8. Kenn Thomas, "Clinton Era Conspiracies!" *Washington Post,* 16 January 1994, C3.

9. Philip Weiss, "Clinton Crazy," *New York Times Magazine,* 23 February 1997, 36.

10. David S. Bennahum, "Techno-Paranoia in the White House," *New York Times,* 25 January 1997, A23.

11. Citizens' Video Press, *The Clinton Chronicles* (Winchester, Calif.: Citizens for Honest Government, 1994). Its production and reception are described in Weiss, "Clinton Crazy," 40–41. On other videotapes and the circulation of materials on Foster by conservatives, see Susan Schmidt, "Two Years after Foster's Death, Conspiracy Theories Thrive," *Washington Post,* 4 July 1995, A1; and Ellen Joan Pollock, "Vince Foster's Death Is a Lively Business for Conspiracy Buffs," *Wall Street Journal,* 23 March 1995, A1.

12. The Western Journalism Center (WJC) has taken out a series of full-page advertisements in national newspapers questioning whether Foster's death was a suicide. See, for example, "A Special Report on the Vincent Foster Case," advertisement printed in the *Washington Times,* 14 March 1994, A9; "Vincent Foster's Death: WAS IT A SUICIDE?" advertisement printed in the *Washington Post,* 16 November 1994, A21. On Scaife generally, see Iver Peterson, "In a Battle of Newspapers, a Conservative Spends Liberally," *New York Times,* 8 December 1997, D1; on Scaife's role in supporting the allegations about Foster through the WJC and his own newspapers, see Trudy Lieberman, "The Vince Foster Factory and 'Courage in Journalism,'" *Columbia Journalism Review* (13 March 1996): 8; and Frank Rich, "Why Foster Lives," *New York Times,* 11 November 1995, A13.

13. Thomas, "Clinton Era Conspiracies!"

14. Ferguson and Bowermaster, "Whatever It Is," 30.

15. *Tragedy and Hope* is currently kept in print by a small publisher, Angriff Press, whose address is a post office box in Hollywood. The book's market seems to be maintained by far-right-wing and conspiracy-related mail-order companies.

16. In fact, Clinton had identified Quigley's role in his development during the week leading up to the Democratic convention. See David Maraniss, "Bill Clinton: Born to Run . . . and Run . . . and Run," *Washington Post,* 13 July 1992, A1.

17. John Elvin, "Clinton a Bircher?" *Washington Times,* 22 July 1992, A6.

18. "Who Is Bill Clinton?" *The Project* 9(3) (1992) (Ferndale, Mich.: A-albionic Research).

19. Lacan distinguishes between "need," akin to instinctual requirements for survival, demand, the articulating of need in language that at once demands a particular object and another to whom the demand is made, and desire, which he defines in *Écrits*

as "neither the appetite for satisfaction, nor the demand for love, but the difference that results from the subtraction of the first from the second, the phenomenon of their splitting" (Jacques Lacan, *Écrits,* trans. Alan Sheridan [New York: W. W. Norton, 1977], 287). While necessarily a simplification (Elizabeth Grosz, in *Jacques Lacan: A Feminist Introduction* [London: Routledge, 1990], 58–81, provides a helpful discussion of the relationship between need, demand, desire, and the symbolic order in Lacan), the analogy that I make between the interpretive drive of the conspiracy theorist and Lacan's notion of desire focuses on the former's repetition and tendency to reproduce itself endlessly, its complex relationship to the seeming object of its desire, and its attempt to enter into the larger domain of the law and language of the Other.

20. Michael Berubé provides a useful discussion of interpretation in Pynchon's work in *Marginal Forces/Cultural Centers* (Ithaca, N.Y.: Cornell University Press, 1992), 219–21.

21. In Slavoj Žižek's words, the "drive's aim is to reproduce itself as drive, to return to its circular path, to continue its path to and from the goal" (Slavoj Žižek, *Looking Awry* [Cambridge: MIT Press, 1991], 5).

22. "[T]he impeded desire converts into a desire for impediment; the unsatisfied desire converts into a desire for unsatisfaction; a desire to keep our desire 'open'; the fact that we 'don't know what we really want' — what to desire — converts into a desire not to know, a desire for ignorance" (Slavoj Žižek, *For They Know Not What They Do* [London: Verso, 1991], 143–44).

23. One exception to this is fundamentalist Protestant apocalyptic eschatology, in which the final culmination of a conspiracy is expected and, somewhat problematically for some fundamentalists, desired. Of course, such an end is easier to predict and to desire to represent in narrative form. See chapter 6.

24. Slavoj Žižek, *The Sublime Object of Ideology* (London: Verso, 1989), 91–92.

25. Jacques Lacan, *The Four Fundamental Concepts of Psycho-Analysis,* trans. Alan Sheridan (New York: W. W. Norton, 1979), 62.

26. Žižek, *The Sublime Object of Ideology,* 94–95.

27. In this sense, as Baudrillard notes, the details of "history" are marked by contradictory tendencies. On the one hand, "every event is granted its own liberation; every fact becomes atomic, nuclear, and pursues its trajectory in the void" — the detail is a particle that can flow free from a larger mass. On the other hand, every detail "is no longer able to transcend itself, to envisage its own finality, to dream of its own end; it is being buried beneath its own immediate effect, worn out in special effects, imploding into current events." The detail, in other words, is invigorating and stupefying, its meaning shorn by movement (the interpretive "freedom" of creative conspiracy theorizing) and its ultimate deceleration (within the paralyzing interpretive chain of conspiracy) (Jean Baudrillard, *The Illusion of the End,* trans. Chris Turner [Stanford, Calif.: Stanford University Press, 1994], 1–5).

28. Lacan, *The Four Fundamental Concepts of Psycho-Analysis,* 62–63.

29. Keith Thompson, *Angels and Aliens* (Reading, Mass.: Addison-Wesley, 1991), 97 (emphasis in original).

30. The Lacanian concept that this most resembles is known as the *point de capiton,* or quilting point. Once again, Žižek's usage of the concept is most helpful in this context, as he describes anti-Semitic theories of a "Jewish plot" for control as "an inversion by means of which what is effectively an *immanent,* purely textual operation — the 'quilting' of the heterogeneous material into a unified ideological field — is perceived and experienced as an unfathomable, *transcendent,* stable point of reference concealed behind the flow of appearances and acting as its hidden cause" (Žižek, *For They Know Not What They Do,* 18). Similarly, Ernesto Laclau and Chantal Mouffe employ the notion of "nodal points": the "privileged signifiers" within a discourse that constitute "an attempt to dominate the field of discursivity, to arrest the flow of differences, to construct a centre," and, ultimately, to "fix the meaning of a signifying chain" (Ernesto Laclau and Chantal Mouffe, *Hegemony and Socialist Strategy* [London: Verso, 1985], 112).

31. Conspiracy theory thus shares with a similarly masculinist domain of human knowledge, mathematics, this construction of a mastered cognitive rationality. See Valerie Walkerdine, *The Mastery of Reason: Cognitive Development and the Production of Rationality* (London: Routledge, 1988), 199–200.

32. Carl Freedman, "Towards a Theory of Paranoia: The Science Fiction of Philip K. Dick," *Science Fiction Studies* 11 (1984): 15–24.

33. Fredric Jameson, *The Geopolitical Aesthetic* (Bloomington: Indiana University Press, 1992), 3.

34. Fredric Jameson, "Cognitive Mapping," in Lawrence Grossberg and Cary Nelson, eds., *Marxism and the Interpretation of Culture* (Urbana: University of Illinois Press, 1988), 356.

35. Žižek, *The Sublime Object of Ideology,* 126.

36. C. W. Spinks, "Semiotic Shell Games: Foucault's Pendulum and Conspiracy Theory," *Romance Languages Annual* 3 (1991): 597.

37. Lawrence Grossberg, *We Gotta Get Out of This Place: Popular Conservatism and Postmodern Culture* (London: Routledge, 1992), 81.

38. John Johnston has provocatively analyzed Pynchon's novels as a semiotic regime of paranoia ("Toward the Schizo-Text: Paranoia as Semiotic Regime in *The Crying of Lot 49,*" in Patrick O'Donnell, ed., *New Essays on The Crying of Lot 49* [New York: Cambridge University Press, 1991], 47–78).

39. Gilles Deleuze and Félix Guattari, *A Thousand Plateaus: Capitalism and Schizophrenia,* trans. Brian Massumi (Minneapolis: University of Minnesota Press, 1987), 112.

40. Ibid., 112–13.

41. Brian Massumi, "The Autonomy of Affect," in Paul Patton, ed., *Deleuze: A Critical Reader* (London: Basil Blackwell, 1996), 222–25.

42. On Deleuzian notions of decoding and recoding and their relation to deterritorialization and reterritorialization, see Eugene Holland's essays "Schizoanalysis and Baudelaire: Some Illustrations of Decoding at Work," in Patton, *Deleuze: A Critical Reader,* 240–56; and "Schizoanalysis: The Postmodern Contextualization of Psychoanalysis," in Grossberg and Nelson, *Marxism and the Interpretation of Culture,* 405–16.

43. Deleuze and Guattari, *A Thousand Plateaus,* 113.

44. One similarity between Deleuze and Guattari's notion of productive desire and Žižek's reading of Lacan's notion of desire is this metaphor of capitalism, signification and desire. Žižek compares "the fundamental blockage which resolves and reproduces itself through frenetic activity" in the *objet petit a* with the similar processes of capital (Žižek, *The Sublime Object of Ideology,* 52–53).

45. Deleuze and Guattari compare their theory of desire with that of Lacan by discussing what they see as the two poles of the latter's work on desire: the *objet petit a* as a desiring machine and not as the result of need or fantasy, and the "great Other" as signifier, "which reintroduces a certain notion of lack" (Gilles Deleuze and Félix Guattari, *Anti-Oedipus: Capitalism and Schizophrenia,* trans. Robert Hurley, Mark Seem, and Helen R. Lane (Minneapolis: University of Minnesota Press, 1983), 27. They praise the former pole as representing the part of Lacan's work that describes the productive role of desire, while they dismiss the latter as demonstrating Lacan's — and psychoanalysis's — role as an agent of Oedipalization. See also Elizabeth Grosz's comparison of Deleuze and Guattari and psychoanalytic theory in her attempt to articulate a feminist theory of the sexually specific body in *Volatile Bodies: Toward a Corporeal Feminism* (Bloomington: Indiana University Press, 1994), 164–73.

46. Deleuze and Guattari, *Anti-Oedipus,* 7.

47. Grosz, *Volatile Bodies,* 165.

48. This is not to say that many such conspiracy theories do not germinate from the unethical and scandalous acts for which the Clinton presidency has become so justly notorious.

49. Umberto Eco, *Foucault's Pendulum,* trans. William Weaver (New York: Harcourt Brace Jovanovich, 1989).

50. Spinks, "Semiotic Shell Games," 595.

51. Charles Sanders Peirce, *Collected Papers* (Cambridge: Harvard University Press, 1931–58), 2: 643.

52. Umberto Eco, *A Theory of Semiotics* (Bloomington: Indiana University Press, 1976), 132.

53. Umberto Eco, *The Limits of Interpretation* (Bloomington: Indiana University Press, 1990), 59.

54. See ibid., 156–60, for a discussion of "abduction" as kidnapping and analogy.

55. Umberto Eco, *Interpretation and Overinterpretation* (Cambridge: Cambridge University Press, 1992), 47.

56. Ibid., 50.

57. Eco, *The Limits of Interpretation,* 24 (emphasis in original).

58. Georg Simmel, *The Sociology of Georg Simmel,* trans. and ed. Kurt H. Wolff (New York: Free Press, 1950), 330–33.

59. Leonard C. Lewin, *Report from Iron Mountain* (New York: Simon & Schuster, 1996).

60. See, for example, Robert S. Boynton, "A Lefty Reunion," *New Yorker,* 13 May 1996, 36, 38; and Scott McLemee, "Irony Mountain," *[Village] Voice Literary Supplement,* June 1996, 7.

61. Doreen Carvajal, "Onetime Political Satire, Adopted by the Right, Becomes Internet Copyright Arena," *New York Times,* 1 July 1996, D7.

62. Francis X. Clines, "First Lady Attributes Inquiry to Right-Wing Conspiracy," *New York Times,* 28 January 1998, A1.

63. "Excerpts From Interview with Mrs. Clinton on NBC," *New York Times,* 28 January 1998, A22.

5. *JFK, The X-Files,* and Beyond

1. William Grimes, "What Debt Does Hollywood Owe to Truth?" *New York Times,* 5 March 1992, B1, B4.

2. John Leo, "Oliver Stone's Paranoid Propaganda," *U.S. News and World Report,* 13 January 1992, 18. See also the unsigned editorial " 'JFK': The Movie," *Wall Street Journal,* 27 December 1991, A10, which strongly implies that Stone and Warner Brothers, which produced and distributed the film, were deliberately playing on the American public's "hatred for the U.S. government and institutions" — the latter in order "to get Time Warner stock somewhere within shouting distance" of two hundred dollars a share to ward off a takeover attempt by Paramount. Apparently, some far-fetched theories are more acceptable than others.

3. Brent Staples, "Hollywood: History by Default," *New York Times,* 25 December 1991, A30. Staples's commentary appeared as an "Editorial Notebook," a short, signed essay that appears under the general editorials and is written by members of the *Times* editorial board. Another essay that appeared just a week earlier, John P. MacKenzie's "Oliver Stone's Patsy" (*New York Times,* 20 December 1991, A14), made a similar argument that Stone had exceeded "even the questionable liberties [of presenting speculative theories as truth] enjoyed by television 'docudrama.' " See also Kenneth Auchincloss, "Twisted History," *Newsweek,* 23 December 1991, 46–49, which cites film critic Leonard Maltin as a source for the argument that "young people" in the current "media age" are especially vulnerable to movies that can erase the "difference" between "facts" and "dramatic embellishments."

4. David Denby, in his review of *JFK* in *New York* magazine, liked the film precisely because "Stone the moral relativist gave way to Stone the Capraesque hero-worshiper" ("Thrill of Fear," *New York,* 6 January 1992, 50–51).

5. A. M. Rosenthal, "Movies, Drugs, Election," *New York Times,* 11 September 1992, A15, and "America the Terrorist," *New York Times,* 30 March 1993, A15.

6. For example, during the adaptation of John Grisham's best-selling novel *The Firm* to film, screenwriters Sydney Pollack and David Rayfiel "toyed with introducing a BCCI [Bank of Commerce and Credit International]-inspired cabal of international bankers." Interestingly, Rayfiel had written the screenplay for the 1970s conspiracy thriller *Three Days of the Condor* (Greg Kilday, "A Film So Nice They Rewrote It Twice," *Entertainment Weekly,* 23 July 1993, 36–37).

7. This generalization would exclude science-fiction novels whose plots utilize future conspiracies. Even in the novels of Philip K. Dick and William Gibson, however, which often include a conspiratorial corporate, governmental, or, in Dick's case, otherworldly power, the parallels between present and future are clear.

8. Fredric Jameson, *The Political Unconscious* (Ithaca, N.Y.: Cornell University Press), 82.

9. Ibid., 34–35.

10. Michel Foucault, "Truth and Power," in Colin Gordon, ed., *Power/Knowledge* (New York: Pantheon, 1980), 114.

11. This chapter is indebted to models of scholarship on postwar American culture that both discern dominant attempts to frame or contain social narratives about the Rosenbergs and about nuclear war, and describe the ways in which such narratives are continually challenged by competing attempts to reframe history and the social. See Virginia Carmichael, *Framing History: The Rosenberg Story and the Cold War* (Minneapolis: University of Minnesota Press, 1993); and Alan Nadel, *Containment Culture: American Narratives, Postmodernism, and the Atomic Age* (Durham, N.C.: Duke University Press, 1995).

12. I am borrowing the term "classical" from David Bordwell, Janet Staiger, and Kristin Thompson's notion of the "classical Hollywood narrative," a relatively unified system of production, causality, realism, visual and aural style, time, space, shot, and sequence on which most mainstream, commercial American cinematic storytelling has been based since 1917. Although the "classical style" enabled some variance in specific genres (such as film noir) and individual "auteurs" (such as Alfred Hitchcock), and has existed alongside alternative modes of craft-oriented experimental film production, it has organized the production and reception of American (and most European) commercial film. See David Bordwell, Janet Staiger, and Kristin Thompson, *The Classical Hollywood Cinema: Film Style and Mode of Production to 1960* (New York: Columbia University Press, 1985). Similarly, the formulas of popular literary genres have long been organized through their commercial mode of production, marketing strategies, underlying narrative structures, and recurring types of characters and themes. The best-known general work on popular literary formulas is John G. Cawelti, *Adventure, Mystery, and Romance* (Chicago: University of Chicago Press, 1976). A work that is more focused on a conspiracy-related genre and more influential on the present

work is Michael Denning, *Cover Stories: Narrative and Ideology in the British Spy Thriller* (London: Routledge & Kegan Paul, 1987).

13. Bordwell, Staiger, and Thompson, *The Classical Hollywood Cinema,* 12.

14. Millicent Manglis, "Paranoid Fictions: Psychoanalysis and Politics in Cold War Hollywood Cinema," unpublished paper, 1993. As George Wead has argued (using the term "paranoia" instead of conspiracy): "Paranoia is interesting as an esthetic device... [because] it fits precisely nowhere. It overlaps the customary boundaries. And yet it is something we recognize as having a structural unity" ("Toward a Definition of Filmnoia," *Velvet Light Trap* 13 [1974]): 2). See also Paul Jensen, "The Return of Dr. Caligari: Paranoia in Hollywood," *Film Comment* (winter 1971): 36–45.

15. Hans Zukier provides a psychoanalytic analysis of the conspiracy narrative's internal logic, likening its efficacy to that of the analysand's interpretation of past events and psychoanalytic therapy's attempt to provide a narrative of past events whose rhetorical appeal and plausibility for the patient prove therapeutic. See Hans Zukier, "The Conspiratorial Imperative: Medieval Jewry in Western Europe," in C. F. Graumann and Serge Moscovici, eds., *Changing Conception of Conspiracy Theory* (New York: Springer-Verlag, 1987), 87–103, 91–92.

16. Stephen Neale, *Genre* (London: British Film Institute, 1980), 19, 48–50. In describing Robert Ludlum's novels, John Frow refers to the thriller's "formal solution of how to write a novel: it delivers certain resources of story and plot construction, a repertoire of *topoi,* a ready-made thematics of conspiracy and paranoia, and so on" (John Frow, *Marxism and Literary History* [Oxford: Basil Blackwell, 1986], 146).

17. Roland Barthes, "The Discourse of History," in *The Rustle of Language,* trans. Richard Howard (New York: Farrar, Straus and Giroux, 1986), 137–39.

18. Michel de Certeau, "Making History," in *The Writing of History,* trans. Tom Conley (New York: Columbia University Press, 1988), 43.

19. Hayden White, *Tropics of Discourse* (Baltimore: Johns Hopkins University Press, 1978), 70–73.

20. Hayden White, *Metahistory* (Baltimore: Johns Hopkins University Press, 1973), 286–87.

21. Ernest Keen has analyzed the personal narratives of clinical paranoids in similar ways. See Ernest Keen, "Paranoia and Cataclysmic Narratives," in Theodore R. Sarbin, ed., *Narrative Psychology: The Storied Nature of Human Conduct* (New York: Praeger, 1986), 174–90.

22. Barthes, "The Discourse of History," 130.

23. Ed Branigan, *Narrative Comprehension and Film* (London: Routledge, 1992), 3.

24. This search for the "meaning" of history and the individual subject becomes even more significant in popular Christian eschatology, in which "history" is merely pretext and a series of signs to be interpreted in order to discern the imminence of Christ's return. See chapter 6.

25. On the James Bond novels, see Tony Bennett and Janet Woollacott, *Bond and Beyond: The Political Career of a Popular Hero* (London: Methuen, 1987); on the "New War" texts, see James William Gibson, *Warrior Dreams: Violence and Manhood in Post-Vietnam America* (New York: Hill and Wang, 1994).

26. Fredric Jameson, *The Geopolitical Aesthetic* (Bloomington: Indiana University Press, 1992), 33–34

27. As Michael Rogin has written on the film's obsessive fear of gays, "Homosexual contagion is at once source and result of the killing, making the spread of alternative sexualities one more disaster for which Kennedy's death is to blame" (Michael Rogin, "*JFK*: The Movie," *American Historical Review* 97[2] [April 1992]: 505).

28. Michael Ryan and Douglas Kellner make this point with regard to the liberal pessimism of 1970s "paranoid" thrillers such as *The Parallax View, Executive Action,* and *All the President's Men.* They argue further that the sole solution these films propose — liberal reform — proved a failed one, and the crisis of legitimacy that Hollywood films of the 1970s articulated was harnessed by the New Right in its project of dismantling New Deal social programs and governmental regulation. See Michael Ryan and Douglas Kellner, *Camera Politica* (Bloomington: Indiana University Press, 1988), 95–105.

29. Fredric Jameson, "Cognitive Mapping," in Lawrence Grossberg and Cary Nelson, eds., *Marxism and the Interpretation of Culture* (Urbana: University of Illinois Press, 1988), 353.

30. Jameson, *The Geopolitical Aesthetic, 3.*

31. Jameson, "Cognitive Mapping," 356; Denning, *Cover Stories, 152.*

32. For a full account of the story behind the Gemstone File, as well as an interview with Caruana and an annotated version of the *Key* itself, see Jim Keith, ed., *The Gemstone File* (Atlanta, Ga.: IllumiNet Press, 1992). In addition, Gerald A. Carroll's *Project Seek: Onassis, Kennedy and the Gemstone Thesis* (Carson City, Nev.: Bridger House Publishers, 1994) provides a far less skeptical account of the *Key* and the Files and includes a quasi-liturgical parsing of the document.

33. Brussell is profiled in a chapter titled "There Is No Word for Rational Fear" in Jonathan Vankin's *Conspiracies, Cover-ups and Crimes* (New York: Paragon House, 1991), 86–101.

34. Jim Keith, "Interview with Stephanie Caruana," in Keith, *The Gemstone File,* 46.

35. From the January 1972 entry of "A Skeleton Key to the Gemstone File," in Keith, *The Gemstone File, 26.*

36. Ibid., 6.

37. Ibid., 7.

38. Ibid., 30.

39. Keith, "An Interview with Stephanie Caruana," 43.

40. Ibid., 22.

41. Peter Brooks, *Reading for the Plot* (New York: Vintage Books, 1985), 37.

42. Gérard Gennette, *Narrative Discourse,* trans. Jane E. Lewin (Ithaca, N.Y.: Cornell University Press, 1980), 87–88. Another, equally important, relationship defining narrative speed is between what Seymour Chatman has confusingly called "discourse-time," "the time it takes to peruse the discourse," and "story-time," which is similar to what Genette calls "duration." In media in which different "readers" or audience members can move at their own pace, as with print and as opposed to film and television (notwithstanding the ability to fast-forward videotapes), the act of reading through particular parts more quickly and slowly will clearly affect the "speed" of the narrative. See Seymour Chatman, *Story and Discourse: Narrative Structure in Fiction and Film* (Ithaca, N.Y.: Cornell University Press, 1978), 62–63.

43. I use the term "trajectory" and the metaphor of plotting points within a larger system that is at once chaotic and, at a larger level, ordered to suggest not only Jameson's notion of "cognitive mapping" but also the fascinating connections made between narrative theory and chaos theory in Kenneth J. Knoespel's essay "The Emplotment of Chaos: Instability and Narrative Order," in N. Katherine Hayles, ed., *Chaos and Order* (Chicago: University of Chicago Press, 1991), 100–122.

44. Paul Virilio, *Speed and Politics,* trans. Mark Polizzatti (New York: Semiotext[e], 1986), 133–36.

45. Michel de Certeau, "The Historiographical Operation," in *The Writing of History,* 89.

46. A. J. Greimas and Joseph Courtès, "The Cognitive Dimension of Narrative Discourse," *New Literary History* 7 (1976): 433–47.

47. Ibid., 439.

48. Ibid., 440–42. Michael Denning uses Greimas's distinction between the "cognitive" and the "pragmatic" in his analysis of the British spy novel, arguing that the spy novel foregrounds the former with its emphasis on information and the uncovering of secrets over physical actions (Denning, *Cover Stories,* 135–36).

49. Gary Crowdus, "Clarifying the Conspiracy: An Interview with Oliver Stone," *Cineaste* 19(1) (May 1992): 26–27.

50. In an odd and ironic moment in the annotated screenplay, we learn that one of the names that Ferrie rattles off in this scene, Jack Youngblood, is "fictitious" — that is, unlike those characters in the film who are composites of "real" witnesses (such as Willie O'Keefe, the gay prostitute whom Garrison interviews in prison), this name has no relationship whatsoever to the "real." In this conspiracy film, even the most paranoid character has paranoid fantasies. See Oliver Stone and Zachary Sklar, *JFK: The Book of the Film* (New York: Applause Books, 1992), 91.

51. The annotated screenplay, however, does attempt to support most of Ferrie's assertions. See ibid., 90–94.

52. Art Simon, *Dangerous Knowledge* (Philadelphia: Temple University Press, 1996), 216.

53. Janet Staiger has argued that *JFK*'s attempt to articulate an authoritative representation is largely recognized as such by contemporary viewers, who themselves recognize that "the movie is a subjective version of the past, created through shots put together by some agent." Therefore, she contends, it constitutes part of the larger struggle to produce a satisfying narrative resolution to the tragedy of the assassination. Extending Staiger's argument, one could assert that the film's ultimate incoherence could simply be a triumphant representation of the inability to resolve the historical argument — though I doubt that that was Stone's intent. See Janet Staiger, "Cinematic Shots: The Narration of Violence," in Vivian Sobchack, ed., *The Persistence of History: Cinema, Television, and the Modern Event* (New York: Routledge, 1996), 52–53.

54. For a brief historical account of theoretical discussions of closure in narrative theory, see Wallace Martin, *Recent Theories of Narrative* (Ithaca, N.Y.: Cornell University Press, 1986), 83–88. Martin argues that an "open" narrative form with no, or at least an ambiguous, closure dates back at least to the nineteenth-century novel. Further, he argues against polemical attempts by those such as J. Hillis Miller (in, for example, "The Problematic of Ending in Narrative," *Nineteenth-Century Fiction* 33 [1978]: 3–7) who claim that resolution is impossible. Martin writes: "Even if a philosopher succeeded in convincing the world that all talk and thought of beginnings and ends is a delusion, the source of the delusion, its universality, and its mode of operation would remain to be explained" (86).

55. A. Ralph Epperson, *The Unseen Hand: An Introduction to the Conspiratorial View of History* (Tucson, Ariz.: Publius Press, 1985), 8 (emphasis in original).

56. Brooks, *Reading for the Plot,* 58.

57. Roland Barthes, *S/Z,* trans. Richard Miller (New York: Hill and Wang, 1974), 75.

58. Ibid., 76.

59. *Conspiracy Theory* was directed by Richard Donner and written by Brian Helgeland.

60. Series creator Chris Carter has said about the show's use of strange items culled from news stories: "If there's anything current or topical, I try to use it as an element inside of a bigger story" ("Episode Guide: *The Erlenmeyer Flask,*" *Cinefantastique* [October 1995]: 58). On the show's use of conspiracy theories and especially UFO sources: "I'm taking what is in the current UFO literature about Roswell and MJ-12 [allegedly a secret committee of military, intelligence, and academic elites that controls the "truth" about alien contact] — these are all things I didn't make up — and letting the *X-Files* explain it further" (quoted in Paula Vitaris, "Filming the Fox Show That Has Become a Horror and Science Fiction Sensation," *Cinefantastique* [October 1995]: 78). See also Tim Appelo, "X Appeal," *Entertainment Weekly,* 19 March 1994, 58, 61, for Carter's discussion of the "real-life" inspiration for series episodes.

61. Brian Lowry, *The Truth Is Out There: The Official Guide to the X-Files* (New York: HarperPrism, 1995), 2.

62. "Anasazi," written by Chris Carter with a story by Carter and David Duchovny, directed by R. W. Goodwin, originally aired on 19 May 1995.

63. Dana Kennedy, "The X-Files Exposed," *Entertainment Weekly,* 10 March 1995, 20.

64. "The Erlenmeyer Flask," written by series creator and executive producer Chris Carter, directed by coexecutive producer R. W. Goodwin, was originally broadcast on 13 May 1994.

65. "Fallen Angel," written by Alex Gansa and Howard Gordon, directed by Larry Shaw, originally aired on 19 November 1993.

66. First implied in "The Host," written by Chris Carter, directed by Daniel Sackheim, and originally aired on 23 September 1994, X intially appears on screen in "Sleepless," written by Howard Gordon and directed by Rob Bowman, originally aired on 7 October 1994.

67. Original novels based on the series and "novelizations" of episodes are published by imprints of HarperCollins, News Corporation's book division. *Songs in the Key of X* (Warner Brothers, 1996) is a compilation of songs "inspired" by the series. The official magazine, comic book, and trading cards of the *X-Files* are published by the Topps company. "Official" *X-Files* conventions have been held throughout the country. One held in San Francisco in February 1996 (convened at the Nob Hill Masonic Center — ironic, given the position that Masons hold in many conspiracy theories) included numerous compendiums of clips from the series, trivia contests, an "official" prop gallery, a "blooper" reel, and appearances by some of the actors who portray relatively marginal recurring characters and by series creator Chris Carter. Other than the personal appearances, crowds were most interested in the merchandise booths, which were well stocked with photos, posters, and T-shirts.

68. Don Delillo, *Libra* (New York: Viking, 1988); *Tribulation 99: Alien Anomalies under America* (1991), written and directed by Craig Baldwin; Richard Condon, *Winter Kills* (New York: Dial, 1974); its film adaptation (1979) was written and directed by William Richert. The story behind the adaptation's production and subsequent withdrawal from release is filled with intrigue; see Richard Condon, "Who Killed *Winter Kills*?" *Harpers* (May 1983): 73–80. Other Condon political conspiracy novels (as opposed to organized crime novels based on the Prizzi family — though I recognize that this distinction makes little sense) of note include, most obviously, *The Manchurian Candidate* (New York: New American Library, 1959) on mind control and anticommunism, and *Death of a Politician* (New York: Ballantine, 1978) on Nixon. *The Parallax View* was directed by Alan J. Pakula. Michael Ryan and Douglas Kellner criticize the film for its refusal to make its protagonist, Joe Frady (played by Warren Beatty), into a sympathetic hero, for its curiously detached affect, and for its depressing resolution that leaves Frady dead and the Parallax Corporation of private assassins victorious (Ryan and Kellner, *Camera Politica,* 98–101). By contrast, see Jameson's attempt to read *The Parallax View*'s doubling of hero and conspiracy and the film's cynical,

ironic detachment from Frady's investigation of and resistance to the Parallax Corporation as an allegory of postmodernity (Jameson, *The Geopolitical Aesthetic,* 55–66).

69. Maria Nadotti, "An Interview with Don Delillo," *Salamagundi* (fall 1993): 94.

70. John A. McClure, "Postmodern Romance: Don DeLillo and the Age of Conspiracy," *South Atlantic Quarterly* 89(2) (spring 1990): 353.

71. Craig Baldwin, *Tribulation 99: Alien Anomalies under America* (New York: Ediciones La Calavera, 1991).

72. Frow, *Marxism and Literary History,* 146–47.

73. Dana Polan describes the duality of narrative structure in American cinema of the 1940s: "Power here is the power of a narrative system especially — the power that narrative structure specifically possesses to write an image of life as coherent, teleological, univocal; narrative, then, is a power to convert contingency into human meaning. Paranoia here will first be the fear of narrative, and the particular social representations it works to uphold, against all that threatens the unity of its logical framework" (Dana Polan, *Power and Paranoia* [New York: Columbia University Press, 1986], 12).

74. Patrick O'Donnell, "Engendering Paranoia in Contemporary Narrative," *boundary 2* 19(1) (1992): 204.

6. Millennialism and Christian Conspiracy Theory

1. Hal Lindsey, with C. C. Carlson, *The Terminal Generation* (Old Tappan, N.J.: Fleming H. Revell, 1976), 185.

2. George Gallup and Jim Castelli, *The People's Religion: American Faith in the Nineties* (New York: Macmillan, 1989).

3. Jeffrey L. Sheler, "The Christmas Covenant," *U.S. News and World Report,* 19 December 1994, 62. Although the ability of such polls to index religious and political beliefs precisely is inherently suspect, these kinds of polls at least demonstrate the importance of conservative Protestantism in the United States. See Steve Bruce, *Pray TV: Televangelism in America* (London: Routledge, 1990), 184–89.

4. K. L. Woodward, "The Final Days Are Here Again," *Newsweek,* 18 March 1991, 55.

5. "The Rapture Index," <http://www.novia.net/~todd/>, last visited 5 June 1997.

6. Frank Kermode, *The Sense of an Ending: Studies in the Theory of Fiction* (Oxford: Oxford University Press, 1966), 8–9.

7. One recent example of this was the events in Korea surrounding the prediction by Lee Jang Rim, a Seoul-based Korean pastor, of a rapture of Christians on 28 October 1992. See "World Fails to End; Korean Cult Is Stunned," *Louisville Courier-Journal,* 29 October 1992, A10.

8. Richard Rees uses the suggestive term "popular historiography" in relation to conspiracy theories and particularly the popular obsession with the Kennedy assassi-

nation. See Richard Rees, "Conspiracy Theory: Popular Historiography and Late Capitalism," paper presented at the annual meeting of the Popular Culture Association, Louisville, Kentucky, March 1992.

9. Religious historian Martin Marty has made a particularly effective case for the study of movements such as fundamentalism that can go beyond the often simplistic prejudices of academics and intellectuals against them. See Martin Marty, "Explaining the Rise of Fundamentalism," *Chronicle of Higher Education,* 28 October 1992, A56.

10. Lee Quinby, "Coercive Purity: The Dangerous Promise of Apocalyptic Masculinity," in Charles B. Strozier and Michael Flynn, eds., *The Year 2000: Essays on the End* (New York: New York University Press, 1997), 156.

11. Pat Robertson, *The New World Order* (Dallas: Word Publishing, 1991). See Frank Rich's columns "Bait and Switch," *New York Times,* 2 March 1995, A25; "The Jew World Order," *New York Times,* 9 March 1995, A25; "New World Terror," *New York Times,* 27 April 1995; and Michael Lind's "Calling All Crackpots," *Washington Post,* 16 October 1994, C1, C5; and "Rev. Robertson's Grand International Conspiracy Theory," *New York Review,* 2 February 1995, 21–25. For a general discussion of this exchange between Rich (a liberal editorial *New York Times* columnist), Lind (a former friend and employee of such conservative luminaries as William F. Buckley and Irving Kristol and now a centrist-liberal freelance writer), and Pat Robertson and Ralph Reed (at the time the executive director of the Christian Coalition, the conservative political organization that Robertson founded), see Gustav Niebuhr, "Pat Robertson Says He Intended No Anti-Semitism in Book He Wrote Four Years Ago," *New York Times,* 4 March 1995, A10.

12. See Rich, "The Jew World Order" (comparing Robertson to Farrakhan); and Rich, "New World Terror" (holding Robertson partially responsible for the rise of the militias and the Oklahoma City bombing).

13. Lind, "Rev. Robertson's Grand International Conspiracy Theory," 23.

14. This chapter will not refer specifically to the prophetic biblical texts used by eschatologists; my focus here is on a cultural, rather than liturgical, analysis of popular eschatology. Paul Boyer's *When Time Shall Be No More: Prophecy Belief in Modern American Culture* (Cambridge: Harvard University Press, 1992), and to a lesser extent Robert Fuller's *Naming the Antichrist* (New York: Oxford University Press, 1995), place current eschatology more within the context of the original biblical texts, and also discuss a greater number of eschatological texts.

15. George Marsden, a prominent historian of Christianity in America, defines fundamentalism as a subset of evangelicalism that is more militant in its opposition to liberal theology and changes in contemporary cultural values. It is also important to note that evangelicals, and to a lesser degree fundamentalists, come from a wide variety of Protestant denominations, ranging from Pentecostals and Baptists to Presbyterians and Episcopalians. There is thus a range of beliefs and religious practices among evangeli-

cals (though less so among fundamentalists), and this chapter generally concerns the more conservative among them. See George M. Marsden, *Understanding Fundamentalism and Evangelicalism* (Grand Rapids, Mich.: William B. Eerdmans, 1991), 1–6.

16. Paul A. Carter provides a particularly forceful argument along these lines. See Paul A. Carter, "The Fundamentalist Defense of the Faith," in John Braeman, Robert H. Bremner, and David Brody, eds., *Change and Continuity in Twentieth-Century America: The 1920s* (Columbus: Ohio University Press 1968), 179–214.

17. Marsden, *Understanding Fundamentalism and Evangelicalism,* 4–5.

18. Ibid., 162–68.

19. Ernest R. Sandeen, *The Origins of Fundamentalism: Toward a Historical Interpretation* (Philadelphia: Fortress Press, 1968), 8.

20. George M. Marsden, *Fundamentalism and American Culture: The Shaping of Twentieth-Century Evangelicalism, 1870–1925* (New York: Oxford University Press, 1980), 55–57; Garry Wills, *Under God: Religion and American Politics* (New York: Simon & Schuster, 1990), 130–32.

21. As Martin Marty has argued, contemporary Christian evangelicalism and fundamentalism are practiced within the mobile and affluent lifestyles of postwar America. They have been adopted within and adapted to suburban lifestyles and values of spiritual and material success, and offer help and resolutions to contemporary personal, professional, and social problems. See Martin Marty, *A Nation of Believers* (Chicago: University of Chicago Press, 1976).

22. Nathan O. Hatch, "Evangelicalism as a Democratic Movement," in George M. Marsden, ed., *Evangelicalism and Modern America* (Grand Rapids, Mich.: William B. Eerdmans, 1984), 71–82. Institutionally, contemporary conservative Protestantism is based less on denominational difference than during other eras, although divisions between, say, Pentecostals, who believe that glossolalia, or "involuntary" speaking in tongues during moments of "anointment" in the Holy Spirit, is evidence of a work of grace, and Baptists such as Jerry Falwell, who shun glossolalia, are quite important. Rather, the basic unit of contemporary Protestantism is the individual believer, and the strongest loyalties of many Christians is to specific preachers. Larger national and international denominations and conventions provide some hierarchy, but there is little structure holding together individual churches and larger ministries of those who use the mass media to reach believers.

23. The political economic and public policy circumstances for the contemporary rise of mass-media religion begin with the 1960 Federal Communications Commission (FCC) decision allowing broadcast television stations to sell time to religious programmers rather than to give it away, thus leading to the domination of those denominations that could show profit through broadcasts. Religious broadcasters have often been in the forefront of the development of new distribution systems, including the use of UHF in the 1970s, and satellite and cable delivery systems in the 1980s and 1990 (see Bruce, *Pray TV,* 29–31). As there were no restrictions for religious broadcasters

on the amount of commercial time, and religious broadcasters face a much more favorable tax situation compared to commercial stations and networks, conservative Christian broadcasting had and continues to have a relatively favored economic and political position in the marketplace (ibid., 52–53). See also Quentin J. Schultze, "The Mythos of the Electronic Church," *Critical Studies in Mass Communication* 4 (1987): 249.

24. For example, Pat Robertson's Christian Broadcasting Network adapted some of the conventions of secular entertainment and information programming for Robertson's news/talk/religious show the *700 Club* (and ultimately renamed the entire network "Family Channel") in order to reach a larger audience (Stewart M. Hoover, *Mass Media Religion* [Newbury Park, Calif.: Sage, 1988], 84).

25. Ibid., 87. See also Steve Bruce, *The Rise and Fall of the New Christian Right* (Oxford: Clarendon Press, 1988), 46, 66.

26. Stewart M. Hoover, "The Meaning of Religious Television: *The 700 Club* in the Lives of Its Viewers," in Quentin J. Schultze, ed., *American Evangelicals and the Mass Media* (Grand Rapids, Mich.: Zondervan, 1990), 236.

27. Bruce, *The Rise and Fall of the New Christian Right,* 190. For an example of an attempt by a then-budding member of the New Right to build alliances with the New Christian Right, see Dinesh D'Souza's biography of Jerry Falwell, *Falwell: Before the Millennium* (Chicago: Regnery Gateway, 1984). D'Souza clearly identifies his own dislike for what he would later term the "illiberalism" of academia and the media with what he sees as the fundamentalists' degradation: "So fundamentalists withdrew from involvement with secular institutions of American life to prepare for the end. They were helped along by liberal spurs. Fundamentalist educators were kicked out of the universities. The media proclaimed fundamentalism intellectually discredited.... They were outcasts, shoved out of society, not because of low birth or skin color, but because of alleged stupidity" (29).

28. In addition, as one study of the Moral Majority has argued, many of those fundamentalists who do engage in electoral and issue-oriented politics do so with ambivalence both about the importance of politics relative to spiritual struggles and about the likely success of their actions (Clyde Wilcox, Sharon Linzey, and Ted G. Jelen, "Reluctant Warriors: Premillennialism and Politics in the Moral Majority," *Journal for the Scientific Study of Religion* 30[3] [1991]: 245–58).

29. Rodney Clapp, "Overdosing on the Apocalypse," *Christianity Today,* 28 October 1991, 26; Edwin Yamauchi, "Updating the Armageddon Calendar," *Christianity Today,* 29 April 1991, 50–51; David Neff, "Apocalypse When?" *Christianity Today,* 17 December 1990, 15. *Christianity Today* does not itself espouse a specific type of millennialist view, and has published an extended debate/discussion between various types of premillennialists (including a pre-, mid-, and posttribulationalist), as well as a post- and an amillennialist. It began its introduction to this debate in this way: "Few doctrines unite and separate Christians as much as eschatology. For although we agree that Christ indeed will return to Earth, we differ on the when and how" (*Christianity*

Today Institute, "Our Future Hope: Eschatology and Its Role in the Church, *Christianity Today,* 6 February 1987, 1-I).

30. Charles B. Strozier, *Apocalypse: On the Subject of Fundamentalism in America* (Boston: Beacon Press, 1994), 116–25.

31. Grace Halsell, *Prophecy and Politics* (Westport, Conn.: Lawrence Hill, 1986); A. G. Mojtabai, *Blessed Assurance: At Home with the Bomb in Amarillo, Texas* (Boston: Houghton Mifflin, 1986).

32. Boyer, *When Time Shall Be No More,* 3–4. Indeed, the narratives of many science-fiction and horror novels and films, as well as nonfictional accounts of impending environmental, social, and economic disasters, share a number of elements with popular eschatology, and they appeal to the same secular audience as Hal Lindsey's work. Michael Barkun persuasively argues that although the texts of religious and secular nonfiction accounts of a coming apocalypse are significantly divergent in a number of ways, they share a tendency to organize the contemporary under the apocalypse and within a social pessimism that has become increasingly pervasive in the postwar era. In fact, I would postulate there are many who read both secular and religious apocalyptics (though perhaps at different points in their lives) and that the "bifurcated enterprise" that Barkun describes may not be as bifurcated as it circulates within popular common sense. See Michael Barkun, "Divided Apocalypse: Thinking about the End in Contemporary America," *Soundings* 66 (September 1983): 257–80.

33. The relationship between fundamentalism and the far right that Sara Diamond analyzes in *Spiritual Warfare* (Boston: South End Press, 1989) constitutes the institutional and political links that are the context for the connections between right-wing conspiracy theory and eschatology. Paul Boyer provides some important historical connections between anticommunism and prophecy (*When Time Shall Be No More,* 152–80). A prominent example of this relationship is Pat Robertson's *The New World Order.*

34. Timothy P. Weber, *Living in the Shadow of the Second Coming: American Premillennialism, 1875–1982,* enlarged ed. (New York: Oxford University Press, 1987), 9.

35. Robert G. Clouse, "The New Christian Right, America, and the Kingdom of God," *Christian Scholar's Review* 12(1) (1983): 3–4.

36. The term "dispensationalism" comes from a very precise reading and periodization of human history. According to these teachings, all of which arise from a specific set of hermeneutical principles for the reading of the Bible, God deals with human beings in successive dispensations, or periods of time, in which humanity is tested according to a specific revelation of the will of God. Each dispensation terminates in judgment — for example, the fall from Eden, the flood — because of humanity's continual failure. This systematic periodization of human history provides a specific set of eras in which man's relation to God can be understood, and the overall trajectory of human history across these eras does not progress or change. In each dispensation, humans make the same kinds of mistakes and fail the same kinds of tests.

For a much fuller accounting of the differences among premillennialists, see Weber, *Living in the Shadow of the Second Coming,* 9–12.

37. Clouse, "The New Christian Right, America, and the Kingdom of God," 4.

38. Ernest Lee Tuveson, *Redeemer Nation* (Chicago: University of Chicago Press, 1968).

39. An example of Dominion Theology is Pat Robertson, with Bob Slosser, *The Secret Kingdom* (New York: Thomas Nelson, 1983). The strongest recent summation of the Reconstruction movement is Gary North and Gary DeMar, *Christian Reconstruction: What It Is, What It Isn't* (Tyler, Tex.: Institute for Christian Economics, 1991). For a particularly critical and effective account of the relationship between such postmillennial movements and conservative politics, see Diamond, *Spiritual Warfare,* 134–41.

40. Clouse, "The New Christian Right, America, and the Kingdom of God," 10.

41. Marsden, *Fundamentalism and American Culture,* 112–13.

42. Ibid., 50–55.

43. For a discussion of the strong and complex response that contemporary Adventists have had to the popular success of Lindsey's popular eschatology, see Malcolm Bull and Keith Lockhart, *Seeking a Sanctuary: Seventh-Day Adventism and the American Dream* (San Francisco: Harper & Row, 1989), 52–55.

44. Weber, *Living in the Shadow of the Second Coming,* 52. As Weber argues, premillennialism's success in the period before, during, and after World War I was also a result of the fact that premillennialists' explanations of current events and predictions for the future were remarkably accurate. In reaction to their success, however, some premillennialists began to go too far, foreshadowing many current popular eschatologists by speculating about the precise date of Christ's return and the rapture (ibid., 105–14).

45. Ibid., 16, 26–36.

46. "Watch, therefore, for ye know neither the day nor the hour wherein the Son of man cometh" (Matt. 25:13), and "Watch therefore: for ye know not what hour your Lord doth come" (Matt. 24:42).

47. Hal Lindsey, with C. C. Carlson, *The Late Great Planet Earth* (New York: Bantam, 1970), 170. Parenthetical page references in the next section refer to this work.

48. Lindsey's *The Terminal Generation* (1976) and *The 1980s: Countdown to Armageddon* (New York: Bantam, 1981) seem primarily aimed at persuading believers and nonbelievers that the world is moving quickly and inexorably toward apocalypse, whereas *The Rapture* (New York: Bantam, 1983) gives a detailed description of the scriptural account of that moment in the end times, and *The Road to Holocaust* (New York: Bantam, 1989) is an extended and often bitter argument against postmillennialism and particularly against Christian Reconstructionists.

49. Voice-over narration for the opening credit sequence of *Jack Van Impe Presents,* aired 2 February 1998, WHPX-26, Hartford, Connecticut.

50. *Jack Van Impe Presents,* aired 26 June 1992, Trinity Broadcasting Network (TBN).

51. *This Week in Bible Prophecy,* aired 21 June 1992, TBN.

52. On dispensationalism's ongoing interest in the European Community in the period after World War II, see Boyer, *When Time Shall Be No More,* 275–78.

53. *Jack Van Impe Presents,* aired 19 June 1992, TBN.

54. *This Week in Bible Prophecy,* aired 21 June 1992, TBN.

55. Ibid.

56. For example, in late 1997 Jack Van Impe (on a show aired 18 November 1997, WHPX-26, Hartford, Connecticut) led with a tribute to Red Buttons, who had recently died, and noted the lack of morals in current comedy as emblematic of the current state of civilization and the likely return of Jesus. A show in early 1998 (aired 2 February 1998, WHPX-26, Hartford, Connecticut) discussed the problems computers would face in the year 2000 and plans by the National Aeronautics and Space Administration (NASA) to return to the Moon as further evidence of the coming rapture.

57. Gustav Niebuhr, "The Newest Christian Fiction Injects a Thrill into Theology," *New York Times,* 30 October 1995, A1

58. Boyer, *When Time Shall Be No More,* 7.

59. Bob Summer, "Religion Is His Business," *Publishers Weekly,* 21 September 1992, 46; Ephraim Radner, "New World Order, Old World Anti-Semitism," *Christian Century,* 13 September 1995, 844.

60. Robertson's *The New World Order* also contains such implicit anti-Semitism and explicit bigotry against non-Western religions. This, as well as the connections between his thought and that of earlier, more "secular" conspiracy theorists, is apparent in his unquestioned citation of the work of Nesta Webster, a relatively well-known early twentieth-century British conspiracy theorist who considered *The Protocols of the Elders of Zion* to be a legitimate document and saw Jews as leaders of a master plot to take over the world. See Nesta Webster, *Secret Societies and Subversive Movements* (New York: E. P. Dutton, 1924).

61. Frank E. Peretti, *This Present Darkness* (Wheaton, Ill.: Crossway Books, 1986).

62. For a discussion of Peretti's place as one of the top evangelical/fundamentalist novelists, see Erling Jorstad, *Popular Religion in America* (Westport, Conn.: Greenwood Press, 1993), 143–45; and Niebuhr, "The Newest Christian Fiction Injects a Thrill into Theology."

63. Pat Robertson, *The End of the Age* (Dallas: Word Publishing, 1995). The novel was enormously successful within Christian publishing. See Sara Diamond, "Political Millennialism within the Evangelical Subculture," in Strozier and Flynn, *The Year 2000,* 206–7.

64. Weber, *Living in the Shadow of the Second Coming,* 51.

65. See Diamond, *Spiritual Warfare,* 24–25.

66. Lindsey, *The 1980s,* 139–58.

67. Timothy LaHaye, *The Battle for the Mind* (Old Tappan, N.J.: Fleming H. Revell, 1980), 218–19; Michael Lienesch, *Redeeming America: Piety and Politics in the New Christian Right* (Chapel Hill: University of North Carolina Press, 1993), 227–28. Lindsey himself never fully resolves this dilemma; in his book-length attack on Christian Reconstructionists, published in 1989, he warned against any Christian "political revolution" or party, although he does admit that it is proper to influence politics and to vote. He argues that although the Bible "gives no hope of taking over this present world-system and establishing a Theocratic Kingdom on Earth," Christians can and should "save souls and transform lives of converts into citizens of God's spiritual kingdom" (Lindsey, *The Road to Holocaust,* 278). The controversy surrounding President Ronald Reagan's apocalyptic beliefs during his 1984 reelection campaign provides an interesting, if not particularly enlightening, discussion of the issues surrounding politicians who espouse apocalyptic beliefs. See, for example, Gene Krupey, "The Christian Right, Zionism, and the Coming of the Penteholocaust," in Adam Parfrey, ed., *Apocalypse Culture,* 2d ed. (Los Angeles: Feral House, 1990), 286–98; Wills, *Under God,* 144–51; Larry Kickham, "The Theology of Nuclear War," *Covert Action Information Bulletin* 27 (spring 1987): 9–17; "Critics Fear That Reagan Is Swayed by Those Who Believe in a 'Nuclear Armageddon,' " *Christianity Today,* 14 December 1984, 48–49; Hedrik Hertzberg, "The End Is Nigh," *New Republic,* 12 November 1984, 50; Richard N. Ostling, "Armageddon and the End Times," *Time,* 5 November 1984, 73; "Reckoning with Armageddon," *New York Times,* 5 October 1984, 12.

68. Marsden, *Fundamentalism and American Culture,* 210–11.

69. Lee Quinby, *Anti-Apocalypse: Exercises in Genealogical Criticism* (Minneapolis: University of Minnesota Press, 1994), xv.

70. Hayden White, *The Content of the Form* (Baltimore: Johns Hopkins University Press, 1987), 21.

71. In Joanna Brooks's words, this is a reading in which the text plays a "providential role," positioning the reader "on the text's terms, on the text's times" (Joanna Brooks, "Calling All Radicals: Reading Hal Lindsey's *The Late Great Planet Earth,*" paper presented at Discerning the Right conference, University of Wisconsin-Milwaukee, March 1996, 8).

72. Gabriel Fackre, *The Religious Right and Christian Faith* (Grand Rapids, Mich.: William B. Eerdmans, 1982), 88–95.

73. John G. Gager, *Kingdom and Community: The Social World of Christianity* (Englewood Cliffs, N.J.: Prentice-Hall, 1975), 55 (emphasis in original).

74. Kermode, *The Sense of an Ending,* 25–26.

75. Fredric Jameson, *Postmodernism; or, The Cultural Logic of Late Capitalism* (Durham, N.C.: Duke University Press, 1991), 369.

76. Richard Johnson and his coauthors in the Popular Memory Group of the Birmingham School have described this process operating in working-class popular history and memory. In this sense, popular eschatology displaces the local and tangible aspects of

such remembrances and interpretation of the past for the global and spiritual concerns of prophecy. See Popular Memory Group, "Popular Memory: Theory, Politics, Method," in Richard Johnson et al., eds., *Making Histories: Studies in History Writing and Politics* (Minneapolis: University of Minnesota Press, 1983), 205–52.

77. Boyer, *When Time Shall Be No More,* 270, 421–22.

78. Ernesto Laclau, *New Reflections on the Revolution of Our Time* (London: Verso, 1990), 89–93.

7. The Conspiracy "Community"

1. A parallel set of alternative media and interpersonal networks exists for African-Americans and tends to rely more on rumor and gossip circulated in what Regina Austin has called the "black public sphere," in addition to their circulation through the publications of institutions such as the Nation of Islam. See my discussion of race and conspiracy in chapter 3, as well as Patricia A. Turner, *I Heard It through the Grapevine* (Berkeley: University of California Press, 1993), and Regina Austin, "Beyond Black Demons and White Devils: Antiblack Conspiracy Theorizing and the Black Public Sphere," *Florida State University Law Review* 22 (spring 1995): 1021.

2. When Oliver Stone made a surprise cameo appearance at the April 1992 assassination conference, for example, he was met with a rush of reverent attendees seeking to get his autograph and to talk with him about the recently released *JFK.* Yet, as had been clear throughout the proceedings whenever *JFK* or Stone's name had been mentioned, many of those at the conference also resented the fact that the mainstream media and much of the general public seemed to assume that he represented the cause and theories of Warren Commission critics. Some were particularly disturbed at what they saw as his film's wild and speculative presentation of the evidence and events surrounding the assassination, as well as his virtual canonization of the problematic figure of Jim Garrison.

3. See the discussion in chapter 1 of the vast body of historical accounts of conspiracy theory, produced largely in the 1960s and 1970s.

4. Sara Rimer, "New Medium for the Far Right," *New York Times,* 27 April 1995, A1.

5. See, for example, "Militia of Montana Page," <http://www.nidlink.com/~bobhard/mom.html>, last visited 12 June 1997; "conspire.com," <http://www.conspire.com/>, last visited 12 June 1997, an impressive site promoting the book of the same name by Jonathan Vankin and John Whalen, which provides very extensive and up-to-date links to sites around the Web; "Birch-New American," <http://www.execpc.com/~jfish/na/index.html>, last visited 12 June 1997, a link to *The New American,* the magazine of the John Birch Society.

6. The period between "alt" and "conspiracy" is a convention of the UNIX system on which USENET operates. For a more extensive description of USENET, see Ed Krol, *The Whole Internet Catalog and User's Guide* (Sebastopol, Calif.: O'Reilly

& Associates, 1992), 127–32; and Tracy LaQuey, *The Internet Companion* (Reading, Mass.: Addison-Wesley, 1993), 60–66.

7. Of the USENET gateways that report in this survey, 64 percent received alt.conspiracy, a relatively high proportion for a news group in the "alt." hierarchy, whose news groups tend to be banned from some systems because of their controversial subject matter (Brian Reid, "USENET Readership Summary Report for July 1994, *news.lists,* posted 4 August 1994).

8. Indeed, in July 1994, more than 40 percent of the articles in alt.conspiracy were cross-posted, a proportion that was far above average.

9. Erik Davis, "Barbed Wire Net," *Village Voice,* 2 May 1995, 28.

10. Alt.conspiracy.jfk was the 1,541st most widely read news group (out of 3,121) for July 1994, and approximately 54 percent of the USENET gateways received it (Reid, "USENET Readership Summary").

11. In his study of the rhetoric of British anti-Semitism and fascism, Michael Billig stresses the degree to which conspiracy theory is often an argument against both skeptics and competitors. See Michael Billig, "Arguments in British Fascism," in *Ideology and Opinions* (London: Sage, 1991), 107–21.

12. The very impossibility of articulating "conspiracy" as community is the flaw at the center of Michael Kelly's attempt to identify what he terms "fusion paranoia," the coming together of left and right around a bipolar model of popular politics. To the extent that Kelly is trying to describe an innate pathology of a wider populism (that is, that conspiracy theory is now a mass phenomenon), he misrecognizes as pathological that which is not only an important historical discourse in American politics but a crucial organizing rhetoric for political out-groups that is often based on rational and empirical injustice (see chapter 3). On the other hand, to the extent that Kelly is trying to identify a newly emergent subculture of conspiracy (that is, that conspiracy theory is merely a cult activity), he oversimplifies the often conflicting politics of those who constitute the subculture, as well as the contradictory nature of an enterprise built on collective mistrust of everything. See Michael Kelly, "The Road to Paranoia," *New Yorker,* 19 June 1995, 60–75.

13. The seminal text outlining these allegations is Gary Sick's *October Surprise* (New York: Times Books, 1991).

14. For a full account of the Hamiltons' charges and the intricacies of the Inslaw case, see James Ridgeway, "I Hate Meeses to Pieces," *Village Voice,* 22 September 1992, 19–20.

15. The Judiciary Committee report complained that the Justice Department "delayed and hindered Congressional inquiries into the Inslaw matter over several years," and files that had been subpoenaed by the committee were reported as lost or were denied on the basis that they contained "criminal investigative material." On the Brooks Committee report, see "House Judiciary's Inslaw Report" (unsigned editorial), *Washington Post,* 8 September 1992, A20; Eric Reguly, "House Committee Racks Inslaw

Conspiracy Theory," *Financial Post,* 18 August 1992, 12. On the Bua Committee report, see William H. Freivogel and Steven Casmier, "Inslaw Allegations Rejected," *St. Louis Post-Dispatch,* 18 June 1993, 15A. On the results of the most recent decision in the Inslaw litigation, a determination by a federal claims court exonerating the federal government, see "CFTC v. Free Speech; DOJ Didn't Steal," *National Law Journal* (18 August 1997): A10.

16. Debra Gersh, "Justice Dept. Report Says Journalist's Death Was Suicide," *Editor and Publisher,* 17 July 1993, 9–10.

17. "Inslaw Revisited," *Wired* (November 1995): 86.

18. The information that follows is based on the following sources: Stephen Pizzo, "The Long Arm of Lew?" *Mother Jones* (May–June 1993): 14; John Connolly, "Dead Right," *Spy* (January 1993): 56–65; Phil Linsalata, "The Octopus File," *Columbia Journalism Review* (November–December 1992): 76; James Ridgeway and Doug Vaughn, "Who Killed Danny Casolaro?" *Village Voice,* 15 October 1992, 31; Michael K. Griffin, "A Conspiracy Far Worse Than Watergate," *St. Louis Journalism Review* (October 1992): 1; Kim Masters, "What Killed Danny Casolaro?" *Washington Post,* 31 August 1992.

19. John Connolly, "Dead Right," *Spy* (January 1993): 59.

20. Chip Berlet, "Big Stories, Spooky Sources," *Columbia Journalism Review* 32(1) (June 1993): 67–71.

21. Printed as "Behold a Pale Horse: A Draft of Danny Casolaro's Octopus Manuscript Proposal," in Jim Keith, ed., *Secret and Suppressed: Banned Ideas and Hidden History* (Portland, Oreg.: Feral House, 1993), 169–72.

22. For a full discussion of the problems of the investigation into Casolaro's death, see Connolly, "Dead Right." Judge Bua's report dismissing charges against the Department of Justice in the Inslaw case concludes that there is no credible evidence supporting anything other than that Casolaro committed suicide. See Gersh, "Justice Dept. Report Says Journalist's Death Was Suicide."

23. See Kenn Thomas, "The Octopus Conspiracy: Fictional Tale or Factional Trail?" *Steamshovel Press* 6 (winter 1992): 32. For more information on *Steamshovel Press,* see http://www.umsl.edu/~skthoma/. Subscription rates are $22 for a four-issue subscription or $6 per single issue; inquiries may be sent to Steamshovel Press, P.O. Box 23715, St. Louis, MO 63121.

24. Ibid.; Kenn Thomas, "The Promis Threat: An Octopus Slouches toward Mena, Arkansas, Area 51 and the International UFO Congress in Las Vegas," *Steamshovel Press* 7 (1993): 32–35.

25. Ben G. Price, "Outlaws and Inslaw," in Jim Keith, ed., *The Gemstone File* (Atlanta, Ga.: IllumiNet Press, 1992), 176.

26. Dave Emory, originally broadcast on KFJC on 11 August 1991. Transcribed from side A of "For Whom the Bell Tolls: The Death of Joseph Daniel Casolaro," a cassette tape series available through Emory's Archives on Audio.

27. Thomas, "The Octopus Conspiracy," 29.

28. The host is named as Paul DeRienzo in the transcription posted to alt.conspiracy, and available at a number of file archives throughout the Internet. This was posted on alt.conspiracy on 17 February 1992 as "The Casolaro Murder → Feds' Theft of Inslaw Software, Part XI."

29. Kenn Thomas, "Behold A Pale Horse: A Draft of Danny Casolaro's Octopus Manuscript Proposal," in *Secret and Suppressed: Banned Ideas and Hidden History* (Portland, Oreg.: Feral House, 1993), 169–72.

30. Virginia McCullough, interviewed by Paul DeRienzo on WBAI-FM, New York, 20 September 1991, posted on alt.conspiracy on 17 February 1992 as "The Casolaro Murder → Feds' Theft of Inslaw Software, Part XXII."

31. Thomas, "The Octopus Conspiracy," 32.

32. See, for example, "A Primer on Inslaw," <http://www.copi.com/articles/Inslaw primer.htm>, last visited 13 June 1997; and "The Inslaw Scandal," <http://www. federal.com/6298.html>, last visited 13 June 1997.

33. See "The Homepage of J. Orlin Grabbe," <http://www.aci.net/kalliste/>, last visited 13 June 1997.

34. "Re: Wackenhut et al.," alt.conspiracy, posted 29 February 1992.

8. Conspiracy Theory as Play

1. Deluxe edition, Steve Jackson Games, 1991.

2. Jonathan Vankin, *Conspiracies, Cover-ups and Crimes* (New York: Paragon House, 1991).

3. Adam Parfrey, ed., *Apocalypse Culture* (Los Angeles: Feral House, 1990), back cover.

4. Parfrey, "Preface to the Second Edition," ibid., 8.

5. Jonathan Vankin, "The Gemstone File and Me," in Jim Keith, ed., *The Gemstone File* (Atlanta, Ga.: IllumiNet Press, 1992), 107.

6. Robert Anton Wilson, with Robert Shea, *Illuminatus!* (New York: Dell, 1975). All page references to the trilogy will be based on the 1988 Dell edition, which collected the three novels in one trade paperback.

7. Two USENET news groups, alt.illuminati and alt.discordia, are forums for Wilson fans and Discordians, and the trilogy receives prominent mention in the *New Hacker's Dictionary.*

8. The 1991 editions of all three novels are New York: Roc. Three collections of nonfiction essays and aphorisms are *Cosmic Trigger: The Final Secret of the Illuminati* (New York: Pocket, 1977); *Cosmic Trigger II: Down to Earth* (Scottsdale, Ariz.: New Falcon, 1991); and *The Illuminati Papers* (Berkeley: Ronin Publishing, 1990).

9. Neal Wilgus's *The Illuminoids* (Santa Fe, N.Mex.: Sun Books, 1978) serves as a quasi-historical companion to *Illuminatus!,* providing similarly bemused descriptions of the "real" history of "secret societies and political paranoia."

10. Wilson, *Cosmic Trigger II*, 148; *The Illuminati Papers*, 19. Both Einstein and James Joyce appear as central characters in Wilson's novel *Masks of the Illuminati* (New York: Timescape/Pocket Books, 1981), in which they act as scientific and literary interpreters of a convoluted story of conspiracy and manipulation.

11. Wilson, *The Illuminati Papers*, 2.

12. "Malaclypse the Younger" (Kerry Thornley), *Principia Discordia* (Avondale Estates, Ga.: IllumiNet Press, 1991), 00074 [*sic*]. On the relationship between *Illuminatus!* and *Principia Discordia*, see *Principia*, vi–x.

13. Collected in Wilson, *The Illuminati Papers*, 114–15.

14. National Insecurity Council (Michael Litchfield), *It's a Conspiracy!* (Berkeley: EarthWorks Press, 1992).

15. Cameron Tuttle, *The Paranoid's Pocket Guide* (San Francisco: Chronicle Books, 1997), provides a similar tongue-in-cheek gloss on everyday life, describing such sources of worry as the Illuminati, government wiretapping, the perils of "sex and dating," and plane travel. Compact, handy, poking fun at the ISBN and UPC code on its own back cover (the phrase "I am not a number" sits proudly next to both), and well merchandised (in its first months of publications it was being placed right by the cash register in some bookstores), the book seems destined for bathroom reading in thousands of homes across America. In it, conspiracy theory is merely part of a "guide" that warns its reader to carry it "at all times, since you never know when you'll get stuck in traffic or trapped in an elevator. . . . And remember, just because you're paranoid doesn't mean that someone isn't out to get you" (7).

16. "Turn Left: Make Your Own Conspiracy Theory," <http://www.cjnetworks.com/~cubsfan/conspiracy.html>, last visited 28 June 1997.

17. The "National Conspiracy League," <http://www.infi.net/~knolled/>, last visited 30 March 1997. Interestingly, this site serves as an ironic counterpart to the site noted in chapter 6 that quite seriously tracks current events to estimate the proximity of the rapture. See "The Rapture Index," <http://www.novia.net/~todd/>, last visited 5 June 1997.

18. For a full description of the FBI raid, see Bruce Sterling, *The Hacker Crackdown* (New York: Bantam, 1992), esp. 133–39.

19. Wilson, *The Illuminati Papers*, 20.

20. "Illuminati Game Rules Booklet" (Austin, Tex.: Steve Jackson Games, 1991). A new "collectible card game," called Illuminati: New World Order, was produced in December 1994, with a very similar premise and somewhat altered rules. See Brett Brooks, "It's Time to Take Over the World Again," *Game Shop News* 34 (21 October 1994): 1.

21. Although the majority of games are played in person and at one time, some games of Illuminati are conducted through the mail and over electronic mail.

22. Nigel D. Findley, *GURPS Illuminati* (Austin, Tex.: Steve Jackson Games, 1992). Parenthetical page references in the text refer to this book.

23. Peter Sloterdijk, *Critique of Cynical Reason,* trans. Michael Eldred (Minneapolis: University of Minnesota Press, 1987), 5.

24. Slavoj Žižek, *The Sublime Object of Ideology* (London: Verso, 1989), 33 (emphasis in original).

25. François Roustang, "How Do You Make a Paranoiac Laugh?" *Modern Language Notes* 102(4) (1987): 707–18.

26. Dick Hebdige, *Hiding in the Light* (London: Routledge, 1988), 243.

27. M. M. Bakhtin, *Rabelais and His World,* trans. H. Iswolsky (Cambridge: MIT Press, 1968). See also Peter Stallybrass and Allon White, *The Politics and Poetics of Transgression* (Ithaca, N.Y.: Cornell University Press, 1986).

28. Bakhtin, *Rabelais and His World,* 19.

29. Peter Stallybrass and Allen White, *The Politics and Poetics of Transgression* (Ithaca, N.Y.: Cornell University Press, 1986), 20, 25.

30. Ibid., 202.

31. Timothy Bewes, *Cynicism and Postmodernity* (London: Verso, 1997), 2–8.

Afterword

1. Andrew MacDonald [William Pierce], *The Turner Diaries* (Arlington, Va.: National Vanguard Books, 1978).

2. For examples of similar — though not "fictional" — texts, see the historical and current tracts from white racist groups collected in *Extremism in America,* ed. Lyman Tower Sargent (New York: New York University Press, 1995), 115–90. An exemplary study of the racist right is Michael Barkun, *Religion and the Racist Right,* rev. ed. (Chapel Hill: University of North Carolina Press, 1997); see also the discussion of the racist right and works referenced in chapter 2.

3. James William Gibson, *Warrior Dreams* (New York: Hill and Wang, 1994). On the use of *The Turner Diaries* as a recruiting tool for *Soldier of Fortune* readers, see Philip Lamy, *Millennium Rage* (New York: Plenum Press, 1996), 129–30, and Gibson, *Warrior Dreams,* 212–13.

4. On the use of *The Turner Diaries* by one white supremacist terror group as a treatise on terrorist tactics, see Kevin Flynn and Gary Gerhardt, *The Silent Brotherhood* (New York: Free Press, 1989), 174.

5. John Fiske, "Cultural Studies and the Study of Everyday Life," in Lawrence Grossberg, Cary Nelson, and Paula Treichler, eds., *Cultural Studies* (New York: Routledge), 161; John Fiske, "Popular Discrimination," in James Naremore and Patrick Brantlinger, eds., *Modernity and Mass Culture* (Bloomington: Indiana University Press, 1991), 115; John Fiske, *Television Culture* (New York: Routledge), 358.

6. John Fiske, *Media Matters: Everyday Culture and Political Change* (Minneapolis: University of Minnesota Press, 1994), 191–216.

7. Ibid., 192.

8. Ibid., 216.

9. For a discussion of the ideological processes of articulation and closure within "chains of equivalence," see Ernesto Laclau, "The Death and Resurrection of the Theory of Ideology," *Modern Language Notes* 112 (1997): 320–21.

10. The assumption that *The Turner Diaries* and similar literature are pitched to white working-class readers, and especially to rural males, is made in Joel Dyer, *Harvest of Rage* (Boulder, Colo.: Westview Press, 1997), 150–51.

11. This critique should not be read as an attempt to demonstrate Fiske's "relativism," in the sense that one scholar recently blamed the rise of Holocaust revisionism as at least in part the result of poststructuralist theory's presumed assault on truth. See Deborah Lipstadt, *Denying the Holocaust* (New York: Free Press, 1993), 17–19. Rather than being relativist — indeed, Fiske would firmly assert that black counterknowledge is a search for a truth that is deeply hidden but may still be recoverable — his theory suffers from ill-defined terms and concepts that are resistant to specific historical and social contexts.

12. See Lawrence Grossberg, ed., "On Postmodernism and Articulation: An Interview with Stuart Hall," *Journal of Communication Inquiry* 10(2) (summer 1986): 55.

13. Matt Wray, "Apocalyptic Masculinities," paper presented at Discerning the Right conference, University of Wisconsin-Milwaukee, March 1996, 21.

14. Lee Quinby, *Anti-Apocalypse: Exercises in Genealogical Criticism* (Minneapolis: University of Minnesota Press, 1994), xx–xxii.

15. See Richard Dellamora's use of Kantian notions of the sublime to describe responses to the AIDS epidemic, which he characterizes as a combination of fascination and paralyzing dread. This response, he argues, enables the assertion of regressive constituted authorities, yet can also motivate organized efforts to understand the conditions that produce the sublime itself (*Apocalyptic Overtures* [New Brunswick, N.J.: Rutgers University Press, 1994], 14–16).

16. See Angela Harris's comparison and contrast of critical race theorists in legal academia to the protagonists of conspiracy fiction ("Afterword: Other Americas," *Michigan Law Review* 95 [February 1997]: 1158).

Index

Viper Militia, 239 n.30
Virilio, Paul, 122
vote, right to, 32

Waco, Texas, and raid on Branch Davidian
    compound, 24, 33, 34, 43, 50, 183
Wagner-Pacifici, Robin, 50
Walkerdine, Valerie, 245 n.52, 249 n.31
Wall Street Journal editorial page, 4, 77, 98
Wallace, George, 47
Walvoord, John F., 145
Warren Commission, 28, 105
Washington Times, 98
Watergate, 70–71, 118, 136, 191
Wead, George, 253 n.14
Weaver, Randy, 24
Webb, Gary, 228 n.6
Weber, Max, 4
Weber, Timothy, 154, 174, 63 nn.36, 44
Webster, Nesta, 148, 203, 264 n.60
Weishaupt, Adam, 202
Western Journalism Center, 84, 247 n.12
White, Allen, 218–19
White, Hayden, 176
white supremacy, 221–22

Whitewater, 77, 81, 84
Wilgus, Neil, 269 n.9
Wills, Garry, 260 n.20, 165 n.67
Wilson, Robert Anton, xx, 201, 202, 205, 211.
    See also Illuminatus!
Winter Kills, xix, 138, 257 n.68
Wood, Gordon S., 229 n.14
Woollacott, Janet, 254 n.25
World Bank, 62, 171
World Wide Web, 180, 184, 196–97
Wray, Matt, 272 n.13
Wulff, Erich, 233 n.42

X-Files, The, xii, 106, 132–38, 184
    and closure, 129, 134, 138
    episodic narrative in, 132, 134, 135
    "Erlenmeyer Flask, The" (episode),
        134–38
    "Fallen Angel" (episode), 136
    limits of agency in, 135–37
    serial narrative in, 132, 133–34, 137

Žižek, Slavoj, xviii, 90–91, 94, 217, 248
    nn.21, 22; 249 n.30, 250 n.44
Zukier, Hans, 253 n.15

Mark Fenster has a Ph.D. from the Institute of Communications Research at the University of Illinois, Urbana-Champaign, and a J.D. from Yale Law School. He has taught in communications departments at Indiana University and Shenandoah University.